EXTREME SCREENWRITING: SCREENPLAY WRITING SIMPLIFIED

Copyright © 2014 Barb Doyon

Printed in the United States of America.

INTRODUCTION

Extreme Screenwriting is written in an informal, yet direct way to assist the aspiring screenwriter write a commercially viable product that'll help nail down a sale. The approach taken may, at times, seem controversial - - but what do you have to lose? This material DOES NOT cover the basic "how-to" stuff. **It strictly deals with adding a commercial edge to your material geared towards making a first sale!**

This manual helps the writer maintain the art of screenwriting while learning to write what sells. Like any other instructional information out there, take from it what you will and toss the rest!

Dear Fellow Screenwriter,

Some time ago I wrote a coming of age drama titled "The Yellow Tulip." Out of 1,500+ submissions received in the Writer's Digest Screenwriting Competition it placed in the Top 10. As a result, a WGA agent contacted me and soon after I signed with his agency.

This was mistake #1 in a long list of mistakes, miscalculations and what I consider to be some pretty unnecessary mistakes I've made in my quest to become a professional screenwriter. Had I done my homework, I would have discovered the agent (to remain unnamed) hadn't sold a thing in over 2 years.

My second mistake was not remaining in control of my own career. I turned everything over to the agent figuring he'd make the calls, the contacts and the sales. Isn't this what an agent is for? I soon learned that even with a good agent a screenwriter still has to be involved in selling their material on one level or another.

I didn't renew the contract with the agent. Instead, I solicited producers and got several reads for "The Yellow Tulip." All passed, except one producer. I was so excited about meeting with her I nearly quit my day job. Thank goodness I didn't.

She loved the script. It made her cry. I was elated! Only she wasn't interested in purchasing the script. Instead, she wanted me to rewrite a script she had previously purchased. She was offering a writing assignment! At the time I found this insulting. I don't want someone else rewriting my material, why would I offer to rewrite someone else's material? What I didn't realize is a majority of writers make a living taking writing assignments, and many agents won't sign a writer who refuses to do assignments. It's the bread-and-butter of the industry for writers and agents.

What "commercial" means ***[1]

Why scripts fail ***[2]

I asked the producer why she wasn't interested in purchasing "The Yellow Tulip". After all, she loved it, right? Then she said something that utterly infuriated me. She said the script was well written, but it wasn't commercial.

My next mistake was in believing she was 100% wrong. This script made finalist out of 1,500 scripts! After this, I moved forward in life and went to work at Walt Disney Studios in Burbank, California. I worked in Corporate Communications, otherwise known as the press room.

One day a producer came into the press room and asked if anyone would like to earn extra money doing script coverage for him. I jumped on the Hollywood reader's bandwagon and have been there ever since. This producer, at the time, did family films for Disney. He was a perfect match for my script "The Yellow Tulip." I'm a lousy salesman, but eventually I mustered the courage to tell him about my script and its contest placement.

He read the script and passed. He said it was a good script and well written, but it failed as a commercial product and I should try an independent producer. After I got over the initial shock I realized this was the second time a Hollywood producer had told me my script wasn't commercial.

The biggest mistake I'd made was assuming the contest placement put my script in the running for the big screen. What it did was the following: 1) helped me gain industry attention 2) gave my writing skills credibility. But both the producers were right; the script wasn't commercial.

One day the Disney producer and I were discussing what it takes to make a first sale and what he said profoundly changed my view of what "commercial" means. Up until then commercial was a dirty word that meant compromising my art, selling out or conforming to a formula. This was a huge miscalculation.

Commercial simply means presenting a concept that'll draw a large audience. ***[1] As an artist, don't I want others to see my work up on the big screen? Of course I do and I'm betting you do too.

I read hundreds of screenplays a year for production companies and aspiring screenwriters. Many of the aspiring screenwriters have good scripts. Yet 99% of these scripts, like my coming of age story, fail on a commercial level for one reason.

What the producer told me is scripts fail on a commercial level because they ***[2] fail to deliver a plot-driven and character-driven story in one script. It's either all plot-driven or all character-driven and without Hollywood connections a new screenwriter must demonstrate the ability to deliver material on a commercial level before they'll be given serious consideration.

As a Hollywood reader I knew what he was talking about. For example, I'll read a huge Sci-Fi Action script. It'll have great action, a new slant, crisp dialogue – yet, something seems to be missing. Or I'll read a character-driven script where the plot seems non-existent. The characters might be well-drawn, but the plot seems non-existent.

Looking back on my coming of age story it's obvious why it isn't commercial. It's an all character-driven script. Does this mean it'll never sell? Of course not. What it means is that it's unlikely this script will be a FIRST SALE!

The trick to getting a first sale sounds easy enough. Write a script that has a strong plot and strong characterizations. Yet this is a very difficult thing to do. Why? In my opinion, it's because it forces the writer to be creative in a new way. Did I just imply that writing a commercial script inspires creativity? Yes, I did! Because it does. There's nothing more inspiring than writing a great plot with a great character or vice versa.

I can already hear the arguments where the screenwriter names a character-driven or plot-driven film that was a success. I can name them too, but what we're talking about here is making a FIRST SALE. We're not talking about a character-driven script that happened to get a big star attached or a plot-driven script picked up by a famous director. Unless you have solid Hollywood contacts you're unlikely to have this kind of backing to get your screenplay made into a film. What we're talking about is presenting a commercial product that'll land the writer a FIRST SALE! After that, the sky's the limit!

Once the writer makes an initial sale, Hollywood will be more receptive to other material because the writer has proven he can deliver a commercial product. So, give yourself a chance to write a commercial script. I believe you'll find, like I did, that you love it! Soon you'll never go back to writing the way you used to. Instead you'll be proud to say, "I only write commercial material."

Best Always and Keep Writing,
Barb Doyon
Owner/Founder
Extreme Screenwriting
www.extremescreenwriting.com

TABLE OF CONTENTS

CHAPTER ONE: COMMERCIALIZE FIRST

THE IDEA: Is it Commercial Enough for a Screenplay Sale?

In an episode of *The Apprentice* Donald Trump said the following, "Anyone can come up with a great idea, but if you can't sell the idea you'll never be successful." This statement is especially true of the Hollywood screenwriter because, like it or not, it's the idea that sells the story.

****

You go to the video store and sitting in the doorway is 200 DVDs. The clerk informs you that you must watch all 200 DVDs (or Blue Rays) before making your selection. Is the clerk crazy? Instead you opt to read the back covers and make your decision. After all, you knew what type of movie you wanted before you arrived at the video store.

So, you scan through the back covers and quickly eliminate 90% of the pile. Of the remaining 10% you might select 1 or 2 to rent for the weekend.

This seems like a silly scenario. Why would you go through such a fuss when you knew what you were looking for before you even walked in the door?

This is the dilemma a producer faces. Screenwriters want them to read the entire script, but producers are overwhelmed with requests from various sources to read material. So, instead of reading all 200 scripts they ask for a one-sheet and read this instead. Similar to your trip to the video store, the producer already knows what he's looking for, so why should he read all those scripts? Instead, he'll read the 200 or so one-sheets, quickly eliminate 90% and then out of the remaining 10% will request 1-3 scripts to read.

This may seem unfair to the screenwriter, but it's just part of the business.

This is why the Idea is so Important

Think about this a moment. When you're in the video store scanning the backs of DVDs, don't you know immediately if you want to watch a film or not? You're making a split-second decision based solely on the concept. This is exactly what the producer does prior to requesting a script.

The bottom line is …

1

THE IDEA MUST SELL THE STORY

By Hollywood definition, a commercial idea can be stated in one-line and is an idea whose concept alone will draw a large audience - - this is long before a big star becomes attached.

But how does a screenwriter know right up front if an idea is commercially viable?

#1 The screenwriter must be passionate about the idea or the story will fall flat. Passion shows in material - - only use ideas you are passionate about. Passion is defined as a story that keeps you up late and gets you up early to work on it. You simply can't let it go!

#2 Don't wait until you complete a script or it becomes a movie to see if people like it or not.

Most of us have a group of friends, relatives or co-workers we discuss films with. By the way, during these conversations I don't tell them it's just an idea. I simply hit them with it, usually when we're talking about recent movies we've seen. I once had a friend call me back wanting to know the title of the film I told him about. Well, it isn't a film - - yet! My friends are in habit of asking me, "Is that something you're working on or can we go see it today?" If you tell them up front it's your idea they'll like it automatically (friends don't want to hurt your feelings), so hit them with the idea and watch for their initial reaction.

Note: Don't try out your ideas on Hollywood people. You can't copyright an idea, so keep the Hollywood people out of the loop until you've written the final product.

#3 The idea can be filmed! We've all heard the phrase, "Film's a visual medium."

Yet I'm amazed how many don't understand what this means. It means you can't film hopes, dreams, fears, etc. UNLESS you externalize them. This means you find a way to show them visually. This sounds obvious, but time and again I read scripts where everything is done internally. If you want to write about hopes, dreams and fears from an internal perspective, write a novel.

2

writers needed who recognize the need for commercial material.

What if the idea isn't a big box office draw? Can it still get made? 99% of all screenwriters I work with see their material as making it to the big screen. Yet a majority of what I read is more suitable for the cable network, straight-to-video or as an independent film. There's nothing wrong with these markets. The problem is the screenwriter's ability to determine if their idea is strong enough for the box office. How do you know? Simple. If the idea ALONE will draw a large audience then it's big screen. If not, look to other markets.

#4 Stay away from ordinary ideas. I'm not a numbers person, but I'll give it a shot.

The figures are something like 40,000 screenplays a year registered with the WGA (East and West). Most scripts have been in circulation a few years, times the 40,000 by let's say 3 years = 120,000 scripts on the market at any given time. I've heard the actual number is closer to 250,000. That's a quarter-million scripts circulating per year in an industry that only makes a few hundred films a year!

If you want to know why it's hard to get anyone to read your script...well, out of those 250,000 scripts, less than 2% are market quality!

Are you still interested in doing an ordinary idea?

By market quality, I'm not just talking about the writer's ability to write well - - many are excellent writers. What I'm talking about are writers who ✳ recognize the need to provide commercial material, as opposed to yet another ordinary idea. An ordinary idea can be written so well that it'll make the most critical English teacher smile, but it won't matter in Hollywood if it's an ordinary story. Why? Well, isn't it obvious?

Apparently it is not obvious because I see ordinary ideas every single week!

Unless you know Tom Cruise, Jack Nicholson, Meryl Streep or the head of some big studio the likelihood of getting your ordinary script off the ground is **zero**! The most you can hope for is to use it as a writing sample.

If everything's been done and there's nothing original left, yet I've just told you to avoid the ordinary idea, then what's a screenwriter to do?

Take your ordinary idea and give it 'edge.' What is edge?

<u>Edge is an ordinary idea with a twist.</u>

3

Give a "fresh twist"

Wait a minute! You have a ghost story about a family who moves into a haunted house and all the ghoulish activity starts and somehow they resolve it by uncovering the mystery behind the house. Cliché! Been done before! Ordinary!

So, what do you do? Add a twist.

> The more a subject has been done
> the bigger the twist you'll need
> to make your idea commercially viable.

What if the family moves into the haunted house and the ghoulish stuff starts, only instead of discovering the mystery behind the house, they discover the ghosts aren't really ghosts, but aliens using the house as a base to kidnap humans. Okay, it sounds pretty cheesy, but I'm using this as an "extreme" example so you'll get the point.

> You have to give your ordinary idea a fresh twist!
> Try to make it something we have not seen before!

Original Ideas Versus Adding Originality

I can't tell you how many times a writer has told me their idea is original. Sorry, there are no original ideas. What's original about an idea is how it's executed.

"The Sixth Sense" is a perfect example. I've heard many screenwriters say this film was the most original film they've ever seen. Is it original? You mean there's never been a ghost story before "The Sixth Sense?" Of course there has been. This film is not original. What's original about it is the execution of the idea. Basically, it's just another ghost story with a heck of a twist! The twist makes it seem original because it adds something fresh to the old ghost story that we haven't seen before.

This is your goal as a screenwriter = to give us a fresh take on an old subject because, like it or not, everything has been done before!

A few more examples from actual films so you'll start to get the idea of how this works:

30 Days of Night
Ordinary Idea: Vampires terrorize a small town.
Commercial Twist: The small town is in Alaska where the sun won't rise for a month.

4

Murder at 1600
Ordinary Idea: A cop investigates a homicide.
Commercial Twist: The homicide took place in the White House.

Sphere
Ordinary Idea: A psychologist is sent to assist in the rescue/recovery of a downed aircraft.
Commercial Twist: The aircraft is a UFO.

Identity Thief
Ordinary Idea: A man tries to recover his stolen identity.
Commercial Twist: The thief has no identity of her own.

The Quick and The Dead
Ordinary Idea: A gun fighter faces off with an outlaw high-noon style.
Commercial Twist: The gun fighter is a lady.

Saw
Ordinary Idea: A serial killer taunts police.
Commercial Twist: The serial killer doesn't kill anyone. He gets the victims to kill themselves or others.

Memento
Ordinary Idea: A man investigates his wife's death.
Commercial Twist: The man has short-term memory loss.

While You Were Sleeping
Ordinary Idea: A girl falls for a guy who doesn't know she's alive.
Commercial Twist: She's mistaken for his fiancé while he's in a coma.

The Twist Must Apply to the Entire Plot

Whether or not you liked these films and whether or not they eventually became big box office success, originally their concepts were considered commercially viable and the films got made. This is because the screenwriter took an ordinary idea about a homicide, a monster, a killer, a downed aircraft, identity theft, a gunslinger or a romance, and gave it a twist! This twist wasn't just a big twist ending – these twists applied to the entire plot. A big twist ending isn't enough for a commercial sale. The twist must apply to the entire concept! The idea itself must have a twist!

I'm sure you can list many films that don't have any real twist, but I guarantee for a first sale you MUST have one! Unless of course you already have an extraordinary marketing network of A-list actors, directors, producers and agents at your disposal, but if you did you wouldn't need to read this material.

<u>A twist to the ordinary idea is the commercial edge
that'll help you make a first sale!</u>

How does the screenwriter know if this twist is big enough to make the idea commercial? By doing research of similar material that's already been done.

RESEARCH: Know the story – Know the market

You've come up with a commercial idea, but has it or something similar to it been done already? Don't assume it hasn't. Do your research. This will help prevent the following:

-Writing a script that's already been done.
-Writing a script when a similar story is already in production.
-Writing scenes that are too similar to scenes already done in similar films.

It will also help:

-Inspire you to write new, fresh material because you'll know what's been done, what to avoid and what it will take to add a fresh slant.
-It's also important to know how a similar film got made. If you're writing a vampire flick along the lines of "Twilight", then you might need to start with a best-selling book because that's how "Twilight" got made.
-If the similar film has big A-list stars in all the roles, then that's what you'll need to get it made! If the similar film was done by a studio, then you will probably need studio backing too.

Research Trends – Stay Ahead of the Game

-Also, research trends. Writers see a hot trend in the market, like adult animation and create their own concepts, but fail to take a few things into consideration: 1) these films went into development and production several years ago 2) the trend may be hot right now, but by the time your script gets made the trend will most like be long gone.
-The writer's goal should be to think ahead of the trend by at least 2+ years. You do this by researching trends. We all knew of the upcoming doomsday prophecies before the year 2000 and again in 2012. Plenty of writers capitalized on the upcoming trend. I believe there's a mega-comet threatening the earth in 2042. Do you have your comet story ready?

-We follow trends whether we realize it or not. But being a writer, we have to be familiar with upcoming trends so we can capitalize on them. Start by researching trends and looking for them everywhere you go.

Research Previously Made Films

Consider it a film marathon rather than work you have to do. How do you find these films? Do research on the Internet. Start with www.imdb.com the Movie Database. Look up similar material by genre, plots, etc. Another good location is www.netflix.com . "The hot new way to get videos in your home." They have hundreds of thousands of listings of films in every genre.

What if there are 500 films similar to yours? Am I implying you watch all 500! No. Watch the most popular ones and at least be familiar with the plots of the others. I'd even go so far as to choose a few offbeat ones that didn't do well at the box office. <u>Your goal is to get a feel for the overall market and what's already been done.</u>

Research What's in Production

The industry daily and weekly trade magazines like *The Hollywood Reporter* and the *Variety* both provide periodic listings of what's in production and include the following information: Film's title, studio/company, actor/actresses, and location(s) for filming. In conjunction with reading the daily trades (a must for Hollywood insiders) you should read as many movie magazines as possible, like Premier Magazine, Entertainment Weekly, etc.

Between these two sources you should be able to keep up with what's in production and know what'll be released months ahead of time. If you see a listing in the *Hollywood Reporter* and can't seem to find it in any of the magazines – occasionally the studios will go out of their way to keep a film under wraps – then go to www.imdb.com where a logline of the film in production can be found.

Why Do Research?

If you're not convinced you need to do all this, then here's a story for you...

I've had writers sent scripts in for review bragging about how no one has done a film about terrorists taking over the White House. Had the writers – yes, I said writers as in more than one – done their research and actually taken the time to know this business, they'd know that *Olympus Has Fallen* starring Gerard Butler and Morgan Freeman opened in the of Fall 2013! If you don't already know this story is about terrorists taking over the White

House and kidnapping the President, then I suggest you keep your day job. In this arena, a writer needs to stay ahead of the game if he wants to succeed. Besides, do writers really want to spend weeks, months and even years writing a story that's already in production?

What if you already have a completed screenplay and you're told by a production company, "We already have something like it in production." This means one of two things:

#1 They're politely telling you, "no thanks." It's very easy (see research references above) to see what they have in production.

#2 They really do have something similar in production.

Does this mean you're screwed? No. Remember the two Volcano movies? "Volcano" and "Dante's Peak." Remember the two asteroid movies? "Armageddon" and "Deep Impact." The studios love to compete, and it's possible your material could get picked as a competitor against something already in production. The odds are slim, especially if you're an aspiring screenwriter.

Also, you'd have to make a very quick sale in order for the purchasing company to get it into production fast enough to be in competition for the other company.

Another option is to wait and see if the movie is a hit. Hit movies tend to generate spin-off movies. After the success of "The Sixth Sense" lots of similar films (like "The Others" and "Dead End") hit theaters. Your script could potentially be one of those spin-offs. If, however, the movie flops, you're pretty much screwed!

Most likely, the script will end up being a writing sample. Next time, do your research right up front and avoid this possibility.

Know the Story

Audiences are very savvy. Until your script sells, the Hollywood reader is your audience and most of us are pretty savvy as well.

For example, if you present a script where the CIA hunts down a terrorist in the United States, we'll laugh you out of Hollywood because the CIA doesn't have jurisdiction within U.S. borders - - the FBI does!

Between the TV, the Internet, books and personal interviews there is no reason - - except laziness - - that the script shouldn't be factually accurate. If you don't have the time or means to do personal interviews – I find them to be most effective in developing stories and characters – then go to www.allexperts.com. I've consulted with Navy divers, cops, ambulance drivers, scientists, etc. on this site. Prepare your questions, be brief and professional.

If your character is 30 years old and you indicate her son died 20 years ago, was she 10 when she gave birth? This sounds silly, but I've seen worse.

<u>Scrutinize your own material like you would someone else's.</u>

If it's 1960 the teenage character shouldn't be carrying an iPod around unless the character is a time traveler. This type of researching should include every aspect of the story: dialogue, slang, plot, character attitudes, clothing, setting…everything.

If your idea is commercial and you've done the necessary research and are satisfied your idea has commercial potential then it's time to know…

WHAT NOT TO WRITE: TOUGH & EASY PLOT SELLS

A writer recently mentioned his script was getting good response from agents, but comments were made about how the agents felt like they'd read the same story 5-6 times in the past few months. The agents were correct because the subject matter of the writer's screenplay has been hitting the market lately in droves.

It's weird how people think alike, but it's true because they do. Maybe we're somehow psychologically linked and just don't know it. Maybe it's because we share the same media sources, which often becomes the source material for screenplays. Maybe it's because we share common life experiences. I don't know, but what I do know is that it's easy to spend a lot of time writing exactly the same type of screenplay as hundreds, if not thousands of other writers, with little chance of a successful sale because the market becomes saturated with the same types of stories.

It's tough to give advice in this area, but I'll try my best. First, don't follow current trends. If vampire movies are hot, don't rush out and decide you have a better vampire story. Why not? For several reasons: 1) by the time you finish your screenplay, the trend will probably be dead (no pun intended) 2) movies coming out in theaters today were probably filmed 2-3 years ago and

9

Hollywood already has the next hot trend in pre-production and will be ready to shoot it before you finish your vampire flick 3) a million other writers will be doing the same thing as you! The 'trend' only works in your favor if you have a completed screenplay the moment it becomes hot and your screenplay is so damn original that everyone who reads it goes 'WOW!' If not, you're screwed.

Don't write writer stories! Every writer has a story about a writer. Okay, go ahead and write the damn thing, but don't expect to sell it because all 2.5 million writers out there have one just like it! It's extremely rare to get this made. You'd have better odds at winning the lotto.

Every year, I get dozens upon dozens of similar types of stories. One year, I was inundated with religious snake stories (about folks who pray while holding poisonous snakes). Each writer thought they had an original story that was never before done; wrong! I have yet to see one of these get made. Next it was doomsday stories. I was literally getting several dozen per month! If I'm seeing dozens a month, imagine how many of these types of scripts are circulating around town? Why would a producer purchase a doomsday story today? He wouldn't. It's old news. Pandemic stories are also a dime a dozen lately – they're damn boring to watch on the big screen and only a handful have ever been made – steer clear. I think every writer has tried his hand at his own version of *The DaVinci Code* - I have yet to see a single one of these get made and if I have to read one more my head might explode! You are not Dan Brown, give it up! A recent spec script trend has been zombie apocalypse stories – I've read so many I want to turn into a zombie and eat the writers – just so I don't have to read another one!

If you're watching TV one night, surfing the Internet or reading the morning paper and you see an interesting story and you get an idea for a movie, do yourself a favor – walk outside and scream, "What am I, nuts?" Do not write it because I guarantee dozens of other writers (or more) saw the same TV, Internet or newspaper story and are writing the same thing right now!

How do you avoid these pitfalls? First, learn what's trending in the future. No, you don't have to become a psychic or a time traveler. There are companies and individuals that study and predict trends; keep watch of what they predict. If something catches your fancy, write about it. Just be sure to give it a twist. The stronger the twist, the less likely anyone else has the same idea.

Or, mix ideas! Take that morning newspaper article and open your index file, pick a story idea and combine the two. Take the trending-now vampire story and mix it with your alligator-hunter idea and bam you have a vampire alligator-hunter named Tom living in the Bayou....okay, maybe that's weird, but I think you get the idea.

Stop thinking of stories strictly based on the external conflict and start thinking of stories in terms of irony. Why? Because irony breeds originality. Here's a simple example: A man dead-set against marriage must get married in order to inherit $100 million. Take the media source idea you have and add irony – maybe, just maybe you'll come up with something no one else is writing.

For those of you living in small towns, take the media-derived source material, mix it with an idea from a small town story, then add irony and I'd bet money you'll have a winner. This formula has been used for hit movies like *City Slickers*, *Blair Witch* and even *Con Air*.

Finally, knowing the markets is probably the #1 thing you can do to avoid writing stories similar to thousands upon thousands of other stories. Know what's in pre-production in town, know current trends, know future trends, know what actors and production companies are seeking by reading Hollywood papers like *Variety* and *The Hollywood Reporter*.

Or if you have enough money to make the film yourself, forget everything I said and go for it! Another area a writer should consider before starting a feature-length screenplay is tough and easy sells. There is material that's rarely, if ever, purchased from aspiring screenwriters and is reserved solely for writers with a track record. They often include high budget scripts, period pieces, dramas, etc. Let's take a look at...

Tough Sells...

- **Period Pieces**
  The reason this is a tough sale is because everything must be changed: the clothes, the vehicles, the lingo, the dishes, hairstyles - everything! It's a huge undertaking. Secondly, period pieces rarely attract large audiences - even ones that have won Academy Awards aren't necessarily big box office draws.
  These factors make a period piece a tough first sale.

- **High-Budget Scripts**
  Lots of special effects, big stunts, explosions, exotic locations, bad weather and scenes filmed on the water. These are a few items considered high-budget.
  Does this mean you have to write a low-budget film to get first-sale consideration? No, this is a big misconception of aspiring

11

screenwriters. You can actually keep all the elements listed about by cleverly toning them down to fit a medium-budget.

How? Say you have an explosion scene. Instead of showing the whole thing, let us hear it then see a few remnants of flame and that's it! You still have the explosion but toned down from high-budget to medium-budget geared towards a first sale. This is how a writer takes his art and commercializes it!

Won't this take away from the big action elements and visualization? It really depends on how you handle it, but remember if you've integrated strong character stuff into the story the explosion won't make or break it either way because the audience will be involved in the whole story, not just the action.

- **Dramas**
  Many aspiring screenwriters are unaware that the majority of dramas written for the big screen are written exclusively by A-list writers. Does this mean you shouldn't write dramas? It means you'll really need to have a strong plot/character conflict to make it work as a first sale, but don't be surprised if you receive few, if any, requests for a read.

- **Character-Driven Scripts**
  Too much character study and not enough plot = a tough first sale. Try to keep the ratio 60 % character-driven, 40% plot-driven. If you have a character-driven script, read the section *Commercialize a Character Driven Script* for ways to make it sellable.

- **Plot-Driven Script**
  Too much plot and not enough character stuff = a tough first sale. Try to keep the ratio 60% plot-driven, 40% character-driven. If you have a plot-driven script, read the section *Commercialize a Plot Driven Script* for ways to make it sellable.

Easier Sells...

- **Comedies**
  Comedies have a track record of doing well at the box office because people like to laugh.

12

- **Thrillers**

  Thrillers usually ask the question, "Who did it and why?" This presents a mystery and people love a good mystery almost as much as they love to laugh.

- **Horrors**

  Everyone loves a scary movie! More movies have been made in the horror genre than any other genre, ever!

- **Low to Medium-Budget Scripts**

  These are far more attractive as a first sale because the production costs are less, which equals less risk the studio has to take on a first-time writer.

- **True Stories or Stories inspired by Real Events**

  The influx of reality TV has made true stories and stories inspired by real events a hot commodity. But be careful because a true-life drama will still be difficult to sell.

- **Book Adaptations**

  Assuming you own the rights to a successful book or have cut a deal with the author, this is a good route for a first sale.

Are there exceptions to what's written above? Of course, but they're few and far between. Scripts from first-time writers that have broken this mold have done so for a variety of reasons the screenwriter should be aware of before making a comparison with their own material. For example, if a script was a novel first or required a big-name star to get made, then this is the probable route the screenwriter will have to take in order to get their material to the big screen. Don't assume because a certain kind of movie has been made that your script has a market. This isn't true for first-time writers. Studios and production companies won't take big risks on a writer without a track record. This means the first-time writer is more likely to sell to smaller markets and these sales are usually from the easier-to-sell category noted above.

If, however, you haven't written the novel version of your material and you live in Ohio with no Hollywood contacts, then your material will need drastic commercialization to hit the Hollywood mark.

How to Break the Mold on Your Own

You're still not buying this commercialization stuff? Can you still break in without a commercial script? Sure. There are plenty of other markets available. Let's review a few…

- **B-Movies**
  We've all seen these. We don't recognize any of the actors. The dialogue sucks and the plot, well...you get the point.

- **Straight-To-Video**
  This is a widely overlooked market that many screenwriters don't consider, yet it can be very lucrative for those who write for it. Your stuff is never going to be seen on the big screen, but there are plenty of straight-to-video classics out there. The American Film Market deals with many of them. Check them out at www.afma.com.

- **Slasher Films**
  These are horror films, but ones done with lots of blood and a staggering body count. There's no real plot and a character arc is non-existent because the main character is bound to get hacked up in the process. Most of these are straight-to-video, but many have become cult classics.

- **Independent Films**
  This is the perfect route for those who are intimidated by the entire commercialization process. It's for those who hate the Hollywood stand-on-your-head routine and prefer to express themselves independent of any "rules" they believe will hinder their creative voice. Most fail as commercial products, but some have made the grade and given us remarkable insight into what's possible beyond the commercial realm.

The screenwriter will have to decide what route is best, but the majority of screenwriters I've worked with want to see their stuff up on the big screen and nothing else will do. Before getting started it's imperative the writer knows one thing; the genre.

WRITE GENRE SPECIFIC

More and more producers are seeking genre-specific screenplays, like a Horror with no comedic relief or perhaps an action or Action/Adventure that doesn't try to be a Suspense Thriller.

Roughly seven out of ten scripts submitted to Extreme Screenwriting for coverage list the wrong genre! I start out thinking I'm reading a Suspense Thriller and I realize it's a Crime Drama or the screenwriter indicated the genre is RomCom, but the script reads like a straightforward Comedy. This makes me wonder how the screenwriter could have written an entire script without knowing the genre! A producer will wonder this too and wonder if the writer truly understands the art of screenwriting.

Without fully understanding how a specific genre works, the screenwriter greatly reduces the chance of a sale! Why? Because genres have rules! If a RomCom doesn't have a big kiss scene near the end, then why would a producer buy it? If a Suspense Thriller doesn't establish red herrings, then how can a producer sell it to an audience who love a good mystery and expect to be misled?

What is the difference between a RomCom and a Comedy? How does a Suspense Thriller differ from a Crime Drama or a Mystery? When is a story a Supernatural Thriller and when is it a Horror? When is an Action/Adventure really just an Action flick? When does a story become a Satire?

Here are a few recognizable patterns to help a writer discern which genre a story falls under:

SUSPENSE THRILLER
Usually involves a crime-related mystery with a "Who did and why?" question attached. To sell, this genre should be written with a double twist ending and the audience must be shocked by the identity of the killer because they've been misled by red herrings.

CRIME DRAMA
Unlike the Suspense Thriller, we know who did it and we know why. We're just waiting for the good guys to figure it out and catch the bad guys.

MYSTERY
Unlike the Suspense Thriller or Crime Drama, Mystery doesn't usually involve a crime component, but does pose a question that drives the story and creates suspense by providing the audience with a mystery to solve.

SUPERNATURAL THRILLER
It's a horror with a paranormal mystery attached.

HORROR
No real mystery. We know the perpetrator is a vampire, werewolf, witch, demon, etc. To sell this genre, the threat should remain in the end.

ROMCOM

Story focuses on whether two love interests will get together against all odds. To sell, this genre requires specific rules be met, like a big kiss scene at the end.

COMEDY

Story doesn't center around a romance, but it does have punch-lines, misinterpretation and fun.

ACTION/ADVENTURE

Story takes us to a place we've only dreamed of going before. It travels to the exotic and the unknown.

ACTION

It doesn't travel like the Action/Adventure, but holds us spellbound with non-stop shoot 'em up, bang-bang moments!

SATIRE

Pokes fun at a person, place, or thing by blowing it out of proportion. To sell, Satires tend to be stories surrounding social or political issues.

To learn how to write for these specific genres, see the HOW TO CHAPTER. I'd also like to take a moment to review the two genres I've found that cause the most confusion.

Thriller vs. Horror

I've already noted the general differences above, but let's take a more in-depth look because this is an area I see the most genre confusion from aspiring screenwriters.

Just saying your story is a thriller isn't enough because there are many different types of thrillers; suspense thriller, sci-fi thriller, supernatural thriller, political thriller, crime thriller etc. Sometimes the story isn't a thriller at all, but a horror.

First, determine if the story is a thriller. A thriller tends to have a mystery component. It often asks the question, "Who did it and why?" A horror can have a mystery component, but often deals with a substantial amount of gore and/or blood, which then qualifies the story as a horror. The horror also has other qualifying rules (see below for details).

16

Let's take a look at different types of thrillers and horror.

SUPERNATURAL THRILLER
Limited gore/blood with a story that deals with a mystery and a supernatural component. For example, is there a ghost in the house? The answer is yes and it's come to even the score with the current tenants. The threat doesn't remain in the end, it's conquered.

SUSPENSE THRILLER
No supernatural components whatsoever. Often used for murder mysteries, the suspense thriller keeps the killer's identity secret until the last possible moment. It asks the question, "Who did it and why?" The genre requires a double or even triple twist ending to sell. The twist usually involves the use of red herrings that steer the audience away from the real killer's identity until the last possible moment. We learn the killer's identity, but we're wrong and the real killer is finally revealed.

CRIME THRILLER
No supernatural components whatsoever. In this genre, we know who the killer is and we're waiting for the hero to figure it out and catch the bad guy. The key to selling this genre is to have the killer (or culprit) always be a step ahead of the hero. The hero will have to change (arc) in order to finally outwit the bad guy. This story has a mystery to it. No mystery and it moves from being a Crime Thriller to a Crime Drama.

SCI-FI THRILLER
This thriller takes place in outer space, another world, another dimension, via time travel, etc. It can have any of the components of the other genres, but with the distinct difference of the science fiction angle. A murder mystery aboard a space station isn't a suspense thriller, it's a sci-fi thriller.

POLITICAL THRILLER
Politics or politicians mixed up in a conspiracy involving the unraveling of some sort of mystery. This also includes a politician trying to keep a scandal from the public. There are no supernatural, science fiction, blood or gore involved. However, it can involve a murder. The addition of the political angle shifts the genre from suspense thriller or crime thriller to a political thriller.

HORROR
Gore, blood, a killer on the loose or even a flesh-eating monster. Sometimes there's a mystery, sometimes there's no mystery. Some distinguishing features beyond blood and gore are the following; loss of free will (character trapped or can't escape a killer), unstoppable bad guy (think Jason in Friday

the 13th), the hero might die (only genre where it's okay to kill the hero). The threat remains in the end. Even if the hero wins, the evil is still out there (mandatory for this genre).

MIXED GENRES
It's okay to mix the genres, like a supernatural horror. A word or warning; today's producers have to sell to a genre-specific audience. This means they prefer straightforward genres with little or no mixing of the genres. If it's a supernatural thriller, then it doesn't have a horror ending. If it's a suspense thriller, the killer doesn't end up being a vampire. A genre-specific screenplay is far more likely to sell than one with mixed genres or a screenplay where the writer doesn't clearly understand the genre.

Learn the genres, learn the rules of the specific genres and write a straightforward, easy-to-sell story.

PICK A TITLE

The writer has come up with a commercial idea and done the research. The writer's convinced the story is ordinary with a twist that will sell. The writer knows what not to write and has chosen the correct genre. Now it's time to assign the story idea a title. This will help bring it into focus so the writer can begin the process of preparing the story's concepts, characters, dialogue and scenes to combine into a sellable screenplay.

Don't Use Novel-Like Titles

Titles like "One Flew Over the Cuckoos Nest" only make sense after material is read. This is okay for a novel, but things like the title, logline and synopsis are why producers read a script in the first place. Therefore, the title should paint a clear, visual picture of the story and define its genre. I highly recommend using 1-3 word titles. Why? It's simple. It's because it has to fit on a movie poster, so shorter is better.

Use a Working Title

This is a sappy title you'll change later. It's just a place holder until the script is completed. What if the script's done and the writer still can't come up with a good title? I recommend the writer scan the dialogue. The title is usually somewhere in the dialogue waiting to be used. Also, if the chosen title doesn't appear in the dialogue, it should. And it should preferably be spoken by the hero.

Use Song Titles

Writing a story about a wicked woman, but can't come up with a title? How 'bout the song "Witchy Woman"? Using a song title as the script's title can lock in a potential sound track, which could make the script more valuable. Be careful to pick a song that fits the genre.

Think Genre to Pick the Title

If the script's a horror, then brainstorm scary titles. If it's a RomCom, brainstorm romantic, love titles. Ironically, titles like "The Ring" could be used for a horror or a RomCom. In this case, it's the poster that reveals the genre, but for selling purposes the writer needs a title that reveals the genre. Use the technique mentioned above. But instead of the dialogue, scan the description and pull out words that individually or combined could be used to create a genre-specific title.

Think Movie Poster

What images do you imagine would be on a movie poster for your story? Write each imagine on a single line; Man, Woman, Bloody Axe, Woods, Cabin. This title might be "Axe Cabin" or "Bloody Woods".

Think Irony

Irony sells, so using irony in the title is a great way to attract a producer to the story. Murder stories are a dime a dozen, but writers created irony when they made the crime scene the White House. The irony is showcased in the title "Murder at 1600". Note: This title also reveals the genre and poster.

Think Moving Pictures

Does the title present a visual of the story? That's why I mentioned staying away from titles that sound like novels because they rarely paint a visual picture. Instead of "A Lovely Day Falls Apart" (novel title) - the writer might come up with a title like "Fatal Attraction".

The Hero's Name as Title

We all know "Batman", "Bond", "Mad Max" and "Rambo". The catch to using a hero's title or nickname is to make it cool. A title like "Henry" doesn't say much and will likely be changed by a producer. Note: Producers change movie titles as often as they change their socks, so I wouldn't advise a writer to ever become married to any given title. Extreme Screenwriting client Don Fiebiger's "Border Run" was initially titled "La Linea". The producer later changed the title to "The Mule" and this was later changed to "Border Run". The final title was most likely changed by the distributor because a distributor knows they need a catchy title that quickly draws in an audience.

Antagonist's Name as Title

A title like "Kill Bill" showcases the antagonist. This can be tricky to do because the writer risks upstaging the lead. It'll take a clever 1-2 word title that hits a homerun in the genre department. Also, this usually only works if the antagonist-in-the-title profoundly reveals the hero's goal. In this case, to kill bill!

Use a Catch Phrase

We all hear catchy phrases in our daily lives. Perhaps one of them is appropriate for your story. A spec script sell in town has the title "Rock, Paper, Scissors". We've all heard of this, right? I'm waiting to see the "Let's Roll" movie title – I bet it's coming to a theater near you soon.

Check IMDB

Once the writer selects a title, go to www.imdb.com. This is the Internet Movie Database. Type in the title and see if it comes up. If it does I'd recommend the writer pick another title. Why? Because a producer can't use the title if it's already in the database and he'll be forced to change it. There is an exception: if the title listed in the database is for TV, a short film, documentary or another medium different than the writer's work, like a screenplay (feature film), than it can be used. If the writer isn't sure, then select another title.

The writer has a title. Now it's time to do something amateurs avoid, but pros know is a must:

OUTLINE: Avoid Page-One Rewrites

I know screenwriters who've been working on the same script for 3 or more years. I also know screenwriters who've re-written the same script so many times it makes my head spin. Some of them claim to outline, while others won't hear of it. They'd rather write from inspiration. Then there are the screenwriters who write a script off the top of their heads without giving it a second thought. All I can say is…

...I've never met a professional screenwriter who doesn't outline in one form or another. How you decide to outline is up to you, but thoroughly outlining can save a tremendous amount of time and frustration; and if you really involve yourself in it, it can lead to the best inspiration and creativity you'll ever experience.

Most importantly, you'll be able to tell if your commercially developed idea works as a motion picture. Wouldn't you rather learn this from an outline as opposed to waiting until you reach page 90? Wouldn't you rather identify that something doesn't work before you start writing than when you reach page 72? If you have a drawer full of partially done scripts, most likely it's because you didn't take the time to thoroughly outline. Instead, you allowed inspiration to take over and lead you down the wrong path. Learn to use inspiration wisely and don't let it waste any more of your valuable time.

Outlining can help you spot
gaps and commercial deficiencies
in your material before you put one word to the page.

If you eliminate the gaps right up front and address the commercial issues, aren't you freeing yourself to be as creative once you begin to write? Yes, you are because you no longer have to be concerned about these issues - - you've already taken care of them!
For the sake of this subject, I'm going to use the way I outline as the example. I am, however, in no way advocating that you do it the way I do. I'm only advocating that you OUTLINE!

This is really tough for some because the idea is hot in their minds and they're anxious to get those scenes or dialogue on paper. Okay, here's what you do... get it out of your system. Write that hot scene or piece of dialogue, but write it in Microsoft Word before you commit it to Final Draft or some other screenwriting program. Then set it aside and get to that outline!

I outline in chronological order on index cards beginning with ACT I until I reach FADE OUT. I write every single scene's primary slug indicator....

EXT. HOUSE – DAY

...then I write in 1 or 2 lines what happens in this scene. Sometimes I write a relevant piece of dialogue.

EXT. HOUSE – DAY
-Introduce John's character.

-John tells Mac – "I'm here to make the drop."

Each scene, no matter how long, has its own index card. I usually end up with about 60 + index cards. By doing it in this simple, straightforward step-outline approach, I can instantly see where there are gaps in the material. I can also easily recognize scenes that don't work and even shuffle scenes, if necessary.

Once I have the main scenes on index cards, I type them up in Microsoft Word. I usually end up with around 10 to 15 pages of outlined scenes. I use RED LETTERS to indicate any remaining gaps or areas of concern.

This is still too general to tell if the story works on a commercial level or not, but it's a start. During the course of the remaining chapters we'll be reviewing what it takes to commercialize a script, but here's a list of items you'll be learning to incorporate to assure a script is commercial:

- An external conflict is presented in Act I
- An internal conflict is presented in Act I
- First Ten Pages hooks the reader
- Protagonist has been given a grand entrance
- Story's external event is the most important moment in protagonist's life, not just another day
- The external event forces the character to change
- Protagonist has huge emotional stakes
- Dialogue written to attract A-List actors
- Locations have been commercialized
- Reversals in majority of scenes, not just the big ones
- Every scene contains subtext; visual or dialogue
- Emotional stakes in every scene
- Scene transitions between majority of scenes

How in-depth the outline is up to you, but the more detailed it is the less time you'll spend rewriting later. Feel free to add as much details to each scene and as much dialogue as you like. I know screenwriters who have 1/3 of every scene outlined before they begin. While others keep expanding the outline until it becomes the screenplay.

A Word About the Critical Voice

The critical voice is what stops screenwriters and makes them question a scene, a piece of dialogue, etc. This can be stifling to the creative process, can hinder the best script and frankly gets in the way of completing a feature-length motion picture. This is another reason outlining is so important. Let your critical voice speak during the outlining phase – get it out of the way!

Once you begin to write the actual script refuse to allow the critical voice in and just write, write, write!

Questions Are the Answer

Outlining is the time to ask the tough questions - - NOT AFTER THE SCRIPT IS DONE. I can't tell you how many times I'll submit a review to an aspiring screenwriter with plenty of suggestions due to plots that don't work, etc., only to have the screenwriter ask me if a certain change will work. Their questions usually involve page-one rewrites and had they taken the time to ask these critical questions initially, they wouldn't have to deal with the frustration of having to rewrite a script that doesn't work. Remember, changing one aspect of a script will change everything.

The human brain is an amazing computer. If you ask it a question it will try its hardest to come up with the answer. Have you ever had someone ask you what someone's name is and you couldn't remember? You ask and ask yourself, "What was his name?" Then later when you're not even thinking about it anymore you suddenly remember the person's name. That's because your brain never stopped working on the question you presented.

Ask questions. Even if you don't have an immediate answer you'll be surprised when later you suddenly realize how to make a plot element work, or how to nail down a scene or beef up the dialogue. Let the creative portion of your brain provide the answers for you! Don't feel like you have to get the script done now because the concept is too hot to wait. If it's that hot, it'll sell no matter when you get it done. The goal is to get it done right the first time by asking the important questions BEFORE the writing process begins.

Avoid Problems With the 3-Act Structure

Besides obvious plot holes, character problems, etc., I can easily tell a screenwriter didn't bother to outline from the handling of the 3-Act Structure. I think it's silly to assign certain pages to specific plot points, like plot point I must fall on page 30 and plot point II must fall on page 90.

However, when Act I is 15 pages long or Act II is only 40 pages long or Act III is 5 pages long (I've seen an Act III as short as 2-pages long) then there's bound to be a plot problem that could have easily been avoided by outlining.

Here's what short Acts mean to the Hollywood reader and a producer:

SHORT ACT I
Limited setups have been provided which could easily result in plot points or other relevant information being confusing, misunderstood or unclear later in the story.

SHORT ACT II
Too few obstacles were presented for the protagonist to face. The screenwriter's playing "Mr. Nice Guy" and isn't presenting big enough obstacles with huge emotional stakes for the hero, or worse, the screenwriter hasn't presented a large enough conflict for the big screen.

SHORT ACT III
The external conflict wasn't important enough for the protagonist to have to struggle to defeat it in the end or the protagonist defeats the external conflict in Act II leaving a 2-Act screenplay with one wrap-up scene = a plot that fails on a commercial level. The hero needs a bigger, more important external conflict!

<u>Outlining will immediately identify any structural problems before the writing begins.</u>

FINAL WORD ON OUTLINING

Don't ignore the power of this simple tool, especially if you...

- Have more than one (1) incomplete screenplay
- Have been told the story has plot holes
- Have been told the story is confusing
- Have been told the plot isn't believable
- Have been told the plot requires a better setup or payoff

If any of these apply to you, then SLOW DOWN and take the time to outline. You won't regret it!

<u>Here are just a few of the benefits of outlining:</u>

- Plug up plot holes
- Act I, Act II and Act III are balanced. No more Acts that are too long or too short
- Pacing can be controlled and even manipulated to create suspense
- Major rewrites become a thing of the past
- Plot is cohesive

- Setup and payoffs are nailed down to perfection
- Frees the screenwriter from the critical voice during the writing phase
- The screenwriter will know if a story doesn't work before page 1 rather than on page 90
- A completed screenplay that will beat the competition who didn't bother to outline

The writer has a viable outline that reveals a cohesive plot, strong characters, film-worthy dialogue and unique scenes. Is it time to write? Not yet. It's now time to…

CREATE A ONE-SHEET: Don't Start Without It

I can't tell you how many times a screenwriter has e-mailed me indicating a producer wants to see a one-sheet and why should they bother with this when they have a completed screenplay.

Why are you Marketing a Screenplay Without a One-Sheet?

It's standard practice in the industry for a producer to request a one-sheet before they'll ask for the read. Go back to the first section under "The Idea" and read the "video store" example I give of how producers decide upon material and you'll understand why this is a vital marketing tool YOU MUST HAVE!

I'm truly amazed at how many aspiring screenwriters will market a script without a one-sheet. Being prepared is part of being professional! Treat screenwriting like any job and be prepared. If you're truly interested in selling a screenplay, then having a completed one-sheet is vital.

I'm going to take this to the Extreme Screenwriting level now by telling you that **you should create a one-sheet BEFORE you write the screenplay.** Why? For several reasons:

- In addition to the outline, it can really help you focus on what works commercially and what doesn't work.

- If you can't sum up the story's title, genre, logline and synopsis before you begin, then how can you write the entire script? Something must be missing and it's better to find out what it is now.

- Writing the one-sheet first helps free up your creativity because you've removed the need to constantly question if something works

25

commercially or not - you already know it does. If you want your "art" to shine through, then getting the commercial stuff out of the way right up front will give you all the room you need to be an artist without compromising the commercial viability of the material.

- Most importantly, you won't be up until midnight the night before you have to submit the one-sheet to a producer trying to come up with something that sounds good. Writing something under this kind of pressure will only read like crap!

By having a one-sheet from the get-go you are fully prepared to write the best script ever and you'll be fully prepared at a later date to go to market with confidence....

...or do you want to be in a room with a producer when he says, 'Let me see the one-sheet'. Most producers will ask for this first, so the writer should write it first!

Don't Wait Until the Script's Written

99% of aspiring writers will stop right here and say, "I'd prefer to wait until I finish the script before writing the synopsis". Well, I'm here to tell you this is one reason why you're still an 'aspiring writer' instead of a pro because the pros know that by the time you get done writing the script, you'll be too attached to the details. These 'details' will bog down the one-sheet and result in a writer telling the story instead of selling the story.

The one-sheet's purpose isn't to tell the details. It's to get the producer to ask for the read, so it has to be written similar to a sales pitch where the writer sells the concept. This is accomplished far easier when the writer isn't attached to the story's details and that means BEFORE THE SCRIPT IS WRITTEN, not after.

Before the script's written, the writer still has the 'hot' market qualities of the material fresh in his mind. The writer knows what makes the story original with a twist. Understands the irony. Appreciates one cool aspect of the character. Knows what piece of dialogue rocks. Knows what scene reversals are most shocking, etc. This is the time to write the one-sheet!

What is a One-Sheet?

A one-sheet consists of the writer's contact information, script's title, genre, logline, synopsis and a closing request for the read. It look like this:

GENRE
Horror

LOGLINE:
(1 line only – original concepts with a twist that are truly marketable can be summed up in one line)

SYNOPSIS
(Sell the story, don't tell the story. Keep to a few brief paragraphs – like the back of the old DVD or even VHS covers – provide just enough information to entice a producer to ask for the read).

If you'd like to read "A Great Screenplay", please contact Barb Doyon.

****

The toughest parts will be the logline and synopsis. Here are some shortcuts to help the writer create loglines and synopses that sell the story:

Logline Should Suit the Genre

I've read some fantastic scripts only to read the logline and it sucks! The reason is the writer failed to deliver the genre in the logline. The writer seemed too busy with plot and character; both of which are important, but if the genre isn't clear it's unlikely a producer will ask for the read. Why? Because producers sell material to an audience based on genre.

Think about it. Do you have a friend who doesn't like horrors or RomComs? Sure you do. Audiences tend to lean toward a favorite genre. Producers know this. It means genre is their #1 selling tool. If a logline doesn't reveal the genre, why would they waste their time reading the script? By the way, most producers will assume if the logline doesn't reveal the genre that it's likely the entire script has genre issues.

I'm here to help you avoid this problem. It's simple. If you've written a comedy, then the logline should make us laugh. If it's a horror, the logline should make us cringe. If it's a drama, it should create introspection. Get the picture?

But how? First, be sure the logline externalizes the story. Don't write:

Joe must overcome his fears to live the life of his dreams.

-This doesn't reveal the genre. It doesn't even tell a producer what the story is about. The reason is because the logline doesn't reveal the information externally, it's about internals. Film's a visual medium! Externalizing the logline can help establish genre.

Here's an example:

Joe must overcome his fear of drowning in order to defeat a lake monster and go for his dream of becoming a gold medal winner.

-This logline paints a clearer picture. It sets the story, the tone, mood and atmosphere and it establishes the genre.

Do a test: Pitch your logline to someone who doesn't know anything about your story and has never read the script. DO NOT tell them anything but the logline. Ask if they can guess the genre. If 9 out 10 can't guess it, go back and revise the logline.

If you're still having difficulty with the logline, then start with taglines. Using key phrases that pertain to the story can help the writer come up with a good logline.

Possible tagline for the lake monster story:

A lone swimmer.
A hungry lake monster.
An unclaimed gold medal.

-Work through key phrases taken directly from the story or outline to help write a strong logline that reveals the genre.

Sell the Story – Don't Tell the Story

The synopsis is the second hardest part of writing the one-sheet. It's usually the reason the writer avoids the one-sheet until after the script's written. As mentioned above, this is a fatal error made only by amateurs!

I bet that somewhere in your house, probably the basement, are old VHS cases. Go find them. Or look at the backs of DVDs. Notice how they reveal just enough information to intrigue you to want to rent, buy or watch the movie. They aren't trying to tell you the story. They're trying to sell you the story. The writer needs to do the same thing with the synopsis in a one-sheet. It's a sales tool, not a story tool.

When you write the one-sheet, you're really writing a sales pitch. You're a salesman! Act like you've been hired to write the back cover of your own DVD.

Still struggling with this? Then do an exercise. Repetition is the mother of knowledge. Take movies in your home that you've seen – DO NOT READ THE BACK COVER and write what you think it says on the back cover. You've seen the movie, so give it your best shot. Now turn the DVD or VHS over and read what the distributor wrote on the back. How do the two compare? Is your synopsis too detailed? Does it fail to sell the story? Note how they sold the story. Do this enough times and you'll learn how to write killer synopses that will land reads time after time.

What a One-Sheet Doesn't Include

Do not include bio information on the one-sheet. Do not list contest wins or placements. Do not tell the producer the script is the next summer blockbuster. This isn't the time to sell yourself or make boisterous claims of blockbuster success. Nobody knows what the next big hit is, nobody! The one-sheet is about getting a read. It's not about bragging how you have a BA in Creative Writing. The writer's information comes later.

The one-sheet is the most valuable tool in a screenwriter's arsenal. Take copies with you everywhere you go. Hand them out to anyone who wants to read it. Fax copies to production companies with fax #'s. Email to producers, agents, directors or actors. I personally believe it's a far more effective tool than a query. Many writers no longer bother with a general query and just market with a one-sheet. Be consistent, persistent and always have the one-sheet ready to hand out.

There are other tools a writer can use in his arsenal; phone pitches, treatments, budgets, posters, etc., but nothing is as effective as the one-sheet at getting a producer to ask for the read.

Write the one-sheet first! Don't worry if it isn't perfect. After you write the screenplay, you can always go back and tweak it. You'll be amazed how easy it'll be then.

Need a One-Sheet Written for You?

Extreme Screenwriting writes one-sheet for writers. I'd love to tell you that no one has ever used this service when in fact I've written hundreds of one-sheets for aspiring screenwriters. How many have I written for my pro screenwriting clients (those already making a substantial living writing)? Zero!

I'd prefer you learn to write your own rather than waiting until a producer, agent, director or actor asks for one, then panicking and asking me to write a rush one for you! I can certainly do this and charge for the service, but if you really want to be a pro I'd advise the writer to learn how to write a one-sheet. I've shown you how, now go do it!

CHAPTER TWO – PLOT/EXECUTION

This chapter starts off by teaching an aspiring screenwriter how to commercialize a plot-driven or a character-driven script for a sale; primarily a first sale. The rules for an aspiring screenwriter are different from the rules for an established writer. A movie can hit big at the box office and the aspiring screenwriter can say, "I can write a story like that' and he probably can, but it's unlikely to sell. On the other hand, the established writer with a track record can say the same thing and actually sell the script. Aspiring screenwriters need to understand that until they have a successful track record of sales and/or film credits, they have to write material that provides less risk for producers and/or studios. This will vastly increase the potential for a sale. After the initial sale, the writer will suddenly find doors opening that were previously closed.

The best way to help aspiring screenwriters understand what they'll need to do to break into the fiercely competitive business of screenwriting is to take two highly successful films and show the writer why they could never sell either film as a spec script and what they'd need to do to sell this type of material as an aspiring screenwriter. I've chosen two older, but highly successful films that hopefully everyone has seen. For the plot-driven script, I've chosen the film *Under Siege II: Dark Territory* from the successful *Under Siege* trilogy. For the character-driven script, I've chosen the film *About Schmidt* starring the legendary film icon Jack Nicholson. If you haven't seen these films, I'd recommend doing so before reading these two very important sections of the material.

COMMERCIALIZE A PLOT- DRIVEN SCRIPT

First off, what is a plot-driven script and why is it a hard first sale? A plot-driven script is what's known as a "popcorn movie." It's simply here to entertain us. It doesn't contain some greater meaning and more often than not, it has no real character arc or a very limited arc, which is why it's a tough sale as a spec from an aspiring screenwriter.

Under Siege 2: Dark Territory is the example I'll use for a plot-driven script. This film is the sequel to the successful film *Under Siege* starring Steven Seagal. The story's main character, Casey Ryback, is a former Navy Seal Commander. In the story, he and his niece board a train that's taken over by terrorists and Casey's the only one who can stop them.

31

<u>Let's look at some of the plot-driven elements in this film and discuss why they don't work as a first sale by reviewing how this plot-driven story would be perceived on the spec market:</u>

1) Casey, a former Navy Seal Commander and counter-terrorism expert, just happens to be on a train taken over by terrorists.
-This would be considered too convenient to the plot.

2) The terrorists just happen to be former Navy Seals who Casey trained = Casey knows their tactics and they know how good he is.
-This would be considered too convenient and coincidental to the plot.

3) The terrorists are experts who check every detail – they leave nothing to chance – yet they missed that their former commander is on board.
-Again, a convenient and unbelievable plot element.

4) It's *Die Hard* on a train.
-The comparison could be enough to get it knocked off the market as a cheap rip-off of "Die Hard." After all, "Die Hard" has a good emotional core and this story doesn't. This factor could work for or against a spec script.

5) Casey Ryback is a larger-than-life character, meaning he can get shot at a hundred times and never get hit. Okay, he gets a shoulder wound during the film, but I think you get the meaning.
-Larger-than-life characters are tough to sell because they have few flaws and seem infallible.

6) Casey Ryback has no internal conflict. This character has no real flaws. He's a perfect killing machine.
- A personal issue with his niece is presented, but it's hardly the kind of internal conflict you'd need to sell a spec script if you're an aspiring screenwriter.

7) Casey uses his Navy Seal tactics to take out the terrorists.
-No real setup is presented. We only hear about it in dialogue, and then we see him take on the bad guys. This is a sequel, so we are dealing with an established character. Yet, I've seen many scripts that go straight for the gusto with little or no setup to the character's abilities. These setups are a must.

It's obvious this film got made because of the success of the first *Under Siege*. Actually, I liked *Under Siege 2: Dark Territory* better than the first *Under Siege*. It was a fast-moving, techno action thriller. It presented lots of cool techno satellite stuff, crisp dialogue and interesting - even in a stereotypical way - characters, and if you blink you're bound to miss something. Frankly, it was a fun movie. It is a "popcorn movie."

The convenient plot devices, lack of setup for the protagonist's military ability, no internal conflict and no character arc are a few of the reasons a story like this, presented as a spec script from an aspiring writer, would be a hard first sale. Think of it from a Hollywood reader's perspective. One of the primary things they're looking for when they read a script is a character arc, but an all plot-driven story isn't going to deliver it = a pass.

Then why do I keep seeing similar plot-driven scripts on the spec market? Because screenwriters see these types of movies and think they can sell a similar plot-driven story...

When, in fact, they'd need a much more in-depth story – less popcorn, more character stuff – for a first sale.

Once a writer has broken in and has some successes under his belt he'll find it much easier to convince the studio to go for his "popcorn movie," but in the meantime he'll need to deliver something more in-depth.

A script can still be plot-driven, but it must rise above the "popcorn movie" level before it'll get serious consideration for a first sale.

What if you've already written a "popcorn movie?" Here are the choices:

1) Keep it! After you make a first sale it could suddenly draw attention and get made.
2) Add more character-stuff and create a better balance between plot/character and greatly enhance the potential for a sale.

Be aware that adding a better balance could greatly shift the dynamics of the plot-driven story and make it completely different from what you started out with. In other words, you could potentially be looking at a page-one rewrite. By commercializing FIRST you'll avoid this problem later.

If *Under Siege 2: Dark Territory* were written as a spec geared towards a first-sale what would be different about it? Almost everything.

First, a larger-than-life character is an extremely difficult first sale. Casey wouldwork better as a wanna-be Navy Seal. Maybe a guy who tried to make it as a Seal several times, but failed. The reason he failed would be linked to a HUGE INTERNAL FLAW. Maybe he lost a brother during a home

33

invasion robbery because he failed to take action (he acted cowardly). This character now has a courage issue. This creates a strong internal conflict.

This internal conflict is what has been holding him back all along. This would all be established in Act I. Along come the terrorists. Okay, we'll let our newly-flawed character board the train with his niece and keep the coincidence that he boards a train with terrorists intact. We can get away with it now on a spec level because we've established a flawed character and the reader will be anticipating that he'll end up in a do-or-die situation. Keep the family issues, but make them even more personal. The family blames this character for his brother's death as much as he blames himself.

I'd probably make the niece a nephew. The reason is coming up.

Instead of the terrorists discovering their former commander is aboard, they'd discover a wanna-be Navy Seal is aboard. Maybe one of the terrorists knows him from training camp. The terrorists consider him to be nothing more than a nuisance loose on the train.

Now you have an external conflict that forces the character to deal with his internal conflict. In other words, he must find the courage to act! He must become the Navy Seal he's failed to be so far in order to save the day. Since he didn't save his brother, I'd have him save the nephew. See the connection? This brings his character full-circle. This change should come about slowly. He wouldn't simply step up to the plate like the Casey Ryback we've seen in the "Under Siege" movies - he'd change gradually and his character arc would be intact.

This version would be a far more likely candidate for a first sale.

<u>Integrating internal characterization</u>
<u>to a plot-driven script makes</u>
<u>it more commercial!</u>

Example of a Commercial Plot-Driven Script

Let's take a brief look at a "popcorn movie" that would work on a spec level. That film is *Lake Placid* (the first one). In this story, a crocodile is on the loose in a lake in Maine. It's a monster movie. A female scientist played by Bridget Fonda goes to investigate, but wait a minute - notice how her character is introduced.

We meet her at her day job where she works as a scientist in a museum. This is her safe zone. She's even dating the boss. She comes off as timid and as someone who lets others walk all over her. She finds out her boss is having an affair with a co-worker, then they ship her off to the wilds of Maine. They want her out of the way and she's not a strong enough character to stand up to them.

The film opens with a teaser where an unknown monster kills a diver. Then the protagonist is given her grand entrance where we're introduced to her internal conflict. Then she's forced into an external situation that forces her to change.

By the end of the story, she's completely different. Her hair's wild around her shoulders, no longer tucked tight against the base of her neck. Heck, she wants to go for a beer and is no big hurry to return to her safe museum in the big city of New York. She's no longer timid and she's become a real risk-taker in life and in love.

Lake Placid is without a doubt a "popcorn movie" but it rises above the plot-driven ranks and provided a balanced film. This type of popcorn movie written as a spec from an aspiring screenwriter is far more likely to sell than a spec written along the lines of *Under Siege II: Dark Territory.*

MORE PITFALLS AND HOW TO AVOID THEM IN REGARDS TO A FIRST SALE:

Screenwriters often mistake external conflicts as internal conflicts. For example, if a character's afraid of the water this isn't an internal conflict. It's an external conflict. An internal conflict is a deeply emotional problem the character must come to terms with. It's a personal flaw and we'll be discussing how to properly commercialize it for a sale. Now, let's take a look at how to.....

COMMERCIALIZE A CHARACTER- DRIVEN SCRIPT

First off, what is a character-driven script and why is it a hard first-sale?

A character-driven script is a character study. It's not necessarily here to entertain us as much as to enlighten us on some aspect of the human condition.

About Schmidt is the example I'll use for a character-driven script. This film is based on a novel. The story deals with Warren Schmidt, a retired insurance salesman, and his life after his wife's death. This character is a tightwad with his money, comes off as selfish at times and doesn't appreciate what he has until it's gone.

1) Warren Schmidt's innermost thoughts are conveyed primarily through voice over (V.O.).
-Stories told through voice over (V.O.) are a major red flag for Hollywood readers because film's a visual medium and voice overs should be avoided as much as possible. This is a guaranteed PASS for a spec script being marketed by an aspiring screenwriter.

2) Warren deals with his dilemma internally, not externally. Instead of learning to cook, clean and take care of himself he deals with it internally.
-The lack of external conflict is a tough sell no matter how interesting the character.

3) Nothing external is at stake. Warren won't lose his home with his wife gone. He doesn't try to kill himself. His entire dilemma is internal.
-A story with all internals is a tough sell. Film is a visual medium!

4) The dialogue is real-life verbatim.
-This might seem to work on one level because an audience might relate to certain dialogue. Maybe it's something they've heard their own relative say. However, film-quality dialogue is real-life dramatized, not real-life verbatim.
-Many readers would probably indicate the dialogue is too "on the nose."

5) The scenes and overall plot are predictable.
-No real surprises. Everything happens pretty much the way we'd expect it to happen in real life. This would be extremely hard to sell to Hollywood.

It's obvious this film got made because Jack Nicholson became interested in the project. It was an interesting character study with some entertaining moments, like when Warren falls asleep atop his motor home or when Kathy Bates' character does the nude scene in the hot tub. It's a "character study."

The lack of a visual, external conflict, "on the nose" dialogue, nothing external at stake, predictable scenes and plot devices are a few of the reasons a story like this, presented as a spec script from an aspiring screenwriter, would be a hard sale. Think of it from a Hollywood reader's perspective. One of the primary things they're looking for is a visual film – one that's told via the externals, but an all character-driven story isn't going to deliver = a pass.

Then why do I keep seeing similar character-driven scripts on the spec market? Because screenwriters see these types of movies and think they can sell a similar character-driven script...

<u>When in fact, they'd need a more external plot added to a story like this in order to make it a first sale.</u>

Once a writer has broken in and has some successes under his belt he'll find it much easier to convince the studio to go for his character-driven piece, but in the meantime he'll need to deliver something with more external plot.

A script can still be character-driven, but it must rise above the "character study" level before it'll get serious consideration as a first sale.

What if you've already written a "character study" piece? Here are the choices:

1) Keep it! After you make a first sale it could suddenly draw attention
   and get made.
2) Add more plot/external stuff and create a better balance between plot/character, which increases the potential for a spec sale from an aspiring screenwriter.

Be aware that adding a better balance could greatly shift the dynamics of the character-driven story and make it completely different from what you started out with. In other words, you could potentially be looking at a page-one rewrite.

If *About Schmidt* were written as a spec script geared towards a first-sale what would be different about it? Almost everything.

First off, the voice over (V.O.) - all of it - would need to be eliminated. The screenwriter would have to find visual ways to present what's spoken in the voice overs.

Examples:
-When Warren's writing a letter to his sponsored child he goes off on a tangent about the nitwit who replaced him in his job after he retired. Later, there's a scene where Warren visits the office. Here's an opportunity to present Warren's feelings visually and to eliminate the use of a voice over.

But what about all those great letters Warren wrote to the boy and that final scene where Warren receives the hand-drawn picture? Should they be eliminated? For a first sale the answer is YES because <u>the overall plot would require visualization to work as a first sale.</u>

How would you visualize this? Warren could reluctantly agree to sponsor an inner-city kid one day a week then get stuck with the kid on a road trip. Let's take a look at how this would work:

Warren retires. He signs up to sponsor an inner-city child while watching a TV commercial. Soon after his wife dies, the inner-city kid runs away from his home and shows up at Warren's house.

The inner-city kid has been taking care of himself since he was 5. He knows the ropes and becomes a mentor to help Warren change. A change that's now external and visual = no more voice over.

The kid convinces Warren this 'stay-over' was part of what he signed up for and Warren gets stuck taking the kid on a road trip. Imagine the possibilities for external conflict. Warren's entire character arc would become externalized.

We watch the inner-city kid act as a mentor to teach Warren to cook, clean and loosen up with his money enough to enjoy what's left of his life. The kid could side with him on getting rid of the future son-in-law. Later, their plight would be defeated, but the defeat would help them both grow and change and realize they must accept things about who they are and who others are - rather than the way they'd like them to be.

This type of integration of plot/character in a story like *About Schmidt* would be a far more likely candidate for a first sale.

Example of a Commercial Character-Driven Script

Mystic River successfully integrates a character study with an external plot. This film is also based on a book, but here we have a character study intertwined with a visual external plot.

A devastating case of child molestation happens to one of three boys when they're children. This event is the catalyst that separates them and it remains an unresolved internal conflict until they're adults and an external conflict - the murder of one of the men's daughter - brings it to the surface. It's a character study wrapped around an external plot.

Every scene that points a suspicious finger at one of the childhood buddies in the murder case becomes an external conflict that forces the unresolved issues of the past to the surface.

A story like *Mystic River* is far more likely a candidate as a first sale because it's integrated character/plot without sacrificing one for the other.

MORE PITFALLS AND HOW TO AVOID THEM
IN REGARDS TO A FIRST-SALE

Screenwriters often mistake internal conflicts as being external ones. A character coming to terms with a divorce is facing an internal conflict. This is not an external conflict. The trick here is to create an external conflict that externalizes the divorce. We'll be discussing ways to commercialize the external conflict in upcoming chapters.

UNDERSTANDING INTERNAL AND EXTERNAL CONFLICTS

The writer has learned how to commercialize a plot-driven or character-driven script. All of this knowledge is mute if the writer doesn't understand how internal and external conflicts work in a commercial script and how to use them to greatly increase the potential for a sale.

Every screenwriter is familiar with the internal and external conflicts - - or are they? They're covered in dozens of books. I've never seen a screenwriting book that didn't cover the internal and external conflicts. Then why do I continue to receive scripts with all internal conflict or all external conflict? I believe it's because some writers are better at plot-driven (external) scripts, while others are better at character-driven (internal) scripts.

There's only one major problem with this. The reason all those books explore the internal and external conflicts is because you need BOTH in your script to sell it! Especially for a first sale!

Many of these books do a fine job of instructing the screenwriter on how to develop a character arc or how to make a plot cohesive. What they don't do is tell you how to incorporate BOTH regardless of whether your script is plot-driven or character-driven. In other words, they don't tell you specifically how to commercialize the internal and external conflicts.

First, I want to make sure we're all on the same page with what these two terms mean commercially:

INTERNAL CONFLICT

This is what the protagonist fears. I don't mean a fear of something external like snakes or spiders. I mean internally! This is a flaw they have absolutely no intention of addressing. They may not even recognize they have this problem.

<u>It's an emotional flaw the hero needs to overcome.</u>

We're going to use a very simple example so you see how to develop this on a commercial level. We'll call our character Joe. Joe's a recluse. He fears social contact – developing his reason(s) for being a recluse is part of the job but for now we'll just deal with the straightforward fear: Joe's a recluse (internal conflict).

EXTERNAL CONFLICT

This is the event – usually generated by the antagonist – that FORCES the protagonist to change! The protagonist would never have addressed his internal conflict if this event hadn't happened.

<u>It's a conflict that forces the hero to deal with his emotional flaw.</u>

Both are necessary for the story to work. The trick is to pick an external conflict that will force the hero's flaw out in the open and make him change! A hero should never choose to change. He should be forced to change! Unless the hero's challenged with this conflict, he won't change.

<u>The external conflict drives change in the hero.</u>

Here are a few examples:

Scenario #1 A former cop regains his courage when he's forced to take on a bank robber.
External Conflict: Bank Robbery
Internal Conflict: Lack of Courage

Scenario #2 An ex-con must stop a gang member from his old neighborhood from killing a friend when he discovers there's a contract on the friend's life.
External Conflict: Gang Hit
Internal Conflict: Redemption

****
Joe's a recluse.

What kind of external event could FORCE Joe to change? Force him to no longer be a recluse?

Let's say Joe's lived in the same apartment for 15 years. He has his food, paper and dry cleaning delivered. He rarely goes outside. What if his building's being sold and turned into a parking lot and the only way Joe can stop it is to create a neighborhood campaign against the new owner? Wouldn't this force him to no longer be a recluse? YES – it would!

Do you see how this is done?

The purpose of a screenplay is to develop an external conflict that forces a protagonist to come to terms with an internal flaw that's previously been avoided.

You can't just create an interesting concept OR an interesting character. Both the internal external conflicts need to be present. They need to be intertwined.

Let's take a look at how this is PROPERLY applied to the screenplay structure.

I've picked a film that outwardly appears to be a plot-driven story, yet it has a definite character arc. I chose the film "Speed" because it's an extremely straightforward example.

Speed

External Conflict = A mad bomber's loose in L.A.

Is there an internal conflict for the protagonist (Jack) and does this external conflict force him to come to terms with his internal conflict?

In the opening scene, when Jack and his partner are examining the bomb on top of the elevator shaft, Jack's partner tells him he needs to start making decisions for himself because he's not always going to be there to back him.

Internal Conflict = Jack needs to learn to be the leader. He's a follower!

Both the external and internal conflicts are established in Act I.
Here's how they play out:

41

ACT I

A mad bomber's on the loose in L.A. (external conflict)
Jack must learn to become the leader. (internal conflict)

PLOT POINT I

Jack jumps on the bus! (He's now in a situation where he has NO CHOICE
BUT TO MAKE LEADERSHIP DECISIONS)
-The external conflict puts the protagonist in a scenario where he's forced to
change.

ACT II

Jack's in a cat-and-mouse game with the bomber. (external conflict)
Jack must make split-second leadership decisions while dealing with
obstacles after obstacles = he's changing! (internal conflict)

PLOT POINT II

The bomber tricks the police and gets away with the money. (By this time
Jack's partner has died and the obstacles presented in Act II have forced Jack
to change = Jack's now the leader)
-Jack was NOT emotionally strong enough to defeat the bomber until this
point!

ACT III

Jack's NOW strong enough emotionally to go head-to-head with the bomber
and win.
(Notice in the scene where the SWAT guys realize the money's moving that
Jack DOESN'T wait to be given orders, he bursts out the door and pursues
the bomber = Jack's the leader!)
Jack vs. the bomber in an L.A. subway. Jack wins and gets the girl!

NOTES ON *SPEED*

Jack is a SWAT guy. Certainly he's strong enough physically to take on the
bomber, but Jack's internal (emotional) issues were standing in his way of
defeating the bomber.

Jack was perfectly comfortable being the follower.
He had no plans to change!

The bomber's (antagonist) plan forced him into a scenario where he had no
choice but to make leadership decisions. He must change or he will be
defeated!

It's not until this change is complete that he'll be able to defeat the bomber
and he does!

****

Understanding that the internal and external conflicts are intertwined can help an aspiring screenwriter avoid writing a cool concept where a flaw's thrown in that doesn't connect with the main conflict. This will only result in a PASS from producers.

Finding balance between plot and character is important to a first sale. Knowing how to interconnect the internal and external conflicts is also vital to a first sale. Sometimes, the writer gets both these areas right, but something still doesn't work. Why?

Plot/Character Driven in the Wrong Order

When I do receive a script for coverage that appears to have both an internal and an external conflict regardless of whether it's primarily plot or character-driven, I tend to find that 99% of the time the writer has the protagonist defeat the external problem by the end of Act II, then they defeat the internal problem in the end (Act III).

The problem with this is... how is the protagonist strong enough to defeat the antagonist or central conflict if the hero hasn't resolved his flaw? He can't, and this is why these types of scripts fail as a first sale. The writer must understand how these elements are presented in a commercial structure.

COMMMERCIALIZE THE 3-ACT STRUCTURE

Let's discuss how to commercialize a 3-Act structure. For those of you who balk at working within such a structure, I can only ask the following: Are you really expecting a producer to buy a story without a beginning, middle and an end?

Stop looking at the 3-Act stucture as a formula. Instead, look at it as a way to address commercial considerations right up front which in turn will open up many creative avenues because once you start the actual writing you'll be free to be as creative as you want!

In other words, consider it a tool in helping you make a first sale! Your computer and keyboard are tools also. Do you consider them a hindrance to your creativity? Do you believe they'll destroy the artist within you? Of course not. This is ridiculous. The computer and keyboard are nothing more than tools you utilize in creating your material and do not reflect your ability as an artist - nor should the 3-Act Structure.

Here's how the 3-Act Structure looks from a commercial perspective:

ACT I (Setup)
Internal and External conflict is presented.
It's advisable to introduce the internal conflict first.

PLOT POINT I (Spins Story in New Direction)

ACT II (Confrontation)
The external conflict FORCES the protagonist to change by forcing
him to deal with an internal conflict (flaw) he's been avoiding.

PLOT POINT II (Spin Story in New Direction)

Note: Protagonist must FIRST overcome his/her internal conflict
before
he's strong enough to overcome the external conflict.

ACT III (Resolution)
The protagonist is fully changed and is now strong enough to defeat
the
external conflict and the antagonist.

Reference this structure when developing stories and during the outlining
phase to help assure proper commercial delivery of the script. Once the
writer has mastered these areas, it's vital to start looking at the script the way
a producer sees it. Why? He's the buyer. He's person writing your check and
I'm here to teach you how to get his attention. Let's start with Plot Irony:

CREATING PLOT IRONY

Aspiring screenwriters often believe producers are just looking for great
concepts. I can tell you from experience that most writers are good at coming
up with great concepts, but they still fail to sell; even well-executed concepts.
Don't get the wrong idea. Producers need great concepts to get their projects
funded, but they need plot irony to sell the story to an audience. An aspiring
screenwriter who commercializes a script by adding plot irony has
signifcantly increased the potential for a sale.

Here are two areas to consider when plotting a story:

1) The entire plot must contain irony, not just the end
2) The irony should stem from the hero's internal conflict.

44

Here are a few examples:

In *Identity Thief* a woman who doesn't know her own identity steals the identity of others.

In *Click* a man who's anxious to get the good things in life ends up fast-forwarding, via remote control, past the best parts of his life.

In *Collateral* a man afraid to live his life to the fullest meets a hit man who plans on ending his life that very night.

In *The Wedding Planner* a woman meets the love of her life while planning his wedding.

In case I'm dealing with a writer who doesn't know what irony is – stop right now – go look it up at www.dictionary.com, then resume reading. This material is here to help a writer finally break out of the wanna-be arena and become a bonafide, check-cashing screenwriter!

Still struggling to grasp irony? Start looking for examples of irony in your life. Do you have a cousin diagnosed with lung cancer who can't stop smoking? Does your friend tell you she wants to lose weight while eating a chocolate cookie? Does your brother tell you he's broke while you're driving in his Mercedes?

Irony is all around us. It can be funny, dramatic, cruel, sad, happy....it provides entertainment. It's one of the things that makes life interesting. That's why producers need it to sell a concept to an audience. If you still think I'm nuts, then tell me why your well-written script that has had tons of contest placements is still sitting in a drawer collecting dust? Take another look at it. Does it contain plot irony? If not, it could be the one thing keeping it from selling. If you're just starting to write a script, add plot irony and be ahead of 98% of the scripts on the market because most fail to add it. I just told you how to beat the competition – now go do it!

ESTABLISHING GENRE & THEME

The next major thing a producer looks for is a solid, one-genre story. Ten years ago, producers could easily sell mixed genre stories. But in today's economy, producers are forced to deal with penny-pinching audiences who would prefer a straightforward comedy over a sci-fi thriller/action/adventure/comedy. Producers must sell to a targeted audience and this requires one genre. To grab a producer's attention, an aspiring writer

45

should establish the genre in the first ten pages. I'd recommend establishing the genre on page one with word one.

Ways to Establish Genre

OPEN WITH A TEASER
Movies often open with a teaser to establish genre. In the horror *The Ruins* the teaser shows a woman trapped in the ruins. Something stalks her in the dark, then she screams and the story begins. We have no idea where she is, who or what is stalking her. The story continues on a bright, sunny beach with young adults. The opening teaser established the genre, then moved to the story.

In a suspense thriller, a teaser often involves setting up a mystery, preferably in the opening scene. Perhaps show a murder victim with a knife sticking from his chest.

In comedy, a skit, a gag or quirky event can be used to establish the genre.

For drama, use a life-altering event. Perhaps the teaser is a funeral scene where we see crying nuns.

USE AN ESTABLISHING SHOT
An establishing shot can help create tone, mood and atmosphere and set the genre into motion.

A horror establishing shot shouldn't open on a bright, sunny day. That's why the writer of *The Ruins* chose to open in the ruins rather than on the sunny beach.

In comedy, does the establishing shot appear funny somehow?

In the suspense thriller, we might see a shadow moving across buildings creating an air of mystery.

For drama, we might see a typical house and take a moment to view the rusted mailbox, the broken fence and the unkept lawn. It's the small details of everyday life that separate a drama from the other genres.

OPEN AT THE END
Start with the end scene then continue the story in chronological order until we reach the critical scene and it repeats (or continues to completion). This technique is often used in dramas (see films like *Lolita* and *Ordinary World*).

By showing how the story ends, the screenwriter can easily establish a genre that might not be apparent otherwise. Many screenwriters are against this technique because they don't want to give away the ending. The trick to using this technique isn't to give away the ending, but to hint at it. This is technically a teaser.

USE BACKSTORY

Another technique to establish genre is to introduce the back-story. The trick to this technique is not to overuse it. Only give us enough back-story to clearly setup the genre.

An example is the film *While You Were Sleeping* with Sandra Bullock where we're introduced to the main character as a child. Once the comedy is established, the story starts and we move to present day where the story plays out with the character as an adult.

LET THE HERO INTRODUCE THE GENRE

How a hero is introduced can establish the genre. Indian Jones' swashbuckling attempt at stealing treasure is the perfect way for the hero to introduce an action/adventure genre.

Timing, Editing & Audience

The TV show "America's Got Talent" is fun to watch. It reminds me of the "Gong Show" reruns from the '70s. I've never been a Howard Stern fan, but I appreciated his comment that aspiring talent who never make it big tend to fail in the same three areas; timing, editing and audience. He was judging a magician's act. The act started out okay, then dragged on to the point of becoming boring. The ending was climatic, but it was obvious the magician's timing was off. The act definitely required editing and the whole thing made it seem like the magician didn't know how to entertain an audience.

Timing, editing and audience are major contributing factors to why many aspiring screenwriters never succeed in breaking into the biz. Timing failures are usually a result of not understanding a story's genre, how it works and how it's delivered. It's knowing the perfect moment in a horror to reveal the monster isn't dead. It's knowing how and when to deliver a big kiss scene after a chase scene in a romantic comedy. It's knowing how to keep suspicions away from the real killer in a suspense thriller by misleading the audience with red herrings. Timing goes beyond pacing. Perfect timing delivers! If you think I'm talking about following a formula then think again. Learn the structure of the genre you're writing, then come up with an original way to deliver a story and timing will fall into place. Think of films like "The

Sixth Sense"....it's a supernatural thriller that delivers its promised genre in a very structured way, but it's not obvious because the writer cleverly came up with a unique way to deliver a good, old-fashioned ghost story.

Editing is another contributing factor to writing failures. I'm not referring to editing dialogue that doesn't work or moving a plot point. Pro editing means listening, really listening, to your gut instinct; it means removing a beloved dialogue scene or a grand visual sequence when you know deep down that it doesn't work. Pros don't become emotionally involved in their stories to the point they can't let things go. Oh, they know how to create emotion, but they explore it through their characters and keep themselves out of the story. Don't become attached to any piece of dialogue, scene, characters, etc. It's like having a million pound anchor strapped around your neck. It makes it difficult to function and you'll never get where you want to go.

Audience is the area I believe is the biggest failure of most screenwriters. It's easy to say, "My script is written for a teen audience or a 30+ audience", but that's not what I'm talking about. Understanding an audience means understanding what entertains an audience. Don't be like the magician who got so caught up in his own little 'magical' presentation that he forgot how to be entertaining because entertaining means knowing how to create genre-related emotions.

Think about your own experience as an audience member. I remember going to see Jennifer Aniston and Vince Vaughn in "The Break Up" because I thought it was a RomCom. It was advertised as a RomCom, but I guess I should have known with a title like "The Break Up" that it was actually a romantic drama. I left the theater thinking to myself, "What a piece of shit of RomCom – I wasted my money to watch a sappy drama where the couple doesn't end up together in the end!" We've all had similar movie-going experiences....the producers played an advertising bait-and-switch trick on the audience because they knew a RomCom sells better than a sappy romantic drama. I still want my money back!

Howard Stern it right! In the end, it's all about what you'd go pay money to see. If you paid money to see a RomCom, you don't want Christian Bale flying into a scene in his batman suit in the end. If you paid money to see a scary horror, then you don't want a wise cracking Adam Sandler type character to show up and end the whole thing with a punch-line (unless the punch-line involves a bloody axe). If you paid to see comedy, then you're expecting to laugh, not cry. Get it?!

To truly understand an audience, the screenwriter has to understand the genre he's writing for and what an audience expects from that genre. When an audience pays good money to see a crime thriller, they expect to see a shoot 'em, bang, bang flick. Yet lately, 8 out of 10 writers are sending me scripts for coverage with the WRONG genre indicated for their story!

Guess what, I'm like Howard and I'm giving you a big, giant X! If you don't even know what genre you're writing, then I guarantee you don't know how to entertain an audience, the story's timing is sure to be off and the editing is most likely in poor form.

Get serious! Don't let these factors ruin your potential for a career in screenwriting. This is a biz and in this biz pro writers know how to deliver timing, editing and audience! The aspiring screenwriter can do the same with three simple steps:

1) Timing – Learn how specific genre structures work
2) Editing – Don't become emotionally attached
3) Audience – Deliver the promised genre

Don't even pick up a pen until you know the genre you're writing and you've tossed out the crap you think you can't live without. Get serious with timing, editing and audience and you'll be one step closer to making a sale!

Mistakes to Avoid When Establishing Genre

Don't take more than ten pages to setup the genre. In fact, it should be established on page one with word one, if possible! Isn't this where the story begins?

Don't shift genres mid-stream. If the story's a drama, don't toss in a murder mystery on page 50. If your action flick has comedy, play by the rules of the primary genre = action and use one character to provide a comic relief. This ensures the main genre remains action and doesn't shift to comedy mid-stream.

Don't take the scenery for granted. Keep the tone, mood and atmosphere in each scene consistent with the genre. Watch films like *The Ring* to see how this is accomplished.

Not knowing how the genres work is a huge mistake! Study the genres. Notice how suspense thrillers open with a mystery, how horrors often open with a teaser, how comedy opens with a skit, etc.

Learning how to establish genre and stick with it can save the writer from painstaking rewrites and can help the screenwriter elevate material to a commercial level where it'll appeal to producers.

Establishing Theme

Producers want to know three things when considering purchasing a script; concept, genre and theme. Producers need stories with strong themes; yet 8 out of 10 aspiring screenwriters have no idea what their story's theme is. What this means is that they haven't taken the time to truly learn the craft of screenwriting.

Do you know your script's theme? If not, you either don't understand what it means or the script lacks a strong internal conflict (or both).

This happens because most screenwriters begin with a great concept. Screenwriters often become so enthralled with the concept that they fail to create a great theme.

Here's the easiest way to stick with a great concept while creating a great theme: Ask the following, "What internal conflict does the external conflict help the character overcome?"

Here's an example:

Concept: A security guard helps hostages escape a bank robbery.
-If this is the concept, then let's ask the question, "What internal conflict does the external conflict help the character overcome?" The answer to this question requires a screenwriter to fully understand what "issue" the character is trying to avoid and it'll help the screenwriter develop the concept so it forces the character to deal with the issue.

Character: The security guard is a wanna-be cop who never made it through the police academy. Take it a step further because this needs to be very personal and very internal! Let's say the character was the victim of a crime, like a home robbery, and was afraid to stand up to the robbers and his wife was killed.

Internal Conflict: The security guard has a courage issue.

What internal conflict does the external conflict help the character to overcome? The bank robbery (external conflict) forces the security guard to face his courage issues (internal conflict)!

Theme: Courage

Do the following exercise:

Fill in the blanks:

The _____ conflict forces my character to overcome his
_____ issue.

For example: The robbery conflict helps my character overcome his courage
issue.

If you can't fill in the blanks, then your script might be lacking an internal
conflict and as a result the writer will have a difficult time telling a producer
what the theme is because the theme is closely tied to the character's internal
conflict.

The external conflict should force him to deal with a past issue. There are
many themes to explore, but the best way to discover what your script's
theme is – is to answer the question, "What internal conflict does the external
conflict help the character overcome?" Or ask it a different way: "The
external conflict causes what change in my character?" The answer will lead
you to the theme!

The theme should be the script's driving force and teach us a lesson. The
theme should be evident in Act I as early as possible. Most pro writers
introduce a character and his/her internal conflict upon initial introduction.
This usually sets up the theme. A movie might look like it's about killing
aliens or stopping a bomb, but it's really about courage, redemption, love,
trust, etc. Theme is the emotional core that connects the audience and the
hero.

ESTABLISHING RULES & WORLDS

Regardless of genre, if the writer is creating a world with different rules than
the established real-world or the establishing Hollywood world, then rules of
the world must be clear to the audience.

REAL-WORLD RULES
These are rules where the writer breaks what we expect in day-to-day life.
For example, undercover police aren't allowed to break the law to enforce it.
If the writer wants an undercover narcotics officer to become hooked on
drugs, then he has to establish the special circumstances that either allow the
officer to break the rules or force him to do so. Opening a movie with the
officer already addicted while setting up a sting will be a tough sell to an
audience.

HOLLYWOOD RULES

Well, these technically aren't Hollywood rules, but they're what we've come to expect in certain scenarios. For examples, vampires can't live in daylight, so if the writer has them prancing around a sunny beach, the writer has to establish how this is possible or the audience won't buy into the story line.

Also, doing research will help writers avoid making stupid mistakes. I once read an entire story where the CIA was going around arresting US citizens on US soil for narcotics. The CIA doesn't handle narcotics and their jurisdiction is outside the USA. Knowing the rules and worlds of a story can make it believable, but only if the audience understands it too.

Let's start by discussing stories that bend the rules, take us to foreign territories or allow us to explore alien worlds. If the writer takes us to a place that we've never seen before or bends established rules (like aliens in the old west in *Cowboys and Aliens*), then the writer MUST establish and/or clarify the rules of this unique situation or location. There is one catch; the rules of this world don't have to be established up front. In fact, they can be used as a big twist ending. For example, in the classic film *Planet of the Apes* from 1968, Heston's character believes he's crash landed on an alien world gone amuck with apes who talk. That's the established world and we go with it, then in the end the world shifts in a devastating twist when he learns he never left planet earth. Instead, he'd crash landed in the future.

In *Cowboys and Aliens* the rules are learned as the story progresses. We learn how Daniel Craig's character came to have the metallic bracelet on his arm, what happened to him and how he ties in with the aliens and why they've come to earth. Learning the 'rules' gradually is a necessity for this story to work because it helped build suspense. If the writer had laid out the circumstances of this unique world up front, the story would have lacked suspense.

In the *Twilight* saga the vampires are running around during the daytime. Aren't vampires supposed to sleep during the day and only come out at night? In the first movie of the trilogy, the writer establishes how this story breaks the rules by establishing new rules; the vampires can be out in the daylight, but must refrain from direct sunlight. While direct sunlight won't kill them, it will expose what they really are. By knowing this, the audience accepts the daylight scenes and the vampires' world.

What if the writer hadn't visually and verbally revealed this information? Then the audience would be shouting; "No way, vampires can't live in daylight!" The entire movie would have lacked believability. While vampires, zombies, ghosts, werewolves and other horror creatures are make believe, they have established rules audiences accept. If these rules are broken, then the writer must provide an explanation. I recommend a visual explanation, if possible, but even a dialogue one will suffice. A word of caution regarding horror; the screenwriter can bend the rules to suit the story's unique world, but don't take it too far or the audience won't accept it.

Remember the first *Jurassic Park* and the stunning scene where the characters first see the living dinosaurs? Notice how we're taken from that scene immediately to the laboratory where the 'rules' of how this came about is explained in scientific detail. While even I think this scene was a bit dry, it was vital to the believability factor of the audience. In *Honey I Shrunk the Kids* we learn up front that the father is a mad scientist and we learn of his potential to shrink objects (and eventually kids) before the event happens, thus setting up the believability factor when it happens.

The problem I'm encountering with aspiring writers is they make the assumption the audience will fill in the blanks, so they never establish the rules of the world. While I'm a huge advocate of subtext and layering screenplays with underlying meaning, the writer can NOT leave the audience in the dark as to the rules of the world they've created or they'll risk alienating the audience. The audience must know how, why and must be given a viable explanation that will allow them to suspend their disbelief.

If the writer is taking us to a futuristic setting, then we need to know how the world ended up in its current state, whether a high tech Mecca or humanity has reverted back to caves. Fill in the gaps to establish believability for the story's timeline. We've never been to the future, so we don't know this world or its rules. If the world hasn't changed at all – it should have – we need to know why. Same goes if we're traveling to the past with a unique scenario, like in *Cowboys and Aliens*.

This doesn't mean if you've written a ghost story that you need to try to explain ghosts. The writer only needs to establish the world and its rules when it is outside the norm. By outside the norm, I mean the audience has never seen it before or it breaks the established rules. If the audience expects zombies to eat flesh, but in your story the zombies only eat the flesh of platinum blondes and guys named Steve, then you better explain why.

The rules of the world can be setup early, layered into the story or even postponed for a big twist ending, but the information MUST be there or the screenplay doesn't stand a chance at a sale! I recommend adding the rules to the story based on which way creates the most suspense or provides the biggest shocker. But be very careful as to the placement of this information. If for example, you wait too long to tell us why the vampires can live in the daylight, then you risk audience alienation. Plot out the rules and unique circumstances of the world you've created. By outlining you can see where the information works best to create suspense, yet assures the audience suspends its disbelief. A helpful tip is to consider the genre and how it's been done before and use that as a model to disperse your story's information.

Before I get a nasty email from a delusional screenwriter insisting he or she wants to leave the rules a 'mystery', let me be frank; producers know that what sells a movie more than anything is word of mouth. If an audience leaves a theater feeling cheated due to lack of proper information and the story wasn't believable to them, they won't recommend it to their friends and family. This means the movie will fail! No need to worry because the likelihood a producer would purchase such a script is zero! Go ahead, leave out the rules and don't properly establish the world; maybe you can use the screenplay as a paperweight or a dust collector.

Get real, include the rules to establish the world and leave the audience feeling satisfied.

FIRST TEN PAGES: MAKE OR BREAK A SCRIPT

There's a huge misconception among aspiring screenwriters that producers or Hollywood readers read an entire script. This misconception is because writers believe the party reading the script is obligated to do coverage. This is true for union-backed studios and studio production companies, but that's it. There are only five major studios in town each with a different number of contracted companies. Outside of this are roughly around 900+ independent production companies. It's far more likely that a spec script from an unknown writer would be purchased outside the studio system by one of the independent companies. While many of these companies do coverage on requested material, many do NOT. Case in point: I was asked to read for a production company that makes 5-7 feature films a year. I arrived for the scheduled one day of work and was taken to a room with a stack of roughly 40 scripts. Even Hercules couldn't read 40 scripts in a day. The company didn't have any specific criteria they were seeking. What they said was 'If the first ten pages grab you, then pass it on to the producer". This might seem grossly unfair, but I can speak from experience when I say – and I bet producers will agree with me – that I can tell if a script works in the first ten pages 100% of the time! So if the stack is 40-deep, why should time be wasted? Either the writer grabs the reader or he doesn't.

But wait a minute…

Doesn't the screenwriter have 30 pages to grab the reader's interest? What happened to the 30-page setup? Here's what the First Ten Pages either make or break your script really means:

The screenwriter has 30 pages to setup the story,
but the screenwriter only has 10 pages to hook the reader!

Television uses a hook called a 'teaser' (or cold open) to nail the audience to their seats. It usually runs 1 to 3 minutes at the opening of a 1-hour dramatic series and presents an inciting incident that demands the audience continue to watch to see what happens. It's followed by the credits and a commercial, then after the commercial Act I begins.

Take a close look at how this is done. From the opening teaser we can tell what the basic story is going to be about. We don't have to know the details. We just have to be intrigued enough to continue watching.

Most screenwriters are familiar with the term 'inciting incident' in regards to screenwriting, yet I continue to read script after script where I'm on page 12, 20, 25, 32, 44 or even 57 before anything really happens!

The comparison between TV and screenplays seems unfair. TV is reduced to 1-hour while the feature-film writer has 2-hours (120 minutes) of time to consume. This is true, but…

What would you do if you started to watch a TV show and twenty minutes into it nothing had really happened yet? I'll bet you'd change the channel. We all would! If you wouldn't tolerate this sort of boredom from the TV, why would you chose to bore a captive audience who paid money for any longer than 10 minutes to get them interested in the story? TV only takes 1-3 minutes to grab their audience, so at 10 minutes to grab a feature-film audience (or a reader/producer) the screenwriter has 7 minutes longer to grab the viewer than a TV show, which is a generous amount of time.

But my story builds up to a big moment and I
don't want to give it away in the first 10 minutes.

There are many commercial techniques that can be used to grab the reader in the first ten minutes. Review the section Establishing Genre for a complete list. The writer can use a teaser, back-story, open at the end, etc.

But my story opens with a character at his day job.

Imagine if *Raiders of the Lost Ark* had opened with Indiana Jones in his university classroom teaching archaeology. Boring! Instead we see him swiping a treasure from its historic resting place only to have him race through a maze of deadly traps. He's still at his day job. It's just been presented in a far more intriguing way that acts as an inciting incident and keeps the audience watching.

In the introduction I talk about how commercializing material can actually aid creativity. Well, here's one of those moments because coming up with a creative way to introduce your story/character that grabs the reader will help commercialize the material and will guarantee you "hook " the reader in the first ten pages. So when your script ends up in a stack of 40-screenplays, the writer will know he'll end up in the 2-5 script stack headed to the producer!

Finally, the writer has learned how to interconnect the internal and external conflicts, create plot irony, establish genre and grab the reader in the first ten pages. The writer also learned how to commercialize a 3-Act structure, but now we're going to take an in-depth look at how to idiot-proof the 3-Act structure to assure the writer gets the Hollywood gatekeepers (readers) and gets their script into the hands of the buyers; the producers.

FOOLPROOF ACT I

I'm reading a screenplay and it's looking pretty good, then I get to the end of Act II and a character comes along – out of nowhere - who provides a vital piece of information that helps the hero save the day. The script gets a pass! Why? The character and/or the information wasn't hinted at (setup) in Act I.

Act I can destroy a story's believability. It's like the missing link in human evolution. If we had the vital information, we'd know the whole story. Without it, we're still wallowing around in the dark wondering if our ancestors were really aliens. Obviously, there's more to Act I than just setting up plot elements to pay them off later. Here are the vital components to foolproof Act I:

FIRST TEN PAGES
The following should be accomplished in the first ten pages:

Establish the genre
Introduce the hero
Introduce the hero's internal conflict FIRST
Introduce the external conflict (or hint at it)

56

Grab the reader
Set the tone, mood and atmosphere for the entire story

The writer may have 30 pages in Act I to setup the entire story, but he only has ten pages to grab the reader. That's accomplished by making sure you have all the components I listed above in the first ten pages.

FIRST THIRTY PAGES
For the remaining 20 pages, make sure to do the following:

Setup or hint at anything relevant that happens in Act II or Act III
Introduce the external conflict
Make sure the external conflict challenges the hero's internal conflict
Introduce the theme (or strongly hint at it)
Reveal the major players (characters)
Work toward an incident that spins the story in a new direction (Plot Point I)

MAINTAIN FOCUS
Use the genre as a way to maintain focus in regards to characters, plot, scenes and dialogue.

If the story's a horror, don't start adding punch-lines. Stick with horror. Don't show me bright sunny days if it's a horror. Stick with gloomy, dark shadowy places. Creating dialogue reflective of the focus; a character's words reflect his fear in a horror. Don't start with a hint at Dracula, then show us a volcano exploding.
One plot. One story. Be genre specific helps maintain focus.

PACING
Act I is where the writer can get away with longer scenes because he's setting up the story. This doesn't mean 5-10 page scenes. It means 2-4 pages as opposed to 1-3 pages. The character can also chat more, but watch the length. Film's a visual medium, not a talking heads medium – that's TV. Keep in mind that as the screenplay progresses into Act III, scenes should become shorter and faster to give the feeling that the story's coming to a conclusion.

SETUPS & PAYOFFS
Everything that happens in the entire story MUST be setup in Act I. Don't think this means you have to reveal vital information. Just showing a nail clipper on a bathroom sink may seem irrelevant in Act I, but could end up being the murder weapon in Act III. It's also vitally important to remember that the audience tries to anticipate a story – it's human nature. Therefore, anything you introduce in Act I, the audience will be seeking its payoff. The

trick here is to give them the payoff, but with a twist they didn't see coming. For example, if you show the nail clipper in Act I, the audience will suspect it's the murder weapon. In Act III, it appears it is indeed, but come to find out it wasn't murder after all, but self-defense. Adding a twist is the trick to payoffs.

THE INTERNAL CONFLICT

This is the #1 error writers make in regards to Act I. I can't tell you how many screenplays I've read and I'm on page 31, 52, 80 and I still have no idea what the hero's internal conflict is. The entire story should be about a flaw that the external conflict forces the hero to change! The easiest way to avoid this script death trap is to introduce the hero's internal conflict the first time we meet him. In fact, it should be introduced BEFORE the external conflict. Show us his weakness first! In *Night at the Museum*, we meet a guy who can't hold a job long before he ends up at a job where everything in the museum comes alive at night.

THE EXTERNAL CONFLICT

Believe it or not, 99% of writers are pretty damn good at coming up with unique concepts. Where they fail is coming up with a concept that forces a hero to change! These two, the internal and external conflicts, should be intertwined or the plot won't work as a film. A unique concept isn't enough. The audience wants to care about the hero. They want to identify with him and the only way to accomplish this is via the internal conflict. Take a look at the unique concept you've come up with and find a way to use it to force the hero to change a flaw. Remember, the story's about changing a hero not about the cool aliens that landed on someone's front lawn....it's about how the guy whose front lawn they landed on is going to have to change his ways in order to deal with the aliens.

RELUCTANT HERO

If the hero knows his flaw and is determined to fix it, then the story fails in Act I. Whether he knows what his flaw is or not, he should be reluctant to change. Reveal his reluctance in Act I. Like in real life, something major needs to happen before people change. How many drug addicts have had to hit rock bottom before they finally put down the narcotics? Same goes with your hero. His drug of choice may be something like cowardice. It may not be flattering, but it's what he's comfortable with. It's your job to knock him out of his comfort zone. No one wants to watch a hero who they know will succeed because he's already determined to change his cowardice. They want to watch him struggle to do so because he's refused to change. The reason this is so appealing to audiences is because they don't know how to change in real life. They want to watch someone struggle and overcome a major flaw because it gives them hope. Think I'm nuts? What was your New Year's resolution? Was it the same as last year? Yep, I thought so. Audiences want a hero who can do what they can't, change. Watch films like *Anger Management* where the hero never sees himself as an angry guy until the very end – also note how the hero in this film had to be forced to change!

TEASE 'EM GOOD

Here's where that unique concept can really help the writer. Open the movie with it! Show the aliens landing on the front yard. Grab the reader ASAP! When I said to introduce the hero's internal conflict first, I didn't say you couldn't introduce the unique teaser first, then let us meet the hero. The goal is to grab the reader in the first ten pages and the easiest way to do this is with a teaser or an inciting incident.

CREATE SUSPENSE

I really hate the word 'setup', especially when I tell writers everything must be setup in Act I. I hate the word because it can often be misconstrued to mean 'tell all'. When, in fact, the opposite is true. The word setup should be changed to 'hint'. Drop hints in Act I. These tidbits of information, like showing a nail clipper for no reason (paid off in Act III), builds audience suspense. Writers often make the mistake of believing they don't need suspense unless they're writing a suspense thriller or a genre that involves mystery, but this isn't true. EVERY genre should contain suspense in its plot. If we don't wonder what's going to happen to a character or a situation, then we won't want to watch the movie. Suspense starts in Act I by dropping hints.

CONFLICT

If the writer has properly setup the internal and external conflicts, then conflict should come naturally. The key to conflict is to make sure it's in every scene in every Act. No conflict equals a failed story. For the record, I'd like to note the producers do more than red pen scenes with no conflict, they completely delete them. Or more often than not, they simply don't buy the script in the first place.

KNOW THE THEME

Introduce the theme when you introduce the hero's internal conflict. Do you know how producers can tell if you're really a professional writer or a hack or got lucky with one script? They ask a simple question; "What's your story's theme?" If you can't answer the question, you're a hack or maybe the proper word is quack. Okay, I know what you're going to ask, "What the heck is a theme?" Simple, it's the lesson learned by the hero. It's how the external conflict forced him to change a flaw. For example, John found courage to return to the police force after he saved hostages during a bank robbery. Internal conflict = lack of courage. External conflict = bank robbery.

Theme = finding courage. Get it? If not, what can I say except, if it looks like a duck, quacks like a duck.....quack, quack.....quack....keep your day job!

PLOT POINT I

The easiest way to write plot points that work is to think of the three Acts as individual stories, each with its own beginning, middle and end. Something should happen around page 30 that spins the story in a new direction. In *Night at the Museum* it's obviously the moment the dinosaur comes alive and chases the hero through the museum – new story! The story's taken on a new direction.

Act I is the steering wheel to a story, don't build a story's car without it.

FOOLPROOF ACT II

This is the area most writers get stuck or never get past at all. I'd like to tell you it's because this Act is the longest, but that isn't the real reason. The real reason is because writers have never been properly taught how to commercialize a script so their art becomes a Hollywood movie. Let's change this status quo.

If you get stuck in Act II there are three ways to move forward: 1) Go back and look at Act I. What hasn't been paid off yet? What hasn't been resolved? What questions haven't been answered? Make a list and use it to help you move forward in Act II 2) The hero. Stay focused on resolving his internal conflict. Most writers make the mistake of focusing Act II entirely on resolving the external conflict, when Act II is really about resolving the hero's internal conflict via the external conflict 3) Focus on Scenes. Break down Act II into individual scenes. Go back to the list you made for Act I and create scenes for each of the unresolved areas.

These three things will help the writer fill in Act II, but the writer may still find that Act II is running short. A short Act II means the writer hasn't given the hero a strong enough internal conflict to resolve and/or the writer has spent too much time focused on the external conflict at the expense of the hero's arc. This happens for two reasons: 1) the writer gets excited about the cool concept he's come up with and forgets about the hero's flaw 2) the writer's identifying too closely with the hero and instead of making the hero confront an ugly flaw, the writer keeps him out of emotional trouble.

ARC IS #1

In Act II, the writer's main focus should be on the hero's arc. Every scene, subplot and every move made by the antagonist should force the hero to face a flaw; a flaw that the hero must change in order to defeat the nemesis. The hero can't decide to change. The key is to force him to change. People don't change easily or shows like *Intervention* wouldn't be on the air.

Arc Scenes

Take a look at the scenes in Act II. Does each scene move the hero toward his arc? This doesn't mean the hero has to be in the scene. An antagonist preparing a bomb is something the hero will have to deal with later, thus the bomb prep scene contributes to the external conflict, which in turn should be helping the hero change a flaw, like cowardice. For example, the hero may have to find the courage to diffuse the bomb and save the day.

Subplots and the Arc

Subplots are obviously going to be different from the main external and internal conflicts, but the way to make this contribute to the hero is to make it reflective of the hero's internal conflict. For example, if the hero has a commitment issue (he's 40 and never been married), a subplot might revolve around his brother who's struggling to keep his marriage together. The contrast between a commitment phobic hero and his committed brother reflects the hero's internal conflict.

Antagonist and the Arc

No time to send the antagonist on a vacation. He's here for one purpose; to take on the hero. He should be stronger, faster, smarter, more street-smart, savvy, etc. If he's the hero's equal, the story fails! The reason he should be stronger is because it forces the hero to rise to the occasion and fix his flaw in order to defeat the nemesis. Everything the nemesis does should challenge the hero's flaw (internal conflict).

ARC HAPPENS FIRST AND LAST

The hero shouldn't change until as close to the end of Act II as the writer can possibly make it happen. If the hero is a changed guy on page 50, it's too soon....but by page 80-90, it works. The hero MUST change before he's emotionally strong enough to take on the antagonist. This is where most writers go wrong. They have the hero take on the nemesis and make the victory the arc moment. This doesn't work because how could the hero defeat an antagonist who is stronger, faster, etc., if he hasn't changed his flaw first? The hero must change in order to be strong enough (emotionally) to confront and defeat the nemesis. DO NOT start Act III until the hero's arc is fulfilled and do not write the final head-to-head hero/nemesis confrontation until the hero's a new man!

ARC IS THEME

I keep harping on the arc in Act II because most writers totally ignore it, which in turn means their story has no theme. Theme and arc are interconnected. A hero who must find the courage to defeat an antagonist leads to a theme involving finding the courage to overcome the worst-case scenario. No arc = no theme. A producer won't buy a story without a theme. If the writer can't tell a producer what his story's theme is, then the writer has failed to deliver a sellable screenplay!

ARC DIALOGUE

I know, you're getting tired of me hounding you about the arc. Too darn bad! I'm getting tired of reading stories with no arc because they suck! Few writers consider how the dialogue in Act II is contributing or failing to contribute to the hero's arc. We all have relatives or even so-called friends who make snide remarks regarding something 'bout us they don't like. It's done via subtext and it's annoying as hell! My favorite is when the relative mentions how great you look by saying, "Did you lose weight, you look great?" Worse is when you answer, "No, I haven't lost weight". Subtext from relative: You were fat. Subtext from fatty: "Yep, I'm still fat"! If we get this type of underlying subtext in real life from people who'd change us if they could, why isn't the hero getting it too? I'm not saying every piece of dialogue has to do this, but the overall dialogue should contribute to the arc.

THE ARC SCENE

Oh no, more arc stuff! Yep – more arc stuff. I want a producer to be able to point out the arc scene in the writer's screenplay. A reader (or producer) should be able to identify the arc by a specific scene and the writer should be able to pick it out too. Yes, the hero will have obstacles along the way (external conflict) that contributes to his arc, but he also needs one, big defining moment. Maybe we meet a frumpy heroine who later comes out dressed to kill in a power suit, briefcase, carrying a latte and ready to take on Wall Street…we hear her address people differently, with more confidence, etc. All done in one pivotal arc scene! This scene should happen at the end or close to the end of Act II. The key to this scene is it should be visual. Don't have the hero tell us he's changed, show us.

WORSE CASE SCENARIO

I hate to tell you this, but 9 out of 10 writers still don't get this! Before you start writing a screenplay, I want the writer to ask, "What's the worst possible thing that could happen to the hero?" The answer should happen to the hero in Act II! If not, you've done him a disservice and probably have a story that doesn't work. The writer's job isn't to be nice to the hero. It's to slam dunk the bastard! If the worst thing that could happen to him is he loses custody of his kids, then he should lose his kids. Shoot his dog, kill his wife, burn down his house, fire him from his dream job, make his dream girl love someone else, etc. This is vital because it tugs at the audience's heart strings by helping them identify and have sympathy for the hero.

THE FALSE ENDING

A trick I like to use to start Act II is to provide a False Ending. The best example I can think of is the scene in the classic film *Jaws* where they think they've caught 'the shark'. Everyone's on the peer taking photos with the giant fish, but we (and the scientist) know this isn't 'the shark'. In a murder mystery, a suspect can be arrested. Later, he or she can be proven innocent. In a love story, there might be a spontaneous proposal that gets crushed with a 'no' and later met with a 'yes'. This technique isn't a must, but it is a great way to spin the story in a new direction and kick-off Act II with a wow factor! Note: A false ending is a technique that can technically be used anywhere in a script, but pros usually like to use it to kick off Act II. It can also be used with any genre.

PAYOFFS

I probably shouldn't have to tell writers this, but Act II (and Act III) is where you payoff the nifty stuff you setup in Act I. If a gun was shown when a character in Act I opened a drawer, then it better go off in Act II (or Act III). Most writers get this, but this is something else to consider in regards to payoffs; introducing new things in Act II. For example, if the character opens a drawer in Act II, pulls out a gun and shoots someone, the scene doesn't work. This requires a setup! Go back to Act I and show him opening that drawer where we casually see the gun. Why is this so important? Setting up things properly in Act I and paying them off later provides a base of believability and it doesn't seem like things happened too conveniently. Don't feel like setups have to be so direct. You don't have to show the gun in the drawer in Act I if you establish the character is known for hiding weapons. There are a lot of clever ways to setup things properly to pay them off later.

SCENE REVERSALS

Every scene in Act II must contribute to the hero's arc and should have a dialogue and/or a visual reversal. If these two areas are not covered in a scene, then edit the scene or delete it. A reversal is nothing more than a mini-twist. Aspiring writers make the mistake of only writing a big twist for the plot points, but pros know every scene requires a mini-twist to make a story work. Other writers follow the 'every 10 pages rule', where a reversal takes place every ten pages. This is okay, but I guarantee the pros have it in every scene! These reversals can be subtle and small, but they must be there. If we're expecting a character to leave via the front door, have him leave via the back door (visual reversal). A character says I love you to one character have the other character say "I hate you too" (dialogue reversal). These mini-reversals keep material fresh because they keep the reader (audience) guessing.

SCENE TRANSITIONS

Every scene in the entire screenplay should have a transition. Failure to add them will stand out mostly in Act II because of the length of this Act compared to Act I and Act III. Transitions are how one scene ends and another begins. A phone might ring in one house, then the next scene opens with someone answering the phone in another house. This creates a visual to visual transition that creates a moving picture in the reader's mind. Transitions can be visual or dialogue and be used in any combination to create a transition. A character might say he'd never fly in a plane (dialogue), then the next scene opens with him flying in a plane (visual). This type of style provides a moving picture, a transition, plus a bonus reversal. That's how the pros do it!

SCENE CONFLICT

I hate that I have to tell writers to add conflict, but I can't tell you how often I see information only scenes, especially in Act II. Sure, information is important to a story's believability, etc., but why isn't the writer clever enough to come up with ways to reveal the information via conflict? Conflict doesn't mean people have to be shouting at one another. A clever technique to create conflict, especially in a softer story that might otherwise have none, is to put the audience in a superior position. For example, perhaps the audience knows the heroine is pregnant, but the story's characters do not! Every scene where we see the heroine lie to try to hide her pregnancy may seem to lack conflict from other character's perspective, but tremendous conflict is created for the audience as they watch to see her house of lies crumble when her secret's finally revealed. Every scene in Act II must have conflict – if not, axe it and stop making up excuses that you needed to provide vital information and start acting like a screenwriter by developing scenes to present information via conflict!

SCENE SUBTEXT

Every scene in the entire screenplay, especially while dealing with the hero's arc in Act II, should have subtext. The subtext should be either visual or via the dialogue. Subtext is nothing more than underlying meaning. Remember the relative who said you look great, have you lost weight? He's really implying you were fat in the first place. He's just not saying it directly. That's called dialogue subtext. Let's say you want to show a character is angry. Rather than having him blurt it out, have him slam a door shut or throw a plate. That's visual subtext that shows anger! It's that simple! If a scene doesn't have subtext, layer it in.

SCENE SUSPENSE

Suspense can be created by conflict, but there are other ways. The easiest way is to withhold information. I don't know why writers feel compelled to answer every question a character asks another character. Leave it wide open. End a scene as soon as the question is asked and come back to it or answer it later – this technique is done in soap operas and they've been around for 30 years because they hold the audience in suspense as they wait for the question to be answered. There's no rule when you have to end a scene.....show a bomb ticking, then go to something else. Leaving us hanging in suspense! Every scene should have suspense and don't make the mistake of believing suspense is only for specific genres like thriller or horror. EVERY scene has suspense or it doesn't work. And stop listening to gurus who tell the scene must have a beginning, middle and an end. Since when? Get in late – Get out early! Nothing's more exciting than entering a room in the middle of a heated argument. Someone throws a plate and before it makes contact another scene starts!

GENRE

Needless to say, the writer needs to maintain the genre in Act II. Shifting from a horror in Act I to a comedy in Act II will only result in a pass. This might seem obvious, but I'd estimate 3 out of every 10 scripts I read have this problem. Or worse, the writer doesn't truly understand how to write for the genre and it becomes painfully obvious during the 60 pages that make up Act II. Learning and knowing the rules of the genres is vital to the writer's story and even to a screenwriting career! Really study genres. Know that horrors end where the threat remains, RomComs require a big kiss scene and action/adventures require a chase scene, etc. Stick to one genre. Multiple genre stories aren't being sold as specs right now and the films getting made as multiple genres are being written by established A-list writers, not you!

OBSTACLES

Needless to say, EVERY obstacle should put the hero in a position where he's forced to resolve his internal issues! He shouldn't resolve the internal issue too fast! He'll probably balk at most obstacles, should fail at first. But as the story progresses he'll grow stronger and stronger until he's changed!

MOVES STORY FORWARD

Heroes should be reluctant to change – at first! It's the fact that we know they have to change to prevail that creates suspense. It's the 'suspense' that moves the story forward. Every story should have this suspense built in – if the audience isn't sure if the hero will succeed or not, they'll stick around to find out! Make sure when you revise information-only scenes they contain conflict that moves the story forward.

65

RISING TENSION

The trick is to slowly have the hero change! This helps maintain suspense! If the hero changes too early, then the suspense is dead and it's suspense in Act II that creates rising tension. While the hero is slowly changing, have the external conflict coming out a 100 miles an hour. That's the easiest way to create rising tension.

THE ANTAGONIST

While Act II is all about the hero and his arc, don't forget the antagonist! In order for the audience to root for the hero to change, the hero must be up against a tough opponent. Far too often, I read antagonists who are equal to the hero. Wrong!!!! The antagonist should be smarter, cleverer, more devious, cunning, etc.! He should be a formidable foe! The only way the hero will outsmart the antagonist is to change! This is important because it FORCES the hero to change! I can't tell you how many times I've read a script where the antagonist is introduced in Act I and doesn't show up again until Act III. If he's not around, then the hero isn't being challenged and this is a sure pass. Also, the writer doesn't have to create an internal conflict for the bad guy. We don't need to know he was abused as a child and that's why he's a monster now. Worry about the hero's internal conflict and let the bad guy be the bad guy.

FOOLPROOF ACT III

Act III is technically the shortest Act. Even if it runs from page 90 to 120, it's still the shortest. How can it be the shortest if it runs roughly the same length as Act I? Because it isn't a matter of page length, it's a matter of pacing. This Act should move shorter and faster, in terms of scene length, dialogue and description, than the other Acts to give a sense that the story's coming to a close. Even if Act III involves a long chase sequence, break it up into bite-size pieces. Keep dialogue short. If there's a long speech, then it better be reserved for the hero and his words better be so compelling they'll resonate for years to come. Otherwise, edit it down to match Act III's pacing.

I'm not going to spend much time boring the writer by reminding him that Act III is the story's resolution, just like Act I is the setup and Act II is the confrontation. What I am going to spend time discussing is the hero. In this Act, the hero MUST resolve the conflict. This should be obvious, but time and again I see a secondary, supporting character take on the nemesis and do the dirty work for the hero. I literally see 4 out of 10 scripts that do this! Let me provide an example of how this is career suicide so those 4 out of 10 writers will stop wasting their money on reviews when they'll never get a recommend for a script where the hero doesn't act like the hero.

Everyone has probably seen the first *Die Hard* movie. Let's imagine in the end, instead of Bruce Willis taking out the main terrorist by killing him – his wife does it! After all, Holly (the wife) was mistreated and her family threatened by the terrorists – doesn't she deserve her due? Yes, and she gets a 'revenge' moment, but it MUST be Willis who takes out the main terrorist or the movie fails. Those 4 out of 10 scripts I read actually have Holly taking out the main terrorist. Does the writer really expect to sell a movie where the hero doesn't take on the bad guy? I guarantee it will NOT sell.

Here's the next hero issue with scripts in regards to Act III: The hero should NOT get what he wants exactly how he wants it or the story fails! If he wants a certain girl in the beginning, he should fall for another girl by the end – he still gets the love he wanted in the beginning, but it's with a different female. He may want a big promotion in the beginning only to learn (grow into an arc) that what he really wanted was more time with his family. The hero should get what he wants, but in a different way than he wanted.

Give the hero the last scene and the last line. Big, name actors want the big moments and there is no bigger moment than closing a film. Give the hero the last scene and the last line. Another tip is to use a repeat-line to reinforce the hero's arc. This is when we hear him say something he said earlier, but it now has new meaning. We'll be discussing all of this in more detail in the chapter on CHARACTERS.

Don't kill the hero! This is one of the toughest sells on the spec market. I know movies have been made where the hero dies, but unless you know Leonardo DiCaprio (*Blood Diamond*) or Joaquin Phoenix (*Gladiator* and *Ladder 49*), then I'd refrain from this approach because it'll take a big, A-list actor attached to get made and in today's economy, audiences don't want downer stories! Plus, it's unlikely this type of script would sell from a writer without a track record.

Check the page length. If Act III is less than 10 pages long, it's too short. A short Act III means the hero wasn't given a strong enough external conflict to resolve. By this point in the story, the hero's reached his arc and has changed internally. Go back and work on Act I's setup and Act II's conflict. Beef it up, stay focused on resolving the hero's internal conflict and leave Act III for the hero to resolve the external conflict.

Think franchise potential. Today's producers are looking to capitalize on material that has franchise potential, which means they can produce part I, part II and part III - maybe even a TV spin-off series. This means to end the story in a way that leaves it open for a potential sequel. A word of warning: this does NOT mean to leave the conflict unresolved! Watch franchise films to see how the first movie in the franchise ended and how it technically leaves open the possibility for the hero to return.

That's it for plot/execution. It's not as hard as you thought, huh? Once you learn the tricks to commercializing a script's plot, you can sit back and let the creative juices flow because you have the knowledge to write a script that will finally land you exactly where you want to be; up on the big screen!

Before moving on to discuss CHARACTERS in Chapter Three, I've provided articles from Extreme Screenwriting's monthly newsletters on how to write the various genres, how to write a subplot, a short script and themes. Reference the sections that apply to you, then move on to Chapter Three.

ACTS STAND ALONE

Screenplays from aspiring screenwriters often start off strong with a solid Act I, then the story falls apart. Screenwriters seem intimidated by the overwhelming length of Act II's 60 pages. They don't seem to understand its structure and how it relates to the hero's arc. By the time the writer hits Act III, it's obvious the story doesn't work and the final resolution is a hodgepodge attempt at a fix. I believe there are two, easy ways to resolve this issue:

1) Take a look at the logline. Does it deal solely with the setup or the entire story from start to finish? Many loglines only tell us the setup. This is a major red flag that indicates Act II and Act III don't work because the writer doesn't know the story beyond the setup. This assessment has never proven to be wrong. If your logline only deals with the setup, then STOP! Go back and outline past the setup and develop the entire story from start to finish or risk writing a solid Act I and a piece of crap Act II and Act III.
2) Start thinking of each Act as its own story. Writers know that at the end of Act I and Act II there is a plot point that spins the story in a new direction. The 'new direction' is like the start of a new story. By thinking of each Act as its own story with its own beginning, middle and end, the writer can free his mind from the daunting task of 120-blank pages staring back at him. Instead, the writer has broken the story into manageable chunks.

I can hear novice writers screaming "This doesn't work!" "I have to think of the story as a whole!" "What about setups in Act I that are paid off in Act II and Act III?" "What about the hero's arc?"

It's time for me to be blunt. The fact that you can't think of your story as three separate stories is the reason you're still an aspiring writer instead of a professional writer. The pros know how to look at story as if it's three separate stories while maintaining the integrity of the whole story. It's no easy task. It's like a puzzle. It looks scattered at first, but it slowly comes together when the writer begins to work with the individual pieces, until finally it's a masterpiece where everything fits together to perfection.

To drive the point home, let's look at the classic film *Jaws*. I'm using a classic film as an example instead of modern film because most you have probably seen this movie. But the three-story structure can be found in any film! Instead of breaking *Jaws* into Acts, I'm going to break it into three stories so you can see what I'm talking about.

Jaws – Story 1: A killer shark terrorizes a small ocean-front town. The shark is eventually caught by local fisherman who put it on display. The town is safe and everybody's happy.

Jaws – Story 2: A marine biologist disputes the capture of a killer great white shark after examining a shark carcass believed to be the culprit. A 3-man team is organized to catch the real killer. Jaws gets the final laugh when it appears he takes out the marine biologist and eats the boat's captain. Story's over; the big-ass fish wins!

Jaws – Story 3: A man afraid to swim goes head-to-head with a killer shark on a sinking boat. Jaws almost wins, but in a twist of fate the man takes him out!

Each one of these is technically its own story with a viable beginning, middle and an end. But take a close look at the length of each story. Story 1 is three-lines long. In the whole story this would be Act I's setup. Story 2 is four long-lines in length, which would be Act II's lengthy 60-pages. Story 3 is only two-lines long, which would be the final resolution or Act III. While each is its own story, the lengths vary.

Here are some techniques to help the writer break the screenplay into three stories while maintaining the integrity of the entire story:

1) Create a false ending at the end of Act I. In *Jaws*, it appears the killer fish has been caught and the story appears to be over. In a suspense thriller, it might appear that a serial killer has been caught. In a romantic drama, it might appear like the leading role has found a soul mate. All of these are going to prove to be 'false endings' that will lead us into a new story in Act II.

2) Literally create a new beginning at the start of Act II. Maybe the hero's been a firefighter all of his life, but a devastating fall from a roof has left him paralyzed and he has to find a new occupation. Act II opens with the wheelchair-bound, former firefighter seeking a new career. This in itself is a story!

3) Make Act II a story about the hero's arc. No, I don't mean to make it an internally-driven story. I mean to make every single scene contribute to the hero's arc, whether the hero's in the scene or not! A scene might only involve the audience seeing a bomber planting a bomb, but it'll still contribute to the hero's arc because the hero must confront his own flaw in order to eventually defeat the bomber. This is what happens in Act II in the classic movie "Speed". The hero is a follower who must learn to be a leader-cop if he hopes to win out against the mad bomber. Like the beginning, middle of end of any story, Act II should start with the hero being put in a position where he's forced to take action and forced to confront a flaw. Then at the end of the story, technically the end of Act II, the hero has overcome his flaw. Beginning of Act II's story = Hero forced to confront flaw. Middle of Act II's story = Hero slowly changes. End of Act II's story = Hero overcomes the flaw.

4) Act III's story is about a hero taking out the bad guy! Unlike the other stories, Act I and Act II, the hero is finally the hero in this story (Act III)! He's learned and grown into a strong-enough character (because he's overcome his flaw) who's ready and able to take on the bad guy and win. Careful! This doesn't mean he just walks up, knocks out the bad guy and wins! Remember, this is its own story and we need to see the hero get knocked on his butt a few times. Make it appear he's lost! Then in a twist of fate he is somehow able to overcome the nemesis. By thinking of Act III as its own story, the writer won't be tempted to write a quickie end where the hero just walks in and wins because this doesn't work. Also, by thinking of Act III as its own story, the writer will be less tempted to finalize the story with the hero's arc because this doesn't work. A hero can't win against a nemesis if he hasn't overcome his own flaw and this should happen at the end of another story (end of Act II).

I've taught the writer how to see each Act as its own story and I've taught the writer a few techniques to develop the Acts individually, while maintaining the integrity of the entire story. Next, I'd like to take this opportunity to mention failures in pacing. Seeing the Acts as three separate stories will help, but many writers don't understand how to pace the Acts. Let's take a look at the individual Acts so the writer will understand how to correctly pace the story as a whole:

ACT I's PACING

The writer might have 30-pages to setup the story, but the writer only has 10-pages to grab the reader (audience). Use teasers, inciting incidents and other techniques to create the best story pacing for those vital opening pages. As noted, above, wrap-up this Act with a false ending or use other techniques to provide a conclusive ending and don't forget the vital spin point (Plot Point I).

ACT II's PACING

Create a mid-point twist or mini-story spin around page 50 (or in the middle of the script). This creates forward momentum and propels the story into the rising tension. Act II, regardless of the genre, should have rising tension as the Act nears its end. Use suspense, misleading information, partial information, reversals, subtext, hero's arc, etc. to build Act II's rising tension. Make sure every scene hits the hero's flaw hard. This will assure suspense and a strong rising tension. This is especially true after the mid-point spin when it's time to up the stakes! End with a changed hero and then spin the story in a new direction into Act III.

ACT III's PACING

This is the Act where most aspiring screenwriters fail in terms of pacing. They just treat it like the other Acts. Wrong! Act III's scenes should be shorter and faster to give the sense that the story is wrapping up. Remember the last time you were at the movies. Didn't the end feel like the end? Why? I bet if the writer thinks about it, he'll discover it wasn't just the story, but the pacing that provided this feeling. Even big, epic battles in Act III will be broken up with INTERCUTS, action, subplots, different scenes, etc. to give a faster feel to the story. Remember, this Act is shorter than the other Acts. Oh, I know it technically has a 30-page, acceptable spread to it, but most writers never use these 30-pages. Realistically, Act III in most scripts is around half this length (or up to 20 pages). Like the Act itself, the scenes should be shorter and faster. Break up longer scenes, as needed. And watch things like lengthy dialogue – keep the lingo short too. I'd even encourage the writer to use shorter description and keep the description/action more toward the left margin. This left-margin look really makes the read fly by and gives a sense of the story moving fast and wrapping up. This technique can apply to all genres and it shows that the writer understands pacing.

Okay, you're no longer a novice writer because you've learned a pro technique. You've learned how to conquer the sagging points in the story by creating three individual stories, while you learned techniques to tackle the story as a whole. It might seem hard at first, but once you get the hang of it, I bet you'll use this technique for all your screenplays. It'll help the writer avoid the pitfall of a lackluster story after Act I.

HOW TO WRITE A SUBPLOT

According to Wikipedia, a **subplot** is a secondary plot strand that is a supporting side story for any story or the main plot. Okay, but how does a subplot work in a screenplay? In my opinion, it serves two purposes in a feature-length screenplay:

1) Provides vital information to the main plot.

Without this information, the story wouldn't be resolved. It usually involves engaging the audience with a character or character other than the hero. The key is that the subplot must be connected to the main plot. This is usually done via the story's events and how they come together to form a cohesive tale. A good example is the film *Magnolia*. There are several stories that at first appear disconnected, each having its own path, but by the end of the film the stories come together to provide vital information that resolves the plot. While I've given *Magnolia* as an example, I'd advise aspiring screenwriters to steer clear of having more than one subplot in a screenplay because multiple subplots can bog down a story's pacing and requires a veteran screenwriter to pull it off without a hitch.

2) Reflects the internal conflict.

This is the area that should be most helpful to aspiring screenwriters because understanding how a subplot can be used to reflect the internal conflict will help identify the hero's internal struggle and enhance it. In addition, by layering in a subplot that reflects the internal conflict, the screenwriter will be adding a layer of subtext (underlying meaning).

The problem is that most writers add a subplot that's a direct reflection of the hero's internal conflict. This is wrong! The trick is to create a subplot that's opposite of the hero's internal conflict because this creates contrast, conflict and pacing. For example, let's say the hero desperately wants to get married, then create a subplot where he has a married best friend. The best friend is opposite of the hero because he isn't desperate to be married, he is married. By creating a mini-story (subplot) around the friend, the screenwriter will be reflecting the hero's struggles and will be creating a subplot that interlinks with the main plot. Don't forget, the best friend must have vital information that helps resolve the plot – perhaps he fixes the hero up with his future wife.

Another plus in using a subplot to reflect the internal conflict is that it often forces the hero to act in a different way. This, in turn, leads to change (hero's arc). Do you see how everything is interconnected? This 'layering' is what

72

makes a screenplay read like a professionally polished story that's ready for the big screen.

Take a look at your subplot. It can't be a stand-alone story. It must be interconnected in a way that helps resolve the main plot and it should reflect the hero's internal conflict. If not, then it's a subplot that doesn't belong in the screenplay.

HOW TO WRITE A LOW-BUDGET FILM

What is a low-budget feature? Most in the industry would say it's any film made for $5million or under. There are variations to this, such as the micro-budget film, but we'll be reviewing the $1million budget and under since this is a market that most screenwriters are either unaware of or avoid. The easiest way to write a low-budget feature script in any genre is to avoid the things that raise a budget. Here are a few examples:

Bad weather
Multiple locations
Large cast
Special Effects
Costumes
Period piece
Alien worlds
Big stunts (car chases, explosions, aerial stunts, etc.)
Filming on or under water

Let's review each and take a look at ways to keep these in a script and maintain a low-budget:

BAD WEATHER
-This one is tough to put in a low-budget script because bad weather is bad weather. Most of us don't even like to be out in it, let alone ask an entire film crew with expensive equipment to film in it.
-Low-Budget Recommendation: Use interior scenes where we only "see" the bad weather from inside. Keep exterior scenes in bad weather to no more than 1-3 short scenes per script – if any).

MULTIPLE LOCATIONS
-Anytime a crew has to move from one location to another location there are costs involved. For a low-budget feature, most producers prefer minimal locations with minimal breakdown. Breakdown is when filming equipment within a location has to be moved. For example, a mansion with scenes/shots that take place in a parlor, bedroom,
bathroom, etc.
-Low-Budget Recommendation: 1-5 locations with minimal breakdown. If you don't think this is possible, then you haven't studied film because Alfred Hitchcock was a master at it. Watch films like *Phone Booth*, *Panic Room* and *Blair Witch* that make use of limited locations.

74

LARGE CAST

-The good news is that if you reduce the # of locations to 1-3, the script can have a larger cast. We're not talking about extras, but the primary players. If the script has one lead who interfaces with 25 different characters, then it's too large a budget for this small arena.

-Low-Budget Recommendation: If 1-3 locations then the total cast can be up to 12. If higher than 3 locations, try to keep total # cast under 12 – this does not include extras.

-The exception is a horror flick where many characters are killed off, like a zombie apocalypse.

SPECIAL EFFECTS

-This is an interesting area because most screenwriters believe that computer generated images (CGI) have made the cost of SPX near to nothing. When's the last time you hired a computer person to do anything for you, even design a website? The costs are substantial.

-Low-Budget Recommendation: Don't use these unless you're the computer guru who'll edit them into the film! Note: If the story is ultra low-budget there might be room for a SPX, but it's unlikely. Computer generated SPX are less costly than creating the SPX, but should be keep to a minimum when writing low-budget.

COSTUMES

-Have you ever rented a costume at Halloween or for the Renaissance Faire? Last time I did the cost was around $125 per day! The average low-budget film shoot runs around 16-25 days. If you have 5 characters to costume (very low estimate) at $125 per day (low estimate) at 16 days minimum that's a cost of $10,000. This may not sound like much, but it can add up quickly.

-Low-Budget Recommendation: Keep costumes to a minimum, if any. Unless you're using a mask, like Jason in the Friday 13th films, with no other costumes, then I recommend avoiding the use of costumes.

PERIOD PIECE

-The problem with making a low-budget period piece is that it's near to impossible for the following reason: EVERYTHING MUST BE CHANGED. Every dish, every vehicle, every item in any room, every piece of clothing....EVERTYHING! Take a look at one room in your home. If you had to change everything in that room to the 1920's what would it cost?

-Low-Budget Recommendation: The only way I can see for this type of script to get made for a $1million or under is if it's one location with a minimal cast. Even then it'll be tough! Try to avoid the period piece if you want to write for the low-budget arena.

ALIEN WORLDS

-Alien Worlds are like the period piece where everything has to be changed. See notes and Low-Budget Recommendation listed above. Exception: Monster flicks where the producer can put an actor in a suit. That's cheap compared to special effects.

BIG STUNTS

-These cost lots of money because special stunt crews have to be brought in, demolish experts, etc., to coordinate the filming.
-Low-Budget Recommendation: Avoid big stunts. How do you get around this? There are several possibilities. For explosions, just write BIG BOOM and show the character's reaction, as opposed to showing the actual explosion. For car chases, keep to under 2 minutes or come up with something less cliché than a car chase, like a unique foot chase.

FILMING ON OR UNDER WATER

-This requires special equipment, special everything and immediately increases a film's budget. It also increases insurance rates, workman's comp and things a producer will be considering before he purchases the script.
-Low-Budget Recommendation: Keep the story dry and try to avoid water scenes. If the story takes place near a lake, keep us ashore.

Reducing or eliminating the areas above will substantially decrease the cost of the film. If you still want a big explosion at the climax, then reduce the number of locations or the total cast. If you want those computer generated SPX in a few scenes, then reduce the location and cast, etc.

Every screenwriter should have at least one (1) low-budget script in his portfolio. It's important for several reasons: 1) most screenwriters make their first break in the low-budget arena because studios aren't likely to take a risk on a first-timer in regards to a high-budget film 2) a low-budget feature sale is the same as any sale and can put the screenwriter in a position to sell larger projects 3) if it's really low-budget the screenwriter might be able to direct it or maybe not

HOW TO WRITE A HORROR SCRIPT

The horror script requires an understanding of how the genre works.

Screenwriters are taught to give their protagonist an arc. In horror, a protagonist's arc might be non-existent. If a flaw is present, the protagonist might be killed off long before he reaches an arc. The killer might be the only one left standing in a horror. What happened to the protagonist with an arc?

There are many standard screenwriting rules that horror turns upside down, making it all the more important to understand how horror works. The first thing a screenwriter needs to do when considering writing a horror is to determine what type of horror they'll be writing. Is it a slasher? A monster flick? A supernatural horror?

THE SLASHER
A slasher tends to have a high body count, lots of gore and usually doesn't have a central protagonist. If there is one, he'll likely be killed off by the slasher. This slasher can be a guy with a big knife or a killer virus with no bounds. See movies like *Texas Chain Saw Massacre* and *Cabin Fever*.

THE MONSTER FLICK
A monster flick involves a physical creature who presents a threat to the story's characters. This type of horror usually has a protagonist who defeats the monster at a great physical and emotional price. See films like *Godzilla* and *Lake Placid*.

THE SUPERNATURAL HORROR
A supernatural horror involves ghosts, demons, witches and other things that go bump in the night. It may or may not have a protagonist, who may or may not have an arc. However, this type of horror is more psychologically demanding and works best as a commercial product if the protagonist has an arc. See films like *Mama*, *The Haunting* and *Boogeyman*.

Here are the primary areas to consider when writing in the horror genre:

-In most stories we're presented with a mystery, then the rest of the story is spent unraveling the mystery. In horror, one mystery must lead to another mystery. This keeps the story in the dark until the last possible moment.

-Slasher horrors tend to open by introducing the cast of characters who will soon become statistics. Monster flicks and supernatural horrors work best when they open with a teaser. A teaser involves seeing a 'glimpse' of the monster; a shadowy figure in the night or something can drag someone into a closet, like in the film *Boogeyman*.

-Screenwriters have been taught to establish the character's "ordinary" world. Not in horror! In horror, it's best, if possible, to remove the character from his "ordinary" world (in every way) because this creates a loss of free will and adds to the fear component.

-In slashers, monster flicks or supernatural horrors, anyone who helps the characters or who the characters ask for help are killed.

There is no help in a horror! Keep the helpers. Just kill them before they succeed in getting the characters out of danger!

-Horror has more films under its belt than any other genre! This makes it exceptionally difficult to come up with fresh material. If the screenwriter has an idea for a horror, he/she should study every possible movie made, especially the more popular ones to make sure their material is different! Putting a fresh twist to the old is the secret to selling horror. I've often heard screenwriters say *The Sixth Sense* was the most original story they've ever seen. Is it?

Isn't it just another ghost story with a heck of a twist? What twist does your ghost story have? In *Shadow of the Vampire* a film director hires a real vampire to pretend to be an actor portraying a vampire – if you haven't seen this horror flick it's well worth the rental to see how to give a fresh twist to a very old subject, vampires! Within the horror genre, more vampire movies have been made than any other kind. It's the most difficult to add a new slant to. It can be done if carefully outlined. Think of films like *30 Days of Night* where the characters are in Alaska where it's always night. Daylight can't save these characters. The vampires hunt 24/7 and that's the new twist to a very old story.

The twist must apply to the entire plot or it won't work. If the story is similar to another horror flick or a combination of horror flicks, it won't sell!

-The threat must remain in horror. This is a key ingredient! The protagonist can get away or succeed in destroying the horror, yet it will remain. For example, in the film *Hocus Pocus* the protagonist succeeds in killing the witches then in the end scene the witches' book opens its evil eye and blinks. The witches are dead, but the threat remains. In the classic film *Halloween*, Curtis' character barely escapes Michael Myers when the psychiatrist shoots Myers and he falls out a second story window, but in a few moments he disappears! Curtis' character escapes death, but Myers is still out there!

Horror can be a great genre to help a writer break into the industry. Give it a try!

HOW TO WRITE A SUSPENSE THRILLER

A thriller asks the question, "Who did it and why?" If the audience knows who did it when the story opens and are waiting for the culprit to get caught, then it isn't a thriller, it's a crime drama. Adding the "Who did it and why?" question creates the genre known as suspense thriller.

The first trick to this genre is to mislead the audience. If the audience guesses who did it and why before the writer reveals the culprit, then the writer hasn't done his job as a screenwriter! Even though the culprit shouldn't be revealed until the end, the culprit and his motive should be in their face the entire time. In addition, subtle hints should be dropped as to the culprit's real identity, but the hints shouldn't be so obvious that the audience guesses it the moment the hint is dropped.

How does the writer accomplish this? The hint should NOT be out of the ordinary. For example, in the film *Along Came a Spider* the female Secret Service agent tells the hero's character what happened up to the point where the girl was kidnapped. This seems routine (ordinary) since he's been put on the case to help her investigate. However, we later learn that this is what leads him to her (she's the conspirator) because her timing was off and he knew she was too good to make such a mistake. This fact is in our faces the whole time, but it isn't obvious until her identity as the culprit is revealed. The goal is to drop the hints, but keep them too ordinary to seem relevant at the time, then later use them to reveal the culprit.

The second trick to this genre is to create red herrings. Creating other suspects takes the focus off the real culprit. Three rules: 1) make sure the suspect is a strong suspect. If the audience can eliminate the suspect then he's not strong enough to keep the audience from guessing who the real culprit is. Remember: the audience is trying to guess the identity of the real culprit. The writer's job is to keep them guessing and guessing in the wrong direction. After giving them one suspect, introduce another one. Keep them guessing. 2) make sure the audience has a number of suspects to keep them busy while the real culprit lurks in the shadows. The writer wants the audience to be surprised when the real culprit is revealed. 3) the hero MUST be directly involved in solving the "Who did it and why?" mystery or the red herrings are irrelevant and the plot has no through-line conflict. What good are red herrings if the hero isn't looking for a killer? The hero must be the one who figures out who the culprit is or provide a wicked twist where the hero is the culprit!

The third trick to this genre is to include lots of reversals! Clues should lead to more mystery, not answer questions. Hold the final reveals as close to the end as possible. This will automatically create reversals because the audience will think one thing and the result will be something else. For example, if the police are sure a suspect killed someone and obtain an arrest warrant, then when they arrive to make the arrest they should discover the suspect died two days earlier and couldn't possibly be the culprit! These kinds of reversals keep the audience in suspense and on the edge of their seats.

The final trick to this genre is to give the audience a big twist ending! Without the twist ending, the suspense thriller WILL NOT SELL! In the above examples, I've shown ways to mislead the audience. These examples will help you create a setup that will give the audience a big twist when the real killer is finally revealed! Remember the great twist in *Saw* when the culprit was the dead guy surrounded by blood lying on the floor – he wasn't dead after all, but was the mastermind behind the whole story. He was in plain sight the whole time, but it wasn't until the very end that we discover it was him! Another example is the film *The Usual Suspects* where the guy being interrogated is in fact the guy they're looking for, but we don't know it until the very end.

Here's a brief overview:
1) Mislead the audience
2) Create red herrings
3) Use lots of reversals
4) Must have a big twist ending

I'd even advocate a double or triple twist ending! It's common to see this in films and could mean an instant sale for the writer. Writing suspense thrillers requires a writer who loves to create a good mystery, loves deception and is good at it (on paper). If you don't love mystery, intrigue, deception or wicked twists, and you want the audience to know who the killer is and have them watch the cops try to catch the culprit, then write crime dramas because the suspense thriller thrives on the unknown to create suspense.

HOW TO WRITE A CRIME THRILLER

Crime is the key word. The story's main plot must revolve around solving a crime.

If we know who perpetrated the crime and we're just waiting for him/her to get caught, then the story isn't a crime thriller, it's a crime drama. A thriller means there is some type of mystery component to the story.

This can be a tricky genre to write because it's often confused with a suspense thriller. Both have mystery components, but the crime thriller doesn't have red herrings and while the clues may lead us in the wrong directions, we probably know or strongly suspect who the culprit is and we're usually right. It isn't such a big mystery. We're just waiting to see if the cops (or good guy) figures it out. In suspense thriller we're most likely to be shocked when the real killer is revealed.

Even though the crime thriller doesn't mislead us the way a suspense thriller does, it usually provides a shocking ending. In *The Departed* DiCaprio's character is shockingly shot and killed at the end of the movie while exiting an elevator after evening the final score with the bad guys. There's no way we could have seen this coming. In a suspense thriller, this ending would have been in our faces the whole time. For example, in the film *Along Came a Spider* the culprit's handling of a case throughout the story was her downfall and lead the hero to discover she was the kidnapper.

In a suspense thriller, the hero ends up in a life or death situation and he's held there for a riveting scene or sequence. Remember the night-vision scene in *Silence of the Lambs*? The opposite is true in a crime thriller. In a crime thriller, the hero is in a life or death situation almost every minute of the movie. Good examples are *The Departed* and *Donnie Brasco*.

Further, the crime thriller tends to lean more toward being a study in how the hero ticks internally, while the suspense thriller delves into the mind of a monster (serial killer, etc.). Both have hero arcs, but one leans more toward the inner workings of the antagonist than the other. There are however, plenty of crime thrillers that are strong character studies in the sense that the antagonists are as interesting to watch as the hero. The trick to doing this successfully is to be sure the colorful antagonist doesn't upstage the hero.

Needless to say, a crime thriller must begin and end with crime. In a strange way, it's as if the crime never really ends. I don't mean an inconclusive plot. What I mean is we get the sense the hero has won 'for the day'. An example is the film *Traffic*. This can be a good way to go with a plot because it promises the hero will be back to fight another day.

HOW TO WRITE A LOL COMEDY

Great comedies tend to border on tragedy. The trick is to give us the tragic (emotional) moments, but keep the LOL comedy going. Often screenwriters make the mistake of creating a dramatic scene that doesn't end with comedy; the result is an attempt at comedy that reads like a drama. Here's a simple rule to avoid this problem: Always follow a dramatic moment with a dialogue or visual punch-line. For example, in the film *While You Were Sleeping* there's a big emotional scene at the end where Bullock's character confesses that she was never engaged to Peter. It's a tear-jerker, but at the end of her confession she turns to Peter and says, "Oh, by the way, I'm sorry about your carpet." This is the dialogue punch-line. It's based on a previously setup scene where she accidentally dumped blue-tinted water on his white carpet. It allowed the screenwriter to give the character an emotional-tragic moment while maintaining the comedy genre.

Visual punch-lines work the same way. There's a big dramatic moment, then something visually funny happens. In the film *Click* the hero's dying. He says an emotional good-bye to his family, then gives his ex-wife's new lover the finger. Tragedy or drama situations should be followed by comedy; that's the key to a successful comedy script.

Next, be sure to let tragedy strike! In the film *Identity Thief* the thief confesses she has no identity. It's a heartbreaking moment where we learn she was raised in foster care, shoved from place to place with a variety of names. She doesn't know who she is and it's tragic. The best comedies know how to handle tragedy by maintaining dialogue and visual punch-lines that keeps the genre from shifting to a drama. It's a gentle balancing act, but you don't have to be a circus performer to pull it off - just study how it's done in films and repeat the technique in your work.

The use of misinterpretation, reversals and subtext make any script, regardless of genre, look professional. But the comedy genre often takes these techniques to a new level to create laughter. This is done by including physical humor. Watch films that star Jim Carrey or Adam Sandler as perfect examples of how this is accomplished. Go through the scenes in your comedy and see if there are ways to include physical humor along with the other techniques. Adding physical humor can take your comedy to a LOL level.

Scene endings can make or break a comedy genre. It's often the mistake of aspiring screenwriters to end a dramatic scene with drama, but as noted above drama/tragedy needs to be followed by comedy. An easy way to achieve this is to double check how each scene ends. If it doesn't end with comedy, then fix it so it does.

The handling of dialogue is vital to selling a comedy. Pro writers know how to use tie-in three lines, repeat lines and punch-lines to create comedy. A tie-in three line is when two pieces of dialogue are spoken by the same or different characters and a third line, delivered by the same or different characters, sums up the situation with a punch-line; watch sitcoms like The

Big Bang Theory and *Modern Family* to see (hear) how this is done. I'm mentioning TV sitcoms instead of films because sitcoms use these techniques every couple seconds to create humor, so it's easier to spot and learn from than comedy in a film.

Contrast can create comedy. Remember the Danny Divito, Arnold Schwarzenegger movie *Twins*? Talk about contrast!

Fish-out-of-water is a common technique used to create comedy because it puts a character into a situation or place he is unfamiliar with. In the hit comedy *Deuce Bigalow Male Gigolo* a fish tank cleaner is inadvertently thrust into the world of male prostitution and becomes a gigolo.

Misinterpretation is another common technique. It's where the hero (or other characters) thinks one thing is happening based on a set of false assumptions, when in reality something else is happening. An example is a commonly used scene where the character walks in on the end of a conversation and misinterprets the meaning. The character then wrongly acts upon this information, thus creating comedy.

The easiest way to learn to write comedy is to study it. Watch a movie and look for use of misinterpretation, tragedy, punch-lines, tie-in threes, subtext, reversals, etc.

HOW TO WRITE A ROMCOM

The Romantic Comedy, often referred to as the RomCom, is the most misunderstood of the genres and can be the most difficult spec script to sell. In 95% of the cases, RomCom are written and sold by established A-list writers. This is usually because they require A-list talent to draw a box office audience. The industry has only purchased three RomComs in a decade that were specs from aspiring screenwriters and none of them made it to the big screen? Why is it so rare for an aspiring screenwriter to sell a RomCom? Besides being the territory of A-list writers, it's because aspiring screenwriters don't like to work with 'formulas' and the RomCom has the strictest, most stringent rules of any genre and if the rules are not adhered to, the script receives a PASS. If even one of the 'rules' are broken, then the screenwriter should refrain from labeling the script a RomCom and call it what it is: a comedy.

How does the screenwriter know if their story is truly a RomCom or just a Comedy?

I've made this as simple as possible with a check-off list:

-Primary plot question is: Will the couple ever get together?

-Plot must have irony (The "Wedding Planner" who's never been married)

-External conflict (entire plot) relates to romance.

-Opens with an establishing shot.

-Both lead roles (male/female) have an internal conflict related to love.

-Both leads MUST change in the end. One more than the other, but both have arcs.

-One of the romantic leads should have a twisted perspective on love.

-The couple has a "cute" meet.

-The romantic lead should get 95% of the screen time! He or she should be in nearly every single scene.

-Every scene must have an emotional core. If you can't answer the question, "What emotion does this scene evoke"?, then it doesn't belong in a RomCom.

-Circumstances prevent the couple from being together and it seems unlikely they'll get together.

-There must be sexual tension between the leads.

-There's a secret and when it's revealed prevents the couple from being together.

-Couple doesn't 'officially' get together until the very end. There should be no permanent relationship (like a marriage) unless it's at the very end (it's okay if they get married – in the last scene).

-No therapy sessions! If there's an intervention style confrontation, keep it brief. RomCom is about dialogue and visual subtext, not about discussing relationships. Note: If the characters finally say, "I love you", it should be brief with no explanations of why they're in-love. See the film *Addicted to Love* for a great scene where it's done via metaphor and the words "I love you" are never spoken!

-There's some kind of chase scene.

-There's a big kiss scene at the end!!!

-Story ends on a high romantic note. The leads get together in the end. If they don't, the story's a Romantic Drama, not a RomCom.

-The lead should get the last line.

-Don't forget to use physical comedy in a RomCom. Like the scene in *Wedding Planner* when she catches her high heel in a crack and is rescued from a run-away dumpster.

-Scenes should be treated like a regular comedy script with punch-lines, comedic puns, subtext and misinterpretation.

If a script doesn't adhere to these specifications, then it's not a RomCom, it's a comedy. For example, it's okay if a couple gets married at the end of a RomCom, but if they get married in the middle of Act II, then it's a Comedy!

If there's no big kiss scene at the end, then it's not a RomCom, it's a Comedy! Get the picture!

Let's go through each of these points in more detail:

PRIMARY PLOT QUESTION

Will the couple ever get together? If the story's about a married couple who split up, then the primary question is whether they'll get back together and it's not a RomCom! RomComs revolve around fresh, new relationships with couples who seem destined to be together, but something is keeping them apart!

EXTERNAL CONFLICT

If the external conflict is the couple will be eaten by wolves in Oregon, then it's not a RomCom! The main conflict MUST relate somehow to love. *The Wedding Planner* is probably the most straightforward example of this. The female lead, played by Jennifer Lopez, is a woman who plans wedding, but has never been married and the guy she's fallen for is her client's fiancé! Everything in the story relates to love.

ESTABLISHING SHOT

RomCom's are famous for their establishing shots. I can't tell you how many times I've seen the New York City landscape, a favorite location for RomCom's. If the screenwriter uses a more specific location (other than a large landscape, like a house), then just make sure the story ends with this scene. For example, in the film *While You Were Sleeping* we're in the train station (Chicago) and that's where the story ends.

INTERNAL CONFLICT

The internal conflict MUST be related to love. This is one of the areas where screenwriters stray from the RomCom formula. No matter what internal conflict the main characters (both male/female) have, it must be related to love. For example, a self-esteem issue could stem from being left at the altar in a previous relationship, a courage issue could stem from not having the courage to leave a previous relationship and take a chance on a relationship that works, etc. The trick is to make sure BOTH leads have an internal issue related to love. If one doesn't, then it's a Comedy, not a RomCom.

THE CUTE MEET

How does the couple first meet? It better be memorable! In *The Wedding Planner* the lead female's high heel gets stuck at the same time a run-away dumpster's headed her way. She's saved by the male lead! This is the fun part of writing a RomCom! The cute meet can involve breaking the physical barrier. Perhaps the male lead has to literally catch the female lead to prevent her from harm and she ends up in his arms. Or the cute meet can be over-the-top, like the runaway dumpster scene in "The Wedding Planner". Coming up with a unique and fun way to have the couple meet.

When the couple meets is also important. A huge mistake screenwriters make is not having the couple meet until pg. 20 or after, often at Plot Point I! The couple should meet ASAP, preferably within the first ten pages!

CIRCUMSTANCES

The story's main conflict must prevent them from being together and be related to love. In the film *While You Were Sleeping*, the female lead can't be with the man she's fallen for because she's supposed to be engaged to his brother. Create circumstances related to love that prevent the two from being together.

THE SECRET

Every good RomCom has one! It doesn't have to be a big secret and it can be revealed at any point in the story. Here are three examples:

In *The Wedding Planner* the secret is that the guy she's fallen for is her client's fiancé.

In *While You Were Sleeping* the secret is the female lead isn't really engaged to the comatose brother.

In *10 Ways to Lose a Guy* the secret is the female lead is writing a magazine article and really isn't so neurotic.

Notice how the 'secret' is related to love! Create a secret, reveal it at anytime during the story and have it threaten to keep the couple apart!

TOGETHER AT LAST

This is probably the biggest mistake made when writing a RomCom! Do NOT get the couple together until the very end. If they do hook up mid-way through the story, destroy their bond and keep them apart until the end!

Wait a minute! In films like *Shallow Hal* the couple's together almost the entire time! Are they? Hal's really with the woman he 'sees', not the 'real' woman and when the secret's revealed, it shatters the relationship! If you want the couple to be together during the story, create irony and a secret that can and will temporarily destroy the relationship.

THE CHASE SCENE

Many RomCom's rely on physical comedy for the chase scene where the male or female has to race across town to stop a wedding or stop their love from leaving town. It's the best way to go, but an implied chase scene will do. In the film *While You Were Sleeping* a physical chase scene is replaced by the entire family showing up while the male lead proposes. Because the male lead shows up on the last day of her job - before she has a chance to leave – it's an implied chase scene.

The key is creating a sense of urgency! Have him race to stop her from marrying someone else. Have her rush to the airport to stop him from boarding a plane, etc.

THE BIG KISS SCENE

This is the #1 requirement for a RomCom! The screenwriter MUST add a big kiss scene or the genre shifts to comedy! It should be as close to the end as possible and is often the final scene. In *Shallow Hal*, they kiss in the convertible and depart for their new lives! In *10 Ways to Lose a Guy* they kiss on the bridge! In *While You Were Sleeping* they kiss as the train pulls out! In *The Wedding Planner* they kiss in the park!

This doesn't have to be their first kiss, but it has to be the kiss that seals the deal! A RomCom will receive a PASS without this vital scene even if it adheres to the other rules! Why? Because RomCom's have a very specific audience who expect to see it and if the screenwriter doesn't recognize that, then the script doesn't deserve to be purchased under this genre!

HIGH ROMANTIC NOTE

The reader (audience) should be swept away at the end. This story is about romance, destiny and we should be swept away in how great it feels to be in love! If the story ends with a couple that do NOT get together, then it's a comedy, not a RomCom!

Writers are always advised to outline, but it's especially important when tackling a RomCom because there are so many factors that must be in the script before it'll get serious attention from Hollywood.

HOW TO WRITE A HOLIDAY SCRIPT

What is a holiday script? There are many holidays in a calendar year, like Easter, Fourth of July, Yom Kippur, Memorial Day, etc. However, if a producer indicates he's seeking a holiday script, he's referring to the period that falls from Thanksgiving to New Years. This includes Thanksgiving, Hanukkah, Christmas Eve, Christmas, New Year's Eve and even New Year's Day. Almost all holiday films open during this time and involve characters in a story that takes place during the holidays. Producers like these stories because they have a built-in audience for two years; the first year the audience views the release in the theater and the second year they give the DVD as a gift.

While these movies can encompass any genre, most are family-oriented, comedies or RomComs with an occasional drama. Regardless of the genre, they have one thing in common; a strong theme. What most screenwriters don't understand is that unlike other scripts, the holiday story's theme is handled differently. First, holiday films have the strongest themes among stories written for the big screen. Secondly, the theme is handled directly, as opposed to a more subtle exploration via subtext (underlying meaning).

A classic example of how the theme is handled directly can be found in the holiday film *The Grinch*. A community is consumed with acquiring presents and upstaging their neighbors with holiday decorating. They've forgotten the meaning of Christmas. A little girl named Cindy Lou directly asks why they need the presents at all. Throughout the story she continually confronts the issue head-on; Christmas isn't supposed to be about presents. It's supposed to be about family. In a holiday film, there's no need to cleverly conceal the theme in subtext dialogue or metaphoric visuals, etc. The screenwriter can state the theme outright and explore it in a very direct manner.

For screenwriters who struggle with identifying the theme in their stories, writing a holiday story is an excellent way to practice nailing down the theme before moving to another type of script that requires a more subtle approach to the theme.

The holiday script starts with a theme! Next, pick the type of story. Holiday films fall under two main categories that I'll label "Dysfunctional People" and "Holiday Magic". A story can focus on one or be a combination of the two categories. Let's take a look at each category:

DYSFUNCTIONAL PEOPLE

In *The Ref*, it's Christmas when a burglar takes a feuding husband and wife hostage and inadvertently solves their marital difficulties, while learning a few lessons himself.

In *Bad Santa*, an alcoholic safe cracker befriends a chubby kid and learns empathy and how to be less selfish.

In *Four Christmases*, an anti-family couple gets stuck with their families for the holidays and learn they want what they feared most; a family.

The key word is 'learn'. Each story involves a theme where the dysfunctional person or persons learn a valuable lesson. This lesson MUST change their lives for the better. It should be a lesson that inspires an audience to want to change their lives. The holidays are about inspiration and getting the chance at a fresh start.

HOLIDAY MAGIC

A story encompassing the magic of the holidays involves learning to believe in something. I'm not just talking 'bout believing in Santa Claus, although this theme has been explored many times and often isn't really about believing in Santa, it's about believing in the magical possibilities of our own lives.

Themes under this category often deal with a need to belong, a need for acceptance or recognition. It's learning one's own self worth. Films that have explored this magic include *Fred Claus*, *Home Alone*, *Jack Frost*, etc.

Again, the key word is 'learn'. It's all about learning to believe in yourself, your world, your family, your career, your abilities, etc. This keyword directly relates to the theme. Remember, the theme is the hero's arc. The hero changes as a result of the story's conflict and the lesson he learns becomes the theme.

How do you pick a theme to explore? The best way is to use your personal experiences. What frustrates you about the holidays? Do you find the holidays stressful? Do you cringe at the thought of the in-laws coming over? Do you dread seeing Uncle Buck and his drooling tobacco habit? Do you hate the mess, the dishes, the crowds, the traffic and the expensive gifts? Do you despise the cousin who brags of his latest six-figure purchase while you struggle to find enough money to put a turkey on the table? Do you dread digging out the ornaments and even procrastinate to the last minute? Do you dread shopping and put it off until Christmas Eve, then rush to pick up gifts for twelve people? Is New Year's Day just another day?

The best way to pick a theme is to start by writing a paper on your holiday woes. Explore the holiday areas that push your buttons emotionally. Don't look at the good stuff – holiday films explore the negative side and turn it into the good stuff. Let's take a look at how this can be done:

Let's say you dread visiting with Uncle Buck (as noted above). He's a filthy pig, especially at the dinner table. His tobacco habit is disgusting. He drools and doesn't care who sees him. You fear him being around the kids or that a pet will get into his tobacco stash. Can this negative experience be turned into a comedy? Can Uncle Buck and the family learn a valuable lesson about acceptance and can Uncle Buck learn to respect other's viewpoints and leave the tobacco stash at home?

Start with a theme, pick a story category (or combine the two), explore your personal holiday experiences and finally, be aware of two important areas:

1) The A-List Factor
Because holiday films have a limited theatrical window between Thanksgiving and New Years, producers often want to attach big stars to help draw in an audience. This means the producer must be able to solicit the star on the strength of the script. This, in turn, means that the screenwriter must be able to compete with the best writers in town to make this cut. The script can't be good, it has to be great!

2) The Santa Factor
Santa has been explored in books, music, animation, films, video games, etc. It's a tough subject to tackle in a holiday film because it's been overdone. If you decide to go with a story pertaining to Santa Claus, it must be 100% original without straying from things we've come to know that relate to Santa Claus. For example, a story where Santa becomes a biker isn't likely to sell, but take a biker, hit him on the head and have him believe he's Santa Claus and you might have a hit on your hands.

The exception to the A-List Factor and The Santa Factor is holiday scripts written as MOW for cable channels like Hallmark and Lifetime for Women. This market doesn't require a big-star and often stays within a specific formula of storytelling. MOW's in the category includes movies like *The Christmas Card*, *Meet the Santas* and *Mr. St. Nick*. If writing for this market, be sure to do plenty of research because a lot of areas have been thoroughly covered and you'll want to assure that you're bringing something unique to the table.

Writing a holiday script can be inspirational on many levels and can even help a screenwriter improve their craft by learning to explore a theme in a movie. Other holiday movies to consider viewing include: *The Santa Claus, The Family Man, The Holiday, A Perfect Holiday, Planes, Trains and Automobiles, A Christmas Story, This Christmas, Surviving Christmas, Deck the Halls, Prancer, Elf, The Family Stone, etc.* See www.netflix.com or www.imdb.com to reference additional holiday picks.

HOW TO WRITE A TRUE LIFE STORY

True life stories appeal to producers and are often easier to sell because they tend to have a built-in audience. Recently, quite a few of these scripts have come across my desk. None have received a recommend to date because they tend to have the same common problems.

Let's review the problems associated with writing a true life story and what to avoid:

A TRUE STORY
If the finished screenplay was 'a true story' it would be real-life verbatim, which is nearly impossible to mimic. The screenwriter isn't actually writing a beat-by-beat, true-life story. The writer needs to understand that what he's writing is 'based on a true story'. The word 'based' allows the flexibility to write original dialogue, change names, locations, details, etc. It allows the writer the room to fictionalize.

TOO TRUE
The writer tries too hard to stick with the facts. Movies are meant to be dramatized and DO NOT stick to real-life facts because real-life is boring in comparison. In the film *Crimson Tide*, based on a true story (although disputed), the submarine captain and first officer were in direct conflict resulting in a near mutiny. This never happened in real-life and subsequent interviews with crew members revealed the captain and first officer were in total agreement and life-long best friends. However, they claim that a radio outage did nearly start a nuclear war.

LACKS CONFLICT

Following real-life too closely will definitely lead the writer down a path where entire scenes will lack conflict – I guarantee it! Film characters don't sound or act like real-life characters. They've been dramatized to create conflict, which creates emotional effect. Without conflict, the project won't sell.

TOO MUCH DETAIL

Sticking to the facts and failing to dramatize the true-life stories often results in a story bogged down with details. The writer has spent months, maybe years studying every aspect of the story, its location, the details, etc. He's fallen in love with the project and you know what they say about love – LOVE IS BLIND. Less is more. Keep those beloved details in a desk drawer and only write what's necessary to the story.

LACKLUSTER DIALOGUE

The writer's need to stay true to the story often results in the writer attempting to create word-for-word dialogue. He literally tries to write exactly what was said when the real-life story happened. The problem with real-life dialogue is that it lacks conflict. Do people you know and interact with daily really talk like movie characters? Film has dramatized the dialogue for effect, so trying to stick to real-life verbatim dialogue will sink the writer's true-life story faster than the Titanic.

What if there's a transcript involved, like from a court? It DOES NOT MATTER! It still requires dramatization!

SCREENWRITING 101

A true life story needs to measure up to ALL the rules of a screenplay. There should be plot points, character arcs, visual and dialogue subtext, reversals, etc. If not, then you're wasting your time.

FALSE FEAR

The writer fears if he strays too far from the facts, he won't be staying true to the story he fell in love with in the first place. Here's the cruel reality: The story you fell in love with in the first place will NEVER sell unless you dramatize it! Here's a way to eliminate your fears; stick with the 'event' surrounding the story and dramatize everything else. This will help you stay true to the story while dramatizing it enough to make a sale.

MARKETING

To help entice producers to the story, be sure to include the phrase 'Based on a True Story' on the title page of the screenplay, in queries, logline and in the synopsis. It's a major selling point that shouldn't be ignored.

HOW TO WRITE A SHORT SCRIPT

Unlike the feature film script, the short script isn't used to attract a large audience who'll purchase tickets and popcorn. Instead, it's used as a promotional tool for a director (filmmaker). It showcases his or her ability to deliver a finished product. Therefore, filmmakers will pick a short screenplay they can shoot that captures their individual style or preferred genre.

With this in mind, short scripts need to be given special consideration. First, a filmmaker wouldn't be making a short screenplay to showcase his talent if he had the big bucks required to make a feature; he'd just make the feature. This means the short screenplay should be treated like an ultra low-budget feature film with limited locations, limited cast, no SPFX, no costumes, no period pieces, no fires, no car chases, no stunts, no animals, no kids, etc. Secondly, it needs to stand out from the crowd. Most likely, the short screenplay will be produced to go to film festivals and be shown on the filmmaker's reel. There are thousands of these submissions a year to festivals. It needs to grab the viewer and be something the viewer will remember long after leaving the theater.

How do you grab the viewer? Just like in a feature film, start with a unique concept. Next, end with a twist. Regardless of the genre, a twist is imperative for a short film to really captivate its viewers. Why? The viewers aren't audience viewers, they're really judges who'll decide if the filmmakers' work is good enough to render considering him for a feature film deal or other work. A twist ending makes the short memorable. At the end of a film festival or after watching dozens of reels, a 'judge' (could be a festival judge, agent, sales agent, producer, studio, etc.) remembers that comedy with a twist or that horror that shocked him, etc., he's more likely to cut a deal with the filmmaker.

Why should you care? You're just trying to sell a script. Well, if the filmmaker gets a feature film deal to expand the short into a feature-length script, guess who gets to write the feature? You! Plus, you'll get the credit for the short and potentially the feature. This could jumpstart a career in screenwriting.

Are there drawbacks? Yes. Don't expect the short to sell for very much and don't nitpick at the price. Selling a short is really 'bout going for the credit, not the money. The money will come later. It's about getting your name out there. So, what do you charge? I'd say the range is between $200 to $2,000 or even just for the credit. The credit is the most important part! Also, be sure to write up a brief contract that states you get the rights to write the feature-length screenplay should the short get picked up. Last, be sure that the contract states you get a copy of the short film's DVD. To recap, for a sale go for a $0 to low amount to sell, credit is most important, do a brief contract to assure your place as writer of the feature-length film and request a copy of the short film's DVD. Don't expect to be invited to the film festivals, unless you are invited, then go!

For those who've written a short based on a spec feature-film script. I'd advise to include in the contract that the director (or producer) understands the short is based on a copyrighted feature-film script that would be produced should the film become a feature-length production. Be sure the filmmaker knows this when you first submit the short. Add this information to the cover page – 'Based on the feature-length script ABC'.

CHAPTER FOUR - CHARACTERS

CREATING COMMERCIAL CHARACTERS

Screenwriters are focused on creating identifiable heroes. Producers are focused on a hero they can sell to an A-list actor or name talent. If the role isn't strong enough, the producer won't be able to attach talent and secure funding. Screenwriters should be asking, "Will the character attract an A-list actor to the role?" Even if the film is headed to an indie, cable or art-house market, most require recognizable talent, especially in the lead role, before the project can sell.

This DOES NOT mean a screenwriter should only write scripts for specific actors. It means that the quality of the lead role should be worthy of an A-list actor. With this in mind, let's take a look at what makes a commercial character:

THE GRAND ENTRANCE
There's nothing an actor loves more than a grand entrance! It's the #1 way to attract talent to a role. Audience's love the grand entrance too. Remember the way we're introduced to the female lead in *Kill Bill – Vol. 1*? Or the way Johnny Depp's character sails into his introduction in the first *Pirates of the Caribbean*?

What if your character is an ordinary guy with an ordinary life and an ordinary job? You plan to put him in an extraordinary situation, but not until well after he's been introduced. For this type of character, I'd recommend using a teaser opening to give the hero a more film-worthy, memorable introduction. Even an ordinary character deserves a grand entrance. Changing the one factor in a screenplay could result in an A-list talent becoming attached, which means the script's heading to production.

THE BEST LINES
Does the hero get the best lines or do secondary characters get all the great puns? This is a common mistake among aspiring screenwriters. Creating colorful supporting roles is important, but the hero should get the juicy lines. Go through the script. If good lines are going to a supporting role, give them to the hero and revise the supporting roles' lines to a secondary position. Make sure the hero gets the best lines.

MOVIE-TRAILER CHARACTERS
Can a majority of the hero's scenes be used in a movie trailer? If not, then the script requires a major rewrite because the hero should be getting the biggest visual moments, have the most memorable dialogue and be in a majority of

the film. If the hero doesn't have 'trailer moments' in the script, a producer can't sell the movie to an audience! A producer will know he can't sell the script's hero to an audience and he won't buy the script.

CHARACTER'S ARC
Every screenwriter I've ever met seems to know what the term 'arc' means, but few know to commercialize it or even how to make it work in a script. I'm going to simplify it: The plot's main event MUST force the character to change!

That's it! That's what an arc means. The character's safe in his house and you burn it down! You force him to do something he NEVER would have done if you hadn't burned down his house!

This means that characters that volunteer to change or decides to change on his own is NOT commercial! Frankly, they're boring to watch! If all the screenwriter has to do to get the character out of his 'safe' house is to knock on the door and ask the hero to leave, then what's the point of the story? Heroes shouldn't be along for the ride. They should be taken for one!

SLAM-DUNK THE HERO
The writer has to stop playing Mr. Nice Guy with the hero. He isn't your BFF. He's your enemy. He's standing in your way of making it to Hollywood and the only way to move him is to blow him up. Kill his dog. Sleep with his wife. Burn down his condo. Steal his car. Wreck his credit. Kidnap his kids. Bury him alive. Throw him in a cage with a hungry lion. The writer should ask the question, "What's the worst thing that can happen to the hero?" If the answer doesn't happen, then the story and the hero fails.

HERO VERSUS VILLAIN
A common mistake is to create a villain equal to the hero. Wrong! The villain should be stronger, faster, smarter and cleverer than the hero. The hero will have to change if he hopes to defeat the villain. If the hero doesn't change, he can not defeat the villain. The change then becomes a necessary part of the story. Be careful here. Don't create an arc just for the sake of beating the bad guy. The arc must force the hero to come to terms with a personal flaw. Once the hero overcomes this flaw, he's ready to go head-to-head with the villain. Don't make it too obvious he'll win. Just make it obvious he's changed and leave the audience in suspense as they wait to see if the change is enough to help the hero defeat the villain.

CHARACTER NAME
Finally, commercialize the hero's name. Big action heroes aren't named Bob. They're named Axel, Rambo, Bond, Gladiator, etc. Sci-Fi heroes have names

like Osmosis, Chemo, etc. A comedy lead might have a name like Joe Dirt or Boner. A romance might have a female lead with a whimsical name like Rose, June or Summer.

Enhancing these areas will help commercialize the hero and significantly increase the potential for a sale.

THE COMMERCIAL ENTRANCE

The commercial entrance is how the screenwriter introduces the protagonist. I also refer to it as giving the hero a 'grand entrance'. Why is this character's introduction so important?

- A big entrance helps to commercialize the role.
- The more intriguing the entrance, the more attractive the role to an A-List actor or actress.
- The more intriguing the introduction, the more interested the audience will be in the character.
- Boring characters are boring to watch, especially upon initial introduction.
- A big entrance makes for a memorable character.

Remember the moment we met *Edward Scissorhands*? What about *Indiana Jones*? Have you ever seen James Bond make anything but a grand entrance? And no one's been around longer than Bond!

Over and over again I see typical protagonist introductions. The screenwriter succeeds in identifying the lead, but usually fails to make the hero memorable or give him enough of a commercial introduction to make the role enticing. The character may be interesting, but if it's not discovered until page 20 you don't have a commercial introduction!

Here's a typical, boring introduction. Whether you've seen this done in film or not is irrelevant. A commercial entrance makes for a far easier first sale!

A man awakens to an alarm clock. We watch him shower, shave, get dressed, eat then go to work. Zzzzzzzz....that's me snoring because I've fallen asleep from sheer boredom! Yet I can't tell you how many times I've seen dull protagonist introductions. NO MORE!

I don't care if the protagonist is a mousy secretary. Use your creativity to give her a grand entrance. If done professionally, the commercial entrance will cover lots of areas. It'll establish the character's internal conflict, it'll set the tone, mood and atmosphere of the story based on the protagonist's POV (point of view) and most importantly, it'll make the audience immediately interested in the character.

In *The Mummy* when we first meet the female lead she's the mousy librarian. She's up on a ladder and sends bookshelf after bookshelf tumbling over like dominos. This isn't a character we're likely to forget.

What if you have an ordinary guy thrown into an extraordinary situation? This doesn't mean you can't give him a memorable entrance. In *Collateral* we're introduced to Jamie Foxx's character as an L.A. cab driver. This seems pretty straightforward, but he immediately becomes memorable when he tries to impress the lady District Attorney in his cab with big talk of owning limo companies, etc. We know - and she knows - he's just a cabbie with big dreams, but he's suddenly become far more interesting.

There are plenty of ways to introduce your character, but remember....

The goal isn't to simply identify the protagonist,
It's to make him or her memorable upon first introduction

There are many ways to do this and I sincerely hope you'll use your creativity to explore past the few options we'll review here:

- **Inciting Incident**
- **Interesting Character Moment**
- **External Conflict Introduction**
- **Internal Conflict Introduction**

In *Lolita* we meet the lead character bloody in his car, swerving back and forth on the road.
Inciting Incident – What's happening here?
External Conflict Introduction – This guy's in big trouble...how'd he get this way?
Internal Conflict Introduction – What drove him to this point?

What about the choice of introduction for *Indiana Jones*? The screenwriter could have opened with Jones in the classroom. Which introduction do you find more memorable, Jones in the sacred tomb swiping a relic or Jones in the classroom teaching?
Inciting Incident – When's the last time you saw a guy steal a treasure and dive through a maze in an attempt to get out alive?

What about *Saw* where the protagonist is introduced chained to a pipe in an eerie, blood-filled room?

Inciting Incident - When's the last time you saw someone chained to a pipe in a blood-filled room?

What about *Silence of the Lambs* where we see the protagonist jogging through the woods and going through an obstacle course? This simple opening with absolutely no dialogue makes us intrigued about the character.
Interesting Character Moment – Who is this woman running through an obstacle course and why is she here?

What about the wild party the protagonist throws in the opening of *Mrs. Doubtfire*?
Interesting Character Moment – Not often you see a Dad dancing on a table.
Internal Conflict Introduction – This guy is very immature.

What about the protagonist's introduction in the romantic comedy *The Wedding Planner*? We see the female lead character pull off a wedding on the verge of falling apart and she does it all with her suit full of 'fix-it' items. If she were in the military she'd be considered armed and dangerous.
Interesting Character Moment – Who is this master wedding planner? How do you get a job like that?

Who can forget the visual CLOSE UP introduction of the protagonist in *Kill Bill Vol. 1*? Here's a character we won't soon forget!
External Conflict Introduction – Who tried to kill this woman and why?

In *Cliffhanger* the protagonist is introduced hanging from a cliff. This alone is memorable, but when he loses a fellow climber and she falls to her death the introduction becomes a grand entrance.
Interesting Character Moment – Not often we see a guy hanging from a cliff.
Inciting Incident – What will happen next after he loses the climber?

In *The Quick and the Dead* a sleazy cowboy tries to shoot Sharon Stone's character and finds himself shackled to a piece of wood because she's not a helpless woman. This cowboy just met a woman gun fighter.
Interesting Character Moment – Not often we see a woman gun fighter.

Notice how the majority of these introductions are external = visual
Each one presents some sort of intrigue and raises a question.

1) The goal is to commercialize the introduction. To make it as intriguing as possible; an ordinary introduction does not accomplish this goal.

99

2) Ordinary introductions have been done in film, but they make a tough first sale. Stick with making the introduction as intriguing as possible.

The goal is obvious = to make your character memorable and commercially enticing. However, you must make certain that the introduction directly reflects the plot and sets the tone, mood and atmosphere of the story.

COMMERCIALIZE A HERO'S NAME

Add an extra commercial touch to a character by making his or her name fit the role, like in the Will Smith romantic comedy *Hitch*. This guy helps couples get "hitched" and his name is Hitch. Remember Rocky? What about Joe Dirt? Who could forget Dirty Harry? The name doesn't have to correspond to the title, but it should reflect the character and/or story, if possible.

Ever notice how characters in Sci-Fi films sound like their names were pulled from a Science book? Ever notice how action heroes tend to have stronger names? Or how romantic a RomCom's lead's name sounds?

Avoid Similar Character Names

A common mistake among aspiring screenwriters is to use characters names that are too similar, like Bill, Bob, Betty, Barbara, Brad, Bentley & Bruce; or Stephanie, Susan, Sam, Steven.

This often makes it look like the writer has an "identity" problem with the characters and hasn't developed them enough so they are distinct in every way.

It can also lead to confusion for the Hollywood reader who can easily mix up the close names. Is Bob, Bill or Brad the suspect? Is Susan, Sara or Samantha the easy-going one? If a reader has to backtrack to discover information because the similar names created confusion, the script will likely receive a pass.

It's best to avoid names that begin with the same letter or sound too much alike. The only exception is the comedy genre and only when the use of similar names is meant as a way to create comedic moments of misinterpretation. But still, be careful because it's tough to keep track of a character named Sam and another character named Samantha.

Buy a Baby Book

Ever struggled to come up with a name for your character? Try purchasing a baby book with girl and boy names and their meanings. Then you can rifle through the names and find a name that best suits your character! Of course, you might freak out your significant other, so I'd advise you to explain why there's a baby book lying around the house.

The baby book that lists the meaning of the names is the best one because you want to pick a name that hopefully says something about your character. Another bonus is that a newly published baby book will have modern names, probably a few you've never heard of!

A Christmas story might have characters named Holly, Noelle or Chrissy. A fun in the sun story might have names like Reef, Dune, Sandy…get it?

I've randomly picked a few male and female names from my baby book and listed their meaning as an example:

MALE NAMES

ARIEL
Hebrew: lion of God
-This name might be used in a spiritual story or a drama.

GRANT
French: great
-This name might be used in an action or another genre where the lead shows leadership (great) qualities.

FEMALE NAMES

EILEEN
Irish: life-giving
-This name might be used in a drama about a physician or an organ donor.

NORI
Japanese: belief
-This name could apply to many genres about a character who helps others 'believe' something.

THALIA
Greek: joyful
-This name could be used by a lead female role in a RomCom!

However you decide to use the name, a baby book can broaden your horizon and present names you might not have considered otherwise.

THE MOST IMPORTANT EVENT

Even more important than a commercial entrance and commercializing the hero's name is the most important event in the protagonist's life. **The script should focus on this event.** It isn't necessarily the day they get married, have a child or graduate from college.

It's when an external conflict forces them
to come to terms with an internal conflict!

IT'S THE EVENT THAT FORCES
THE PROTAGONIST TO CHANGE!

It's an event with the highest possible emotional stakes for the protagonist!

IT'S A HUGE EVENT WITH
HUGE EMOTIONAL STAKES!

In the romantic comedy *While You Were Sleeping* with Sandra Bullock, her character lost her father about a year before and has no other relatives. She's all alone. When she saves a man's life on the tracks and is mistaken for his fiancé while he's in a coma, his family takes her in as one of their own.

The story takes place at Christmas and who wants to be alone at Christmas? Bullock's character soon becomes a family member. She loves them and they love her. Then the man she saved wakes up. Bullock's character stands to lose what she values and needs the most – family and love. The emotional stakes are huge!

There are plenty of twists and turns after this point in the story and if you haven't seen it, I'll leave the pleasantries for your viewing. Bullock's character saving the man on the tracks is the most important event in her life - even if she doesn't know it at first!

The best way to accomplish this is to stick with ONE MAIN CONFLICT!

One central conflict assures the focus remains on the protagonist - where it belongs in a commercial script!

THE EXTREME CHARACTER

Extreme characters are the ones who do what we've only dreamed of doing, but probably don't have the guts to do. I'm not referring to the larger-than-life heroes who never seem to get shot even when a million bullets are flying their way. I'm referring to characters who push the edge. Here are my two favorite examples:

1) In the film *American Beauty* Lester quits his job after telling his boss off and blackmailing the boss for money.
-Anyone who's had a lousy day job would love to be Lester and for two hours in a dark theater we can be Lester. Lester's our hero!
-He's done what most of us have only dreamed of doing = telling the boss to go to hell.

2) In *Titanic* Rose gives it all up for love! The money. The fancy clothes. Everything!
-Who among us hasn't dreamed of finding the love of our lives and giving it all up to be with them?
- Maybe it's a youthful gesture, but we've all felt the emotional sway, and for two hours we get to throw it all away for love through Rose's character.

<u>Extreme characters can give a script extra commercial edge</u> because they're characters who do things we all wish we could muster the courage to do.

They're our Personal Heroes

The problem with extreme characters is many aspiring screenwriters attempt to write them without understanding how their presence works in a commercial realm. They simply introduce the character and their extreme behavior then get back reviews with comments like, "the protagonist isn't believable" or is "over-the-top."

These screenwriters often become upset. After all, they can name a dozen film characters who exhibit such extreme behavior; how dare the reader say their character isn't believable.

What the reader should have specified - even clarified - is that an extreme character is only believable if the screenwriter has successfully made the character's behavior believable.

In other words, did you set up the extreme behavior? Most screenwriters are pretty good at setting up plot devices and paying them off later, but fail to recognize that this type of over-the-top behavior requires a setup before you get to the payoff. It's important to nail this down because an extreme character is far more attractive as a commercial commodity than an ordinary character - unless he's put into extraordinary circumstances.

Long before Lester tells off his boss the setup begins. He's sick and tired of his dreary life. He wants change but doesn't really know how to go about it.

Then along comes his teenage neighbor who only holds down a day job so his militant dad won't catch on that he's dealing drugs. In a scene where the neighbor quits his day job in a rather point blank manner, Lester says, "you're my hero," and soon after he tells off his boss and blackmails him for money.

Had the scene with the boss come earlier, Lester's behavior would have been unbelievable or even categorized as over-the-top, but it isn't because it's set up to be believable. He subsequently gets a job at a fast-food restaurant. Without proper set up, this entire scenario would be way over-the-top.

Rose giving up everything for love in "Titanic" is thoroughly set up making her behavior extreme yet not over-the-top, and it remains believable.

Go ahead and write extreme characters; they're a great way to commercialize material! Just be sure their behavior has been set up and is understandable or you'll blow the whole thing!

THE LARGER-THAN-LIFE CHARACTER

The larger-than-life character is the guy who takes extreme risks. He does what most of us only dream of doing. This 'extreme' level usually results in characters like James Bond, Indiana Jones & Rambo. These are guys who can have a million bullets being shot at them and somehow manage to escape! They are the larger-than-life characters.

They make for great popcorn flicks, but it would be next to impossible to sell this type of character to Hollywood as a first sale. Why? These characters often fail to have a strong enough arc (or none at all) to get past the Hollywood reader. Story Analysts are required, when providing coverage, to identify the character's arc and if there isn't one or it's lacking, the script will receive a 'pass'.

Only A-list writers can get away with writing these characters because they have a proven track record and many times their material skips the coverage phase and goes straight to the decision makers, like a producer or a Director of Development.

Does this mean a screenwriter should avoid writing larger-than-life characters? What it means is the screenwriter will have to pay extra attention to developing a strong enough arc to make it through the coverage process. Unlike James Bond, who shows up on the scene as a chiseled professional, your character will have to start out flawed and work his way into a larger-than-life scenario! His arc will have a slow, developmental process to it. We'll be able to visually see a different person than the one we met on page one!

Another pitfall in writing larger-than-life characters is the antagonist. For most specs to work the antagonist needs to smarter, cleverer and perhaps even more physically endowed than the hero. This forces the hero to rise to the occasion and change in order to defeat the antagonist. With larger-than-life characters, the antagonist is usually a clever equal and the two spar wits to see who comes out on top. To overcome this pitfall in the spec script, keep the antagonist stronger until the hero has arced (not a moment before), then make them clever equals who'll play a dangerous cat and mouse game to see who wins. This will usually take place in the final resolution also known as Act III.

Watch the dialogue, larger-than-life characters speak from a position of strength from the moment we meet them. They're confident, brave and willing to do what's necessary to accomplish their goals. Unfortunately, this works against developing an arc. For the spec script, the hero should develop into this confident soul and once the arc is apparent he'll speak from a position of power and confidence.

Writing the larger-than-life hero has its challenges on the spec level. It's an ambitious endeavor that I must say tends to fail more often than not. It's far easier to develop an ordinary hero in an ordinary world than writing a hero who is larger-than-life. Plus, the screenwriter has a far greater chance of selling a spec that's not based on a larger-than-life hero.

If the screenwriter has an existing spec that's based on a larger-than-life hero, the writer can do one of two things: 1) save it to sell later when established as a writer 2) change it to assure the script makes it through the stringent coverage process.

SLAM-DUNK THE PROTAGONIST

This has to be my #1 pet peeve! Again and again I read a script with a great plot and great characterization where the screenwriter nails down the plot elements and character elements without sacrificing one for the other only to watch the screenwriter go easy on the protagonist.

Are you nuts?

I'm going to tell you point blank why screenwriters do this. Because YOU ARE THE PROTAGONIST! If he gets hurt, you get hurt. Don't you write to explore issues and help resolve them? Isn't this what it's all about? Yes, it is! So, no more Mr. Nice Guy!

How can you get to the nitty-gritty of any issue or personal conflict if you don't get your protagonist into deep enough trouble?

In Chapter One we discussed Outlining and I mentioned that "Questions Are the Answer." This is how I want you to come up with the most hideous thing or things you can possibly do to your protagonist. I want you to ask....

What's the worst thing that can happen to this character?

Let's take a look at how this works:

> **FILM: *Identity Thief***
> Question: What's the worst thing that can happen to the thief?
> Answer: The discovery of her real identity.
> What happens: We discovery she's a foster child reject with no identity.

> **FILM: *Mrs. Doubtfire***
> Question: What's the worst thing that can happen to the hero?
> Answer: He'll lose custody of his kids.
> What happens: He loses custody of his kids.

> **FILM: *The Quick and the Dead***
> Question: What's the worst thing that can happen to Stone's character?
> Answer: She won't be able to kill the man who killed her father.
> What happens: She rides out of town a coward.

FILM: *Mama*

Question: What's the worst thing that can happen to the hero?
Answer: He loses one of his deceased brother's kids.
What happens: One of the girls dies.

I could go on and on listing film after film, but these four examples give you enough idea of how this is done. Note: Although the character's worst-case scenario happens, something else happens that gives the protagonist one last chance. The key is to make it seem like all hope is lost.

Even though a character eventually gets what they wanted, they don't always get it the way they wanted it.

Let's look at the film *The English Patient*. An aspiring screenwriter with a tendency to go easy on the protagonist would have done the end scenes as follows:

Jeffrey crashes the plane in the desert in an attempt to kill the protagonist and his wife, Catherine, after he discovers they're having an affair.

Jeffrey's dead. Catherine's alive, but badly injured. Our hero has to get help or she'll surely die. He has to walk out of the desert. He barely manages to get back to civilization after a MONTAGE where we see his struggle. He asks military personnel for a vehicle or a plane or some means to get back to Catherine.

Here is the point where the aspiring screenwriter would do a conflict scene where the hero convinces the military personnel to give him a vehicle. Then we'd watch him frantically drive back to save Catherine.

But that's not what happens in this movie! Things get worse! The protagonist is accused of being a traitor. He's arrested, shackled and thrown onto a train bound for who knows where. All we know is he's to hell and back from rescuing Catherine. At this point he can't even rescue himself!

ALL HOPE SEEMS LOST! Every commercial script should have this moment when the audience has NO IDEA how the protagonist will get out of the dilemma!

There's no Mr. Nice Guy screenwriter in *The English Patient*. The screenwriter slam-dunks the protagonist. He puts this guy through HELL! This is the point where even the audience isn't sure the hero will ever get back to Catherine and the suspense leaves the audience on the edge of their seats!

107

This level of anticipation and involvement with the protagonist on an emotional level will never come about if you're nice to your character because things will seem to come too easily!

I won't go into plot detail, but one of my favorite examples of a screenwriter slam-dunking the protagonist is from "Spider-Man 2." If you haven't seen it, please do. Here's a protagonist that never seems to get a break! He was totally slam-dunked at every single turn! Even I felt bad for the guy!

NO MORE MR. NICE GUY!

After you've asked and established the answer to the question, "What's the worst thing that can happen to this character?", I want you to take this a step further.

The reason you keep being Mr. Nice Guy to your protagonist (assuming you do this) is because, as mentioned above, the protagonist is you! We've all heard this before, but I want you to change the status quo - at least for the sake of slam-dunking the main character.

How? By no longer identifying the protagonist with yourself! You may not even realize you're doing this, but you are! Whether you recognize this or not, if you're being too nice to the protagonist this is the reason and it's time to break the habit!

I want you to think back to an event where someone made you boiling mad. A time when you were so mad your face turned beet red. A time when you could have contemplated murder - well, maybe not murder, but you would have loved to hurt that person (physically or emotionally).

Let's use an event and a person that most of us have probably encountered at one time or another = the insane driver! You know the guy! The one who flies down the road at 100 mph, then cuts through traffic and narrowly misses hitting you and four other cars by mere inches.

He's usually the same idiot you catch up with at the very next light.

I decided to choose someone we don't know in real life to avoid any conflict that may occur by bringing this memory to the surface for the purpose of using it to slam-dunk the protagonist.

Okay, you remember that guy! That idiot! You'd like to get out and pound him one. How can he (or she) be so damn irresponsible?

Now, I want you to create a visual item that signifies this event and the emotions attached to it. I used an index card and wrote in big red letters: THAT IDIOT!

Every time your character's about to get himself out of trouble, I want you to look at that card! I want you to imagine the protagonist has just pissed you off…he's temporarily become the insane driver and here's your opportunity to kick his behind!

I'm not insinuating you make the protagonist an insane driver. I'm merely suggesting you use this anger to stop being nice to the protagonist and to stop identifying the protagonist with yourself. See him as an outside individual – the insane driver - who you want to slam-dunk.

I want you to slam-dunk him so hard that pretty soon you may even start to feel sorry for the guy! That's the moment you'll realize you've really nailed down the commercial character!

A Word of Warning

Slam-dunking the protagonist does not include killing him off in the end! It's an extremely tough first sale and I highly recommend you stay clear of this option.

HERO MUST RESOLVE THE CONFLICT

I'm utterly amazed when I read a fairly good script only to discover the protagonist doesn't resolve the external conflict! I read these every single week! This is Screenwriting 101, yet I'm amazed how often it's ignored. I've even seen scripts where a new character is introduced at the end and he or she resolves the conflict!

Why does this happen? Because the screenwriter is too close to the protagonist. As I've outlined above, get pissed off at this guy and you'll stop identifying with him as yourself and you'll start letting him resolve the central conflict.

If the protagonist DOES NOT resolve the external conflict then you DO NOT HAVE A COMMERICAL PRODUCT and aren't likely to sell the script to anyone, ever!

THE INTERNAL FLAW

Can you answer the following questions? 1) What is the hero's internal flaw (conflict)? 2) What is the script's theme? 3) In what scene does the arc happen in the story?

If you can't answer all three questions regarding your screenplay then the script most likely would fail to sell on the competitive market, especially since these are the first questions producers ask. A screenwriter needs to acquire a mastery level understanding of the internal conflict and how it's directly related to the arc and the theme.

The internal conflict should be introduced first in a story, not second. Nine out of ten spec scripts introduce the internal conflict after the external conflict or not until Act II. The internal conflict MUST be introduced in the first ten pages, preferably when we first meet the hero and hopefully prior to (or at the same time) as we learn about the external conflict.

A lengthy setup for the internal isn't required; we can learn this information in a quick scene, a line of dialogue or even while being introduced to the external conflict. The goal is to introduce it first! Why? Because this is the reason the audience identifies with the hero. He has a flaw and they empathize with him because of it.

The flaw is the internal conflict. By internal, I don't mean a fear of snakes – that's external. I mean a deep-seeded emotional fear that the hero has no intention of changing or is incapable of changing. He MUST be motivated to change or as I like to say, "The hero must be FORCED to change". In order for the change to happen, a life-altering event or the most important event in the hero's life needs to take place, which doesn't mean writing about another ordinary day in a character's life. Stiller's character in "Night at the Museum" finds another ordinary day job, but soon discovers there's nothing ordinary about a museum where everything comes to life at night! It's an extraordinary event; an event that forces him to finish what he starts and this resulted in his change.

Notice how the internal and external conflicts are interwoven. The external conflict MUST be a conflict that will force the hero's internal 'emotional' fears to the surface. It forces the hero to confront this fear and to change in order to succeed. The purpose of a story is to present an external conflict that will force the hero to change his internal conflict. If the hero decides to change on his own, the story fails. If the hero never changes, the story fails.

If the external and internal conflicts are not directly linked, the story fails. If the theme and internal conflict aren't related, the story fails.

What's the theme? The theme is related to the internal conflict. In" Night at the Museum" the theme is "finish what you start". The hero can't finish what he starts. He's presented with an external conflict that forces him to stop running away from his problems and 'finish what he starts'. When he finally does this he's a changed man!

The hero's arc happens when he changes, not a moment before. Most writers have mastered this technique, but I still see scripts where the arc doesn't happen until the very end of the story. Most producers will ask, "How does a hero beat the nemesis if he hasn't changed yet"? After all, he isn't strong enough 'emotionally' to win. In order for the hero's resolution to be believable, we need to see a changed man. A changed man can conquer anything! Therefore, the arc should happen around the end of Act II. Why here? Because Act III is the resolution and the hero MUST be changed in order to be strong enough (emotionally) to resolve the conflict. Be sure the arc doesn't happen too soon in the story or the plot will flat-line, too late and the resolution isn't believable.

I've always believed that the most powerful stories I've read are ones that really push the hero to his limits and challenge his flaw. Ask the question, What is the hero most afraid of? The answer should happen to him. If he's afraid he'll lose his kids, then in the story he should lose his kids. If he's afraid he'll fail, then he should fail (but be given one last chance). If he's afraid he'll be alone then strand him on an island. If the hero's worse-case scenario doesn't happen, the story will seem incomplete, lackluster or could fail completely.

How to Introduce the Internal Flaw

The hero's internal conflict MUST be introduced in Act I, preferably when the hero is first introduced. Here are two ways to introduce the hero and his flaw:

1) Introduce the internal conflict (flaw) before the main external conflict. In *Night at the Museum,* we meet a hero who can't hold a job or an apartment. We know this before he arrives at the museum.
2) Start with a perfect hero and give him a flaw. In *The Call,* Halle Berry's character is a savvy 9-1-1 operator at the top of her game until she inadvertently causes a victim to die. When the killer returns for round two, she gets a chance to redeem herself and get her moxie back.

#2 is the most difficult to sell as a spec, but both are viable ways to introduce a hero's flaw. Make every scene and every moment about dealing with the flaw while overcoming the external conflict. Most writers do this the opposite way and they never sell a script.

CHANGE THE LEOPARD'S SPOTS

Most of you are familiar with the cliché, 'You can't change a Leopard's Spots'. It means that you can't change who a person is or their nature; they will always be the same. It's the reason the film industry is a billion dollar a year business. A few people do change. Most don't, but ALL people want to change deep down inside. Why don't they change? Lots of reasons that we won't go into here, but what's important is the fact they want to change. With this in mind, what happens when a person goes to the movies? At the movies, he meets a hero who changes; who becomes stronger, more courageous, removed from fear, etc. The hero accomplishes want the audience only dreams of doing; he changes!

For 90 to 120 minutes, the audience gets to forget their own shortcomings and experience what it would be like to change. Through the hero this experience is made possible. It's unlikely the person viewing the film really gets that this is why they're identifying so closely with the hero, but it is the core reason we are all so entranced by movies.

The audience wants to be the hero! The audience wants to be a larger-than-life character! The audience wants to change their spots! Movies give the audience the hope that change is possible.

Why is knowing this so important to a screenwriter? Because in real life you can't change a leopard's spots, but in a movie the writer MUST change the leopard's spots or the story fails. Like in real life, the hero has no desire to change. In fact, the film hero is perfectly comfortable in his dysfunctional world. It's his norm. It's his comfort zone. A bulldozer isn't likely to evoke change. He's EXACTLY like the audience; he isn't able or willing to change! This means the writer has to devise a plot (external conflict) that will FORCE the hero to change.

What's the easiest way to do this? By starting with the hero's flaw (internal conflict). What is it that the hero can't or won't change? Once the writer discovers the hero's weak spot, then all the writer has to do is come up with an external conflict that will force change in the hero. Most writers do the opposite – they focus on a cool concept and forget the rest when they should have focused on the hero's flaw first, then worked on coming up with a cool concept. Or the misguided writer comes up with a good concept and a flawed hero, but doesn't link the two together. The internal and external conflicts must be interconnected for the story to work as a film.

For example, we've all seen romantic comedies where the hero has a 'fear of commitment' issue. What happens? He's forced to make a commitment or forfeit an inheritance. Or he's forced to make a commitment or lose his one true love. The external and internal conflicts are woven together. At the core of every successful film is a hero who is confronted with an external situation that forces his flaw out in the open, which causes him to change. He doesn't want to change, he has to change or he'll fail. The key to making this work and making it believable is to set the stakes high. If he can avoid commitment and somehow still gain his inheritance or keep his love, then the writer hasn't set the emotional stakes high enough.

The key words are 'emotional stakes'. This is the part where many writers fail. Even if they've linked the external and internal conflicts together, they don't set the emotional stakes high enough. The writer may think because the hero has to stop a bomb from exploding to save the world that the stakes are set as high as possible. Wrong! If stopping the bomb doesn't force the hero to change somehow (like becoming more courageous), then the writer hasn't set the 'emotional stakes' high enough and the story isn't strong enough to become a film.

The emotional stakes should be driving the hero to resolve the main conflict, which in turn results in the hero's change. This is why the hero who decides to change fails on the page and will never make it to the screen. The hero can't decide to change. He must be forced to change.

Set the stakes high, especially the emotional stakes. Push the mark, which means don't go easy on the hero. Making the audience cringe, scream, cry, become fearful or grip their seats in suspense is what the writer's striving for. Why? Because if the audience feels emotionally involved in the hero's change, the audience will have hope that they too may be able to change. And that's why we go to the movies! We go for the emotional experience and I've just taught you how to make it happen on the page and on the stage.

DEVELOP AN EYE FOR ARC

Aspiring screenwriters are usually good at coming up with cool concepts. The problem arises when they don't back the cool concept with a film-worthy character. A hero has to change. He has to have a flaw. The external conflict should force the hero to change this flaw. Instead, the writer presents a hero who we know will succeed because he's too determined to change or he's a hero who decides to change on his own. How many addicts do you know who decided to change on their own? They've either hit rock bottom, got arrested, a judge forced them into rehab or something so awful happened (like they accidentally killed someone while high) that they finally change! They don't decide to do it. They're forced to do it; either physically or emotionally forced to change!

The way to develop an eye for how to achieve a hero's arc is to look for examples of flaws in people you know. You won't have to look far. You might be able to start by looking in the mirror. Do you have a friend who's been trying to lose weight for years? Do you have a buddy who is 31 and still living with his parents? Do you have a family member living with an abusive spouse? Do you have an out-of-control teenager?

We all have dysfunctional, flawed people in our lives. You might have tried to help these people. You've probably talked until your lips were ready to fall off. Tell me, did it do any good? I doubt it. Results require action. But what if you had the opportunity to evoke change in this flawed person? What if you were given a short period of time to do so? Say a day, week or a month? What would you do? You've tried talking and that was a waste of time. You could take the overweight friend to a gym. Or find an apartment for the buddy who still lives at home with his parents. But what if the overweight friend refuses to go? What if the buddy doesn't want to move into an apartment because he likes mom's home cooking?

You tried to talk. You tried action. The clock is ticking. What now? FORCE! A hero, just like the flawed person in your life who doesn't want to change, must be FORCED to do. Give the overweight friend a heart attack and bet he reconsiders going to the gym. Flood your buddy's parent's basement. Now he has to move! I don't mean this literally – just via your imagination. But just imagine the things you'd do if you could…imagine how you'd evoke change in all the flawed people in your life. Wouldn't it be fun?

By identifying flawed people in your life, using your pen (computer) and coming up with ways to force them to change, you've learned how to create commercialized characters that will sell to Hollywood. Do this exercise everyday – in your mind.

I was in the supermarket one day and was behind an obnoxious woman who was complaining about everything she could think of; the prices, the parking, the dirty shopping cart, the clerk, etc. What a miserable human being! In real life I ignored her. She wasn't worth my time. I'm not Dr. Phil. But in my screenwriter mind, I had an armed gunman bust into the supermarket, pistol

114

whipped her in the mouth and during a hostage crisis she learned to appreciate the clerk, the parking, etc.

Once you've learned how to deal with flawed characters with ease, combine the dysfunctional hero with one of the cool concepts you've come up. Don't model these heroes too closely to the real-life dysfunctional people you know; fictionalize!

Coming up with concepts is easy. Combing the concept with a flawed character and making it work is what sets the amateurs apart from the pros.

THE ANTAGONIST'S PLAN IS KING!

The antagonist's plan is the most important part of a script because it's his (or her) plan that sets the story into motion. Without the antagonist, the hero would go on with his life as usual. The key to the antagonist's plan is that it must seem impossible for the hero to overcome. This is important because it forces the hero to change in order to defeat the antagonist.

Without the antagonist's plan the protagonist would never change because nothing would be forcing him or her to do so! This makes the antagonist's plan a plot element that should not be ignored! Yet it is.

Time and again the antagonist and his plan are introduced and it gets the ball rolling. Then we never see the antagonist again until Act III. Where's he been? If he isn't constantly antagonizing the protagonist then the main character's motive to change has been eliminated! The antagonist should be stronger, cleverer, more manipulative, etc., than the hero. He should be one step ahead of the hero! This forces the hero to change in order to overcome the antagonist. A hero who doesn't change during the course of the story isn't a film-worthy character and he'll need a strong antagonist with a plan to force him to do so.

I mention this because in many scripts I've read the antagonist's plan falls flat. It either fails to keep the protagonist motivated long enough to force change or it's not clearly defined or even confusing. The easiest way to address this issue is during the outlining phase. The tendency will be to spend most of the outlining time focused on the protagonist. This seems reasonable, but I want you to also spend time – at least 2/3 as long as you did with the protagonist – outlining the antagonist's plan because his plan is king!

<u>Without his plan your character will remain steadfast!</u>
<u>Without the antagonist's plan the protagonist will never change!</u>

Know your antagonist's plan from A to Z before you write a single word on paper. If his plan isn't clear then how will the audience believe it's powerful enough to evoke change in the protagonist?

The Antagonist's Motivation

This has been a heated debate lately among Hollywood readers. Some believe a screenwriter must make their antagonist's motivation believable by diving into his underlying motivations to take such actions in the first place. While others, like myself, believe a bad guy can simply be a bad guy.

The stronger the bad guy the better. I'm actually an advocate for making the bad guy stronger and clever than the protagonist. This is a far more interesting conflict. There's nothing wrong with knowing a bad guy is after the money because he feels it's owed to him for losing a thumb, like in the film *Speed*, but one quick scene should cover it and you don't need to go into depths. Why?

Because the antagonist NEVER CHANGES! So, there's no need to explore all of his internal motives in detail. Besides, this takes away from the protagonist. He's the guy we need to dive into the internal arena with, not the antagonist. A simple understanding of the antagonist's motive will suffice. You may disagree, but how you handle the antagonist is up to you. Just make sure his internal conflict (motivation) doesn't take the spotlight away from your protagonist's internal conflict. An A-list actor doesn't want to be upstaged by anyone, especially the antagonist!

Use the Antagonist to Slam-Dunk the Lead Character

We all know how this works. The protagonist stands in the antagonist's way and it is showdown time. Only the antagonist appears to be winning. He's a better fighter, a better negotiator, and a more devious planner. Everything the antagonist does causes the situation to be worse for the protagonist.

What about the Anti-Hero Lead?

This is an entirely different subject. There's nothing wrong with writing a story about a bad guy from his/her point of view. Just be aware that anti-hero leads are very hard first sales.

An example of an anti-hero lead that would work as a commercial first-sale - and there are few of these - is *Identity*. A twisted tale that works as an anti-hero lead because it isn't obvious this is an anti-hero lead until the very end when we discover we've really been inside the mind of a mad killer and his multiple personalities. It's a rare occasion to find an anti-hero lead story that can sell as a spec from an aspiring screenwriter. For the sake of a first sale, I'd advise the writer to stick with the hero leads for now. Save the anti-hero leads for when you're more established as a screenwriter.

PROTAGONIST VS. ANTAGONIST

This section is to help screenwriters identify areas the story may be weak in terms of character development and how an antagonist and protagonist interact.

Let's start with the bad guy, the antagonist:

The antagonist must be all powerful! 9 out of 10 scripts I read have an antagonist who is weaker or equal to the hero. Boring! The bad guy (antagonist) must be stronger, faster, smarter, etc. He must outwit the hero at every turn. This will result in the hero having to change in order to defeat the antagonist. Once he's changed, he's emotionally (and perhaps physically) strong enough to go head-to-head with the antagonist and win.

Antagonist must be present. I've read too many stories where the antagonist shows up in Act I, causes a problem, then disappears until the end of Act II or Act III. This doesn't work. The antagonist should be in the hero's face, in his path and be the hero's ultimate obstacle or the hero won't have any reason to change!

The two must go head-to-head. This doesn't necessarily mean a physical fight. It could be an argument, a chess tournament, a playoff game, winning his girl back, or something as simple as finding the courage to say 'no'. If the story lacks a final showdown between the protagonist and antagonist, then it fails.

Only the hero can resolve the conflict between himself and the antagonist. If someone else takes on the bad guy, the story fails. Would you want to see Money Penny take out the nemesis in a James Bond film?

Antagonist's plan is king! Without his plan there is no story. It's the driving force behind the external conflict and it's what forces the hero to change. Before a writer types a word, he must know the antagonist's plan from A To Z. His plan is what drives the story. No plan. No story. The antagonist's might not know he has a plan on a conscious level or he may have planned it out. Either way, he's the motive for a hero's change. This does NOT mean the antagonist has to be a person. In *The Perfect Storm* the antagonist is

117

technically the weather. It's a man versus nature story. Again, a very tough sell and I'd advocate staying away from this type of story until the writer has a few films under his belt.

Next, on to the protagonist – the hero:

The protagonist (hero) is like a drug addict. He has a problem, but he's in denial. He won't admit he's a coward, has anger issues, suffers from low self-esteem, etc. His flaw is concealed behind his own denial. This is what keeps him from stepping up to bat, from taking charge of his life and from changing. Like the drug addict, the hero's going to have to hit rock bottom before he'll change. He's going to have to nearly die from an overdose or wake up in a dirty alley filled with needles before he'll admit he has a problem and fix it.

A hero who decides to change on his own isn't worth a movie ticket because he's dull, boring and unbelievable. Why? Because people who go to see movies want to find the courage within themselves to change something. Watching a movie hero rise to the occasion gives them hope and encouragement.

Too many writers focus on the story's external conflict and completely ignore the internal conflict. How do you know if you're one of these writers? What's your story's theme? If you can't answer that question in one sentence, then you're a writer who hasn't mastered the hero's internal conflict and aren't likely to make a sale until you do.

It's okay to start with an external conflict. Maybe you'd like to rob a loot of gems being carried on an Amtrak. Okay, that's an external conflict. You create a hero who's a former cop and put him aboard the train. Okay, that sounds good, but that's where most writers go into shoot 'em bang, bang mode and never touch upon the hero's internal conflict. Before the hero boards the Amtrak let the audience get a taste of his internal conflict. Show his marriage falling apart. Show him losing his job. All of this due to an anger or courage issue, then introduce him to the external conflict. You can introduce the audience to the external issue as soon as the movie opens, but hold off on getting the hero in the mix until you've identified his internal conflict.

The external conflict MUST be something that directly challenges the hero's flaw. If he has a courage issue, then the external conflict should force him to be courageous. If he has an anger issue, the external conflict should force him to deal with his anger like in the movie *Anger Management*. This in turn results in the hero's arc – he changes as a result of the external conflict.

118

If the two are not linked, the story fails!

Now that you've learned how to take an external conflict and layer it with an internal conflict to make a viable scenario that forces a hero to change – all via a strong antagonist – let's talk theme. If the hero had a courage issue and the gem heist forced him to be courageous in order to save the day, then the theme would involve finding the courage within ourselves to save the day.

Do you see how the external conflict, internal conflict, theme and arc are tied together? If not, go back and read this again, then take a good, hard look at your work. Does it measure up? Are the conflicts layered? Is the arc evident? Is the theme obvious?

The writer may have noticed that certain areas are being covered more than once. This is intentional. I believe repetition is the mother of knowledge. Remember how they made you repeat your times tables in grade school. I bet you still know that seven times three is twenty-one. Live, experience and learn – then do it all again!

Writing a feature-length screenplay at 90+ pages is a daunting task, so why waste your time with a great concept if the rest doesn't work? Get tough with your writing. Master the skills it takes to learn to layer stories. They don't pay screenwriters what they pay lawyers because it's an easy thing to do. It's tough and (forgive the cliché) but only the tough survive in this business.

Three final questions:
1) What's the antagonist's plan?
2) How does the external conflict force the hero to change?
3) What's the theme?

If you're still writing and can't answer these three questions, then stop! Your script has already failed! Go back. Review this material and revise your screenplay. Make it a powerhouse on the commercial marketplace.

Next, let's get more in-depth with ways to create characters a producer will want to buy, A-list actors will want to play and audiences will remember for years to come.

CREATING SUBTEXT GESTURES

The number one way to spot a pro from an amateur is subtext. Yet, the number one question I'm asked by writers is, "What is subtext?" It's underlying meaning in words and visuals presented in a way that engages the audience emotionally with the story and its characters. Aspiring writers often take this to the wrong level by tossing in what they think is subtext, but forgetting they're writing for a visual medium and the subtext works best if externalized. In other words, show – don't tell.

For example, the writer will write:

Mark's uncertain.

The problem is the writer hasn't shown me anything! Worse, an actor can interpret 'Mark's uncertain' in dozens of ways, all of which could vastly change the meaning of the scene. It's the writer's job to tell the actor how to portray the role, thus creating a subtext gesture that will allow the reader to become emotionally involved in the story. Here's the correct way to write this:

Mark hesitates, uncertain.

By providing a visual (external) action, 'Mark hesitates', followed by delivering the meaning of this action, 'uncertain', the writer has provided a visual for the actor to portray and delivered the subtext meaning behind the action for the reader. Thus, the writer has created a subtext gesture.

This doesn't mean to write every single movement the character makes. That would be ridiculous. The writer needs to look for moments vital to the portrayal of the character and story. Subtext gestures can be used to reveal a character's hidden motive or show us he's lying or spin the story in a new direction.

Probably the biggest challenge in writing this way is in understanding the gestures and the meaning behind them. I'm not advocating you become a psychiatrist, but rather become an expert in body language. Most think they're good at it, but are you? Have you fallen for something someone said and later regretted it by telling a friend, "I knew I shouldn't have trusted that guy?" How'd you know? Probably because 'something' told you. Call it instinct, but shrinks will tell you something in the person's body language was waving a red flag in your face and you ignored it, intentionally or not. Go to Amazon.com and buy a book on body language. I prefer the books with pictures of each gesture. I've used my knowledge from body language books in my screenwriting and in Hollywood meetings.

Let's review a few body language gestures and what they mean, keeping in mind that the full interpretation of a gesture derives from what's taking place at the time.

Hesitation = reluctance or could mean an outright lie. How often has someone hesitated, then said, 'Yes', only we knew they really meant, 'No'?

Looks away = avoidance. A character may be avoiding confronting a flaw, a lie, a lover's quarrel, etc.

Folds arms over chest = stubbornness. A character may be acting like they're open to what's being said, but this gesture says otherwise. Or the character might be cold – the context of the scene should be taken into consideration.

Looks down = intense feeling. A character is experiencing something on an intensely emotional level. This gesture is often seen in sadness and is how actors are able to feel something to the point the audience believes it.

Eyes widen = disbelief or surprise. A character may act like he's buying what you're saying, but this gesture says otherwise. Or the character may be surprised by something he's seen or heard.

Shaky = fear. Unless the character has a physical impairment, this gesture signifies fear. A character's afraid of what he might say or do or by what's happening to him at that moment.

Points = demanding or matter-of-fact. A character using this gesture plans to get his point across or else! Of course it could mean something as simple as showing someone which way to go. The interpretation is based on the scene.

Snarl = cocky, indifference. A character using this gesture isn't a happy camper and will most likely challenge another character's position.

Twirls hair = feels under pressure. A character, usually female, who exhibits this gesture feels pressure to say or do something or is pressured by what's currently happening to her.

Taps foot (or pen) = impatient, anxious. A character using this gesture may speak slowly and act like he's willing to wait for an answer, but his body language says he wants the answer now!

Arms to sky = freedom, exhilaration. A character exhibiting this gestures feels he's either escaped a great dilemma or he's risen above his own expectations (like winning the Superbowl).

Repeats himself = A character who repeats what he just said is lying or unsure. The meaning should come across in the full context of a scene.

Stutters = nervous. A character who doesn't have a speech impairment who stutters is intensely nervous.

Hands on chin = contemplating other's words. A character who does this is thinking about what the other character is saying and taking it seriously.

Rolls eyes = mockery, indifference. A character who acts like he's buddy-buddy with another character, but exhibits this gesture probably thinks the other guy is a dumbass.

I could go on and on, but I think you get the point. Take these actions and deliver the meaning:

John shakes, nervous.
John taps his foot, anxious.

While I advocate delivering the meaning behind the gestures, it isn't always necessary. The scene's dialogue or description may serve this purpose or the writer may deliberately withhold the meaning to create suspense. By only writing 'Mark hesitates', the audience (reader) will wonder why and by withholding the meaning, the writer can create suspense. Take a close look at what you're trying to accomplish within the scene or the story itself and adjust the subtext gestures accordingly.

Bonus Pro Tidbit: Pros take subtext gestures to the next level by creating a specific character gesture, often referred to as a tic, for the character they've created. They might have a character that spits right before he tells a lie or always plays with his tie if he really likes a woman. This 'tic' is repeated during the story to reveal vital character information without having to resort to dialogue. Consider developing a 'tic' for your character. Use your character's unique tic combined with subtext gestures to write like a pro!

CREATING CHARACTER DEPTH VIA REFLECTION TECHNIQUES

Using a reflection technique can create built-in subtext and reversals in a script. The easiest way to utilize the reflection technique is to start with the hero and reflect the other characters off him. Here is an example:

The hero is Josh. He has a commitment phobia and won't ask a long-term girlfriend to marry him. She's prepared to leave him if he doesn't pop the question.

Josh's best friend has been married 10 years and has a solid family relationship – this "reflects" what Josh really wants, but is too afraid to commit to. Josh's boss is reluctant to make him a partner in the firm. This reflects Josh's reluctance to marry and have a life-time partner. Maybe Josh's mother is married to her fourth husband and looking for a fifth. Maybe Josh's college buddy has a different woman every night...etc.

When the other characters reflect the hero's internal conflict the story becomes layered. Subtext seems built-in and reversals are easily accomplished. All the characters, like Josh, have an issue – good or bad – that deals with relationships and each in turn reflects Josh's flaw.

In most stories, the only character the screenwriter uses to "reflect" the hero is often the antagonist. This is done by creating an antagonist with an opposing viewpoint to the hero. This is great, but if you want to create a layered plot and character depth, then try reflecting all the characters off the hero!

Be careful not to overdo the technique in terms of reflecting off the hero. If the hero has a courage issue, the plot could easily become overdone if all the other characters are too brave or too weak.

The trick is to downplay the other character's reflective issue(s).

Josh's best friend isn't likely to have his marriage end soon. Josh's boss won't lose his business if he doesn't make Josh a partner. Josh's problem is the main conflict and the other characters' issues only serve to reflect it.

Another easy technique to create reflection is via "opposite" visuals. Here's an example:

Put a single guy in a room filled with loving couples and the couples will reflect what the single guy longs for; love. The writer doesn't have to tell us the single guy wants love or that he's lonely because we see it in comparison to the loving couples. An audience is likely to sympathize with the single guy and this will help create the audience/hero connection a writer needs to sell the story.

Another easy technique to create reflection is via "the same" visuals. Here's an example:

We have two drinking buddies. One matures and sees his friend as a reflection of the person he no longer wants to be.

123

Another easy technique to create reflection is via "visual metaphor". Here's an example:

Give a hero with a need for redemption for a past mistake a buddy who collects things from the past, like old 8-tracks or records. His buddy's need to hold onto the items from the past reflects the hero's 'past' redemption issue.

Next...

Learn to reflect the hero's visual world.

Another technique is take inventory of every item in the hero's world. Determine how each item reflects the hero's internal conflict.

A great example is the movie *The 40-year old Virgin*. The film's character rides a bike and collects superhero figures. The bike and the toys reflect his need to move beyond boyhood into manhood. Also, notice how this film's secondary characters reflect the hero's issues regarding sex.

A more complex technique is what I'll call the "Psych 101 Technique". This is where one character reflects their issue onto another character. Here's an example:

A husband accuses his wife of cheating with no basis for the accusation whatsoever. It's more likely she wasn't cheating at all and he was. He's reflected his guilt onto his wife. A good example is from the movie *Sideways*. There's a scene where the story's writer character is speaking about wine – how it ages, etc., but he's really speaking about how he feels about himself.

This technique is more difficult to pull off and requires proper setups and payoffs to work.

There are many reflective techniques a screenwriter can develop that will add character depth. The more reflections there are in a script, especially when the reflections involve the hero, the more layered the story becomes.

Supporting Roles

In many stories, secondary characters have their own arcs. While their arcs aren't as pronounced as the hero's, giving them an arc can help the story feel like it's come full circle. By starting with a reflection technique, the writer can easily create a suitable arc for a supporting role that will work to reinforce the hero's arc because it's a 'reflection' of the hero's flaw.

124

Learning to trick the audience with its own preconceived notions is a technique the pros use to win Oscars and get paid seven figure numbers. Don't worry if you're still at the aspiring level of a screenwriting career because learning this technique can crank up your writing and take it to the next level.

Let's take a look at how this works…

My friend Marilyn met a cute guy who followed her in his Mercedes and honked for her to pull over. She did and they exchanged phone numbers. When I asked her why she'd do something so stupid she replied, "Well, he was wearing a suit". To her a 'suit' meant safety. I reminded her that Ted Bundy often wore a suit!

Take two brothers; one is a uniformed cop and the other a dirty street thug. Most people would gravitate to the cop for security. When, in fact, the cop's been stealing from crime victims for years and the street thug is an undercover FBI agent working to stop a terrorist attack.

Allowing an audience to perceive a character one way, then revealing a devastating twist that rocks their perceptions can make for masterful writing. Marilyn justified her dumb behavior by making a vague reference to the guy who pulled her over as 'being in a suit'. As compared to what: an unshaven, greasy guy with an axe? She's blinded by contrast that involves her own preconceived notions of the difference between a serial killer and a nice guy just looking for a date. If he looks nice he must be nice. I'm sure Bundy's victims would laugh at her stupidity. Let's face it - she did get a date, but she could have got a one-way coffin ticket.

Playing upon peoples' preconceived notions allows the writer to create a fresh character, which is why rogue cop movies are always so popular. It goes against the grain. For example, we may draw a clear contrast between a serial killer and a potential date, but if a writer takes this scenario, blinds the audience with its own preconceived notions, then the writer can shock the audience when the date turns out to be the serial killer!

What I don't like is when the blind contrast information is revealed too soon. Withholding that the cop is rogue until late in the story can shock the audience and provide for a memorable entertainment experience.

The key to pulling this off is dropping very subtle hints that there's more to the character than meets the eye. Perhaps we see the dirty street thug help an old lady across the street. It's too subtle for us to conclude he's really an undercover federal agent, but it sets it up because most street thugs don't help old ladies. For the rogue cop, show a moment of anger or a moment that seems out of character for him. It comes and it goes almost unnoticed, but is really a setup for the fact he's a dirty cop.

Last year I optioned a MOW to a Lifetime for Women TV producer. It involved a mother who drags her teen daughter through the beauty pageant circuit. For all intensive purposes, the mother appeared to be trying to live her life through her daughter. I used the audience's own preconceived notions about this type of mother to mislead them while I dropped very subtle hints that something else was amiss; we see the mother hand the daughter an aspirin and water for an apparent headache, we see the mother rubbing the teen's neck and shoulders for apparent stress relieve before a competition, etc. In reality, the teen is dying and it's her dream to win a beauty contest. The mother had no interest in the pageant whatsoever and was only trying to fulfill her dying child's last wish. It's a heartbreaking moment that takes the audience by surprise. The producer hated the mother, but then loved her and cried with her as she tried to fulfill her daughter's dying wish.

I used blind contrast to create a commercial MOW! One that will not only entertain the audience, but provide them with a twist that will guarantee an emotional response. Making audiences cry is a writer's job.

Write a character based on how you know he or she will be perceived or I should say misperceived. Drop very subtle hints that more is going on than meets the eye and then late in the story hit the audience with a big character twist! That's the way to sell a script and maybe even get an Oscar!

Learn to create blind contrast that will WOW the audience with a big twist. This is the way to sell a script and you'll be 99% ahead of the pack because most writers create straightforward stories that reveal too much information too soon leaving no room for a shock factor! Let them write their crap because you've just learned how to use blind contrast to land a sale!

QUICK LOVE

It isn't likely in real-life that people will fall in-love at first sight (although I hear it happens) or in a day, a week...okay, maybe a month. But in the movies, it happens all the time and somehow it's believable. But then a screenwriter writes a spec screenplay where the couple falls in love quickly and the script's rejected as being 'unbelievable' because real-life people don't fall in love so quickly.

Wait a minute! In *Titanic* they fell in love in two days! In *Bed of Roses* a few days! In *While You Were Sleeping* it's only two weeks. In *How to Lose a Guy in Ten Days* – it's 10 days!

Why do these films work, while your spec script continues to get rejected? The key is the setup. I don't mean a 'cute meet' or the couple's first scene together. The key setup I'm referring to is the couple's emotional vulnerability. If the audience connects with the character's emotional vulnerability – defined as their need for love – then they'll believe the character can fall in love quickly. It won't matter how fast it happens. The audience will accept it.

The emotional vulnerability MUST be introduced when the character's first introduced. The writer needs to keep hitting the hero over the head with it as a reminder to the audience; this character needs love – now! In *While You Were Sleeping* the heroine's a lonely lady who lives with her cat. We quickly learn her father died and she has no family. Her love interest happens to be a man who has a big, loving family. Get these two together and the audience will want the heroine to have a family and find love. When it happens in 2 weeks and she marries the love interest, the audience accepts it.

Study films where the love happens quickly. Watch for the emotional vulnerability setup. Pay close attention to how it's setup and how many times it's reinforced in the story.

Everyone wants to find love. Everyone wants to be swept off their feet. In real life, it's unlikely to happen in a weekend, but in the movies we can believe in anything, especially love!

COMMERCIAL DIALOGUE

Have you ever been told your dialogue isn't realistic? Then you go to the movies. Wait a minute! Movies DON'T TALK REALISTIC, so why is your dialogue being scrutinized for being unrealistic?

This is often a confusing factor to a screenwriter. Here's the reason:

Realistic Dialogue Does Not Mean Real-Life Dialogue

What it means is the dialogue isn't realistic to the character. Go back and take a look at the character's setup. If you haven't set someone up as a rebel and they speak like one, then the dialogue will sound unrealistic. However, if you've done a proper job at setting the character up as a rebel his dialogue will sound realistic for his character. You don't have to "take time" to set him up as a rebel if you've given him a commercial entrance where his "rebel" traits are obvious.

How Film Dialogue Differs From Real-Life Dialogue

Film dialogue is real-life dramatized. It has to be or there'd be tons of fillers and junk information that would put most audiences to sleep.

Steer Clear of Dialogue That's Real-Life Verbatim

Real-life verbatim doesn't walk around in a constant state of conflict – film characters do! If we did this in real life we'd all shoot one another! Real-life people avoid conflict – film characters are slam-dunked with it!

> *The trick to realistic,*
> *commercial-quality dialogue*
> *is staying true to the character!*

DIALOGUE FOR DUMMIES

USE COLOR CODING

Have you ever been told your characters sound alike? This could be due to a variety of reasons, but the easiest way to avoid this is through a simple, color-coding system I've created to assure your characters sound different.

There are four basic colors in this system. Each applies to a standard personality type as follows:

BLUE = Sensitive Soul
GOLD = Authority Figure
GREEN = Down to Earth
ORANGE = Risk Taker

These are stereotypes, but it'll give you a base upon which to start because your character is bound to fall primarily into one of these categories. The goal here is to identify a figure of speech for each color. You can expand upon it later, but first…

Let's do a quick exercise to see how this works:

All four characters (Blue, Gold, Green and Orange) are on an airplane bound for Los Angeles when the flight attendant announces the cockpit's been taken over by terrorists. Here's the first reaction we'd hear from the four characters:

BLUE
"Oh my God, we're going to die."

GOLD
"I'm the Air Marshal, stand aside."

GREEN
"We should negotiate with them."

ORANGE
"Bring 'em on!"

If everyone on the plane starts talking about negotiating with the terrorists then you have too many green personalities. If everyone plans to jump the terrorists then there are too many orange risk takers aboard.

The way to create conflict and assure everyone sounds different is to know your character's color (basic personality trait) and write their dialogue accordingly. If you put two blues together you're bound to hear the same type of viewpoint and this can get boring fast, but put an orange with a blue and watch the sparks fly!

Mixing Colors is the Fastest & Easiest Way to Create Conflict

But what if all your characters are cops and you want their scenes to have conflict, but they're all Gold? Add a color to their primary Gold as follows:

GOLD/GOLD
This cop plays by the rules.

GOLD/BLUE
This cop wants to minimize loss of life.

GOLD/GREEN
This cop wants to negotiate first.

GOLD/ORANGE
This cop wants to hit the bad guy hard, now!

Put these four cops in a hostage scenario and watch the conflict. They may all be on the same side, but their viewpoints - based on assigned colors - will come through the dialogue and create conflict in the scene. Conflict can be subtle. It doesn't mean characters have to be shouting at one another.

Let's listen in as the cops try to decide what to do when it appears the bad guy will kill the first hostage in a matter of minutes:

GOLD/GOLD
We stand down and wait 'til S.W.A.T. arrives.

GOLD/BLUE
If we storm the building more hostages could be lost.

GOLD/GREEN
Let me talk to him, buy some time.

GOLD/ORANGE
We gotta move now before he kills the hostage.

The reason the dialogue might sound alike in this type of scene is because the screenwriter is writing dialogue for cops, rather than writing dialogue for cops with different personalities and opposing viewpoints. In other words, they're writing all Gold!

The best thing about writing dialogue from this straightforward, color-coded approach is that it'll pass the "No Character Cue Indicator" test. Just remove the character's name and it'll be obvious who's talking.

What about the protagonist? What if he starts out Blue and by the end of the story you want him to be Orange? Simple. When we first meet him his dialogue reflects his Blue personality. Then, as he's forced to confront an external conflict and change we SLOWLY hear little snips of Orange appear in his dialogue.

Slowly integrating Orange traits into the Blue dialogue will make his transition believable.

Once the transition is complete you can nail it down by marking the character arc by repeating a line of dialogue that shows the transition from Blue to Orange. It can be the exact same line, spoken differently - the same line with something added or an entirely new (Orange) viewpoint.

Let's take a look at a character who's never taken any physical risks and see how this works. The BLUE dialogue will indicate a line spoken at the beginning of the story and the ORANGE will be the line towards the end or at the end that marks their change.

SAME LINE:

BLUE
I'd never jump off a bridge, that's nuts.

ORANGE
I'd never jump off a bridge....

Character leaps off a bridge with a bungee cord attached.

ORANGE (CONT'D)
(on the way down)
...that's nuts!

SAME LINE WITH SOMETHING ADDED:

BLUE
I'd never jump off a bridge, that's nuts.

ORANGE
I'd never jump off a bridge...once, I plan to

131

do it twice.

Character leaps off the bridge with a bungee cord attached.

ENTIRELY NEW LINE

BLUE
I'd never jump off a bridge, that's nuts.

ORANGE
Geronimo!

Character leaps off the bridge with a bungee cord attached.

****

Revealing the character's arc through dialogue is as simple as SLOWLY adding orange to the blue then repeating a line that nails down the change from blue to orange. My personal favorite is repeating the same line with a different action – it's up to you!

Dialogue Tidbit

Still not sure if the characters sound too much alike? Try a hand-held tape recorder. Read the dialogue into it then go have lunch. You need some time away from it before you listen in order to gain a new perspective.

After lunch, play the scene and I guarantee anything that doesn't sound right for any reason will leap out at you.

Extra Tidbit

Color-coding can easily be applied to characterizations. If you're struggling with defining your characters' individual personalities, then apply the Color-Coding Technique and watch them come alive.

DIALOGUE CUE TEST

I've already mentioned using a tape recorder to gauge whether or not characters sound alike, but is there an ultimate commercial dialogue test? Yes and here it is:

❖ Write a brief character description (1-3 paragraphs) for characters with dialogue in a scene you've chosen to use for the test.

132

- Remove the character "cue" indicators = remove the character's names.
- Print the page.
- Give the character description and the printed page to someone. It's okay if they're a screenplay novice. This is a simple test anyone – except you – should be able to complete.
- Ask them to read the character description then read the dialogue and INSERT THE CHARACTER'S NAME who they believe is speaking.
- Don't help them!
- Check what they put and if it doesn't match, ask why they chose the name they did.

This can be a real eye opener! You don't have to do this with every scene. Pick a dialogue scene, preferably with the protagonist and antagonist – maybe with one other character – and use this. Use two or more scenes if you want.

Don't try to take this test yourself! This is beyond cheating because you're cheating yourself out of the opportunity to get some valuable feedback on the dialogue you've written.

FILM-WORTHY DIALOGUE

Most screenwriters have mastered conflict in the dialogue. Most know how to use the scene's dialogue to convey information and move the story forward. If this is the case, then why do so many dialogue scenes fail?

It could be because the writer is trying too hard to write real-life verbatim. Or the writer hasn't developed an ear for dialogue (read how to develop an ear for dialogue in this chapter). Or the writer is trying to mimic movie dialogue without understanding how it's setup and delivered. Regardless, let's look at ways to assure quality dialogue that will enhance the story.

Short & Pithy Dialogue

Keep dialogue short and pithy. The 4-6 line maximum rule stands. This keeps the story moving along and helps maintain visual flow. What if the character has to provide vital information that's lengthy and can't be delivered visually, like a lawyer in a courtroom setting? Then break it up with action and/or description. Does the lawyer pace back and forth? Does he shuffle paper? Or stroll up to the jury box? Add action and description to break up lengthy dialogue.

An exception might be a speech. Maybe the hero is giving a speech at the end of the movie. Or the hero's a politician. Same rules apply as above to break it up with action/or description.

Extra Note: There should be few, if any all dialogue pages in a script. More than 3 means the script relies too heavily on dialogue to deliver information rather than the visuals. This type of script isn't visual enough for the big screen.

Less is More

No, I don't mean shorter dialogue. We just discussed that. I'm referring to writers who insist on telling us everything the character is about to do or has just done. If John's planning to burn down Todd's house, I don't want John to tell me. That ruins the suspense. Show me!

Don't have a character tell us his flaws and shortcomings. Let another character do this. Or have the character reveal this information visually.

Do NOT repeat information already known. If we just saw a building blow up, don't have one character tell another character about it. Keep the story moving forward. But what if character #2 doesn't know about the building blowing up and he needs to know? Then tell him in a different way. Perhaps character #1 asks about the building and character #2 just shakes his head.

Act III's Dialogue

Dialogue should be shorter and faster as the story nears its end. This gives the sense that the story is wrapping up. The exception might be a speech given by the hero. As noted above, keep the speech but break it up with action and/or description. If the pacing is really fast in the end, I'd advise the writer to break up the long speech with other scenes, then come back to it.

Dialogue Reversals

Have you ever been told your dialogue is on-the-nose, too direct, too straightforward or ordinary? What does this really mean? It means the characters are saying exactly what we expect them to say and this creates boring and often flat-sounding dialogue.

The best way to avoid this is to create dialogue reversals. Don't overcomplicate this. A reversal is nothing more than a mini-twist. Some writers add a twist to create a plot point or every ten pages. Both are good, but pros know that every scene should have a visual or a dialogue reversal.

It's just a mini-twist. Have the character say something unexpected. If the audience has been watching a heroine desperate to get married, then her boyfriend finally pops the question and she says 'No', then the writer has create a reversal.

Reversals are important because they keep material fresh, which makes it interesting to read. It also creates suspense and assures a producer won't put down the script for fear he'll miss something.

Dialogue versus Visuals

Film's a visual medium. This means it relies primarily on visuals to deliver the story rather than dialogue. If you don't know what I mean compare how TV delivers information compared to movies. TV is a talking heads, dialogue medium. For example, in the hit detective show *Psych* the fake, psychic detective tells us how the murderer did his deed in one segment at the end of the show. He'll usually say something like, "Let me tell you what happened". This would never take place in a movie! In a film we need to see the murder plot unfold visually without having anyone tell us how the murderer almost got away with the crime.

What does this mean to you? It means you need to look at the information in a scene. Try to find ways to convey the information visually rather than via dialogue. Visuals first, dialogue second. A simple touch can be more powerful than saying 'I love you'. If you find you're more in tune with dialogue and are having a difficult time visualizing the story, then maybe you're a TV writer because you aren't a screenwriter.

Avoid Q&A Sessions

Every question asked doesn't require an answer. Failing to answer a question can create suspicion, conflict and suspense. Besides, do we always answer every question we're asked in real life? Often we either answer the question indirectly or not at all.

What if the scene takes place in a psychiatrist's office? Shake things up! Don't ask and answer back and forth. Break up the dialogue with action. Have the patient or doctor avoid the question or change the subject. Q&A sessions are boring in real life and even more boring to watch on a 35-foot wide screen.

Also, Q&A sessions if too long can literally hurt the script's chance at a sale because film's a visual medium.

Avoid the word 'about'

The word 'about' used in dialogue is passive and often overly used by writers. Actors know this and often change dialogue containing this word. Why? It literally weakens the delivery. Don't believe it? Write 2-pages with two characters speaking with dialogue chalked full of the word 'about', then read one role and have someone else read the other role. I guarantee you'll hear what I mean in an instant and will rarely use the word 'about' in dialogue. If you already have a completed screenplay, do a search for the word and replace its use in dialogue.

Avoid Cliches

What is a cliché? It's an overused expression. Here are a few examples:

His bark is worse than his bite
The grass is always greener on the other side
No good deed goes unpunished

They're phrases we've heard so often that we know the meaning without being told. The problem arises when they're used in the dialogue of a screenplay. Why? Because spec scripts from an aspiring screenwriter need to have a fresh, original voice. Dialogue can't be original if it's filled with overused expressions. Producers see clichés in dialogue as a lazy screenwriter who can't come up with a character who speaks from an original voice.

Cliches are so common in society that a screenwriter may be using clichés in the dialogue without realizing it. The Writer's Store has books to help identify clichés and here's a link to a 'Cliché Finder' that can help: http://www.westegg.com/cliche/

This link allows a screenwriter to type in a phrase or a single word to determine if it's a cliché. If you're not sure, go to this site and do a search. The screenwriter can also look up lists of clichés and even add a cliché. The goal is to eliminate clichés in the screenplay's dialogue.

Is there an exception to this rule? Yes. The exception is the comedy genre where clichés are often used in dialogue for comedic effect. A word of warning: Although clichés are acceptable in the confines of the comedy genre, comedy spec scripts from aspiring screenwriters should keep them to a minimum.

Avoid the Wryly

Use a wryly sparingly. The writer shouldn't be telling an actor how to deliver a line. This isn't the writer's job. The proper use of a wryly is when a scene calls for a different delivery than it appears to. For example, the writer has written a comedy scene, but wants one line to be delivered 'seriously' rather than said like a punch-line. In this case, the writer would have to use a wryly or the actor will deliver the line wrong and change the meaning of the scene.

The Arc Dialogue Line

The arc dialogue line is often referred to as the tie-in line or the repeat line. Its purpose is to reveal change (arc) in the hero. In Act I, a hero might tell a woman he hates her, then in Act III he says 'I love you'. It's the same line said differently to reveal he's changed. The line can be the same line modified, a different line with the same meaning or a whole new way of saying 'I love you'.

Here's an example:

In the movie *Family Man* starring Nicolas Cage the film opens in an airport. Cage's love interest, fearing she'll never see him again, tells him 'I chose us'. He goes on to a life without her. A life of success, money and power...until one lonely Christmas night he falls asleep and awakens in a different life where he's poor with two kids and his former girlfriend is his wife. He wants nothing more than to escape this life, but eventually it grows on him. He wants to stay. Unfortunately, this life was just a glimpse and he awakens back in his old life, which he now hates. He hunts down the girlfriend, stops her from leaving at an airport and says to her what she once said to him, 'I chose us'. It's the tie-in, repeat line that reveals his arc. He's a changed man!

The key to making the tie-in line work is setting it up, then paying it off AFTER the hero has changed or at the moment of change to reveal his arc. If he changes at the end of Act II, the repeat line can happen before he charges off to save the day. Or it can happen at the very end of the story. Most films have a tie-in line. Listen for it. Learn to recognize it in a film and learn to incorporate a tie-line into your writing to give the story and the hero a more professional finish. If you listen closely, the writer will discover a majority of quality films use this technique. Using it can set your dialogue apart from the rank amateurs who have no clue what it is, why it's used or how to use it.

Hero Gets the Last Line

Producers need to attach talent to a project to get it made. I literally know an A-list actor who flips to the last page of the script and if his character (the lead role) doesn't get the last line, he passes! After all, he's the hero and he wants the last line and this won't happen if a secondary role upstages him. Sounds brutal, but if a screenwriter wants to sell a script, the writer needs to start seeing the script from a producer and even an actor's point of view. Why should the writer care? Isn't it the producer's job to get actors attached? Yes, but what do you think the producer is doing when he options your script? He's trying to get talent attached so he can get funds to make a movie. If he can't do this, then the writer is the one who suffers. Make his job easier and guarantee yourself a paycheck by giving the hero the last line.

Hero Gets the Best Lines

Okay, it's time for another actor reality check. I know quite a few actors who ask the producer to indicate what pages they speak on. Why? If the actor is the lead, he wants to make sure he's in a majority of scenes and this is an easy way to tell. Or, more likely, he's going to read only his role to see if the dialogue jumps out at him. Does he get the meaty lines? The best lines? If not, he'll start to scan the script and if he notices a supporting role is getting the good lines, he'll pass on the script.

If the hero isn't getting the best lines, then switch up the dialogue so he does! Who says you have to commit dialogue to one character? If it makes the hero sound too much like the other character, then revise it to suit the hero.

Does this mean the supporting roles should have lackluster dialogue? Don't be ridiculous. Just make sure they don't upstage the hero. A-list actors do NOT like to be upstaged by another role.
Can you imagine a supporting role getting Clint Eastwood's famous line, "Go ahead, make my day." Or Arnold's famous "I'll be back" line?

DIALOGUE SUBTEXT

Subtext is one of the most difficult areas for screenwriters to grasp. After all, screenwriters have been told repeatedly not to write anything that can't be filmed. But subtext is what adds a commercial edge to dialogue.

Subtext is an implied or underlying meaning to the words spoken

138

How do we film this? Shouldn't we steer clear of subtext all together? As a Hollywood reader I can assure you I've never seen a script – first sale or otherwise – sell without it!

Why is it so important? Because it creates deeper meaning within the story and makes us experience the movie rather than just watching the movie. Almost all screenwriters seem to add subtext to at least one scene in their script – whether intentional or not. The problem is the majority of dialogue should contain subtext.

In my screenplay "The President's Assassin" there's a scene where Robert (protagonist) takes Wade (his best friend) to see a fortune teller for his birthday. This is what Wade has to say about his birthday gift:

> WADE
> When you said you were taking me
> to see a lady for my birthday, this
> wasn't exactly what I had in mind.

The subtext "implies" Wade would rather see a different kind of "lady" otherwise known as a prostitute. Wade never says this directly, but the reader will understand the underlying meaning and this is subtext!

How many couples have had arguments 'bout which end to squeeze the toothpaste or how to unroll the toilet paper? These arguments have nothing to do with toothpaste or toilet paper. They're subtext! It's a way for the couple to vent their 'real' frustrations without saying it directly.

Believe it or not, we all use subtext every single day in our real-life dialogue. How many times does someone say something to you and you 'get it' even though they didn't say it directly? I bet a good 2 to 3 times or more a day. Start paying attention! Make it a habit to note when you've inadvertently said something via subtext or you heard someone else say it.

Shortcut to Dialogue Subtext

It's shocking when writers ask me how they can learn to write dialogue subtext. When a writer asks me this question it's obvious the writer isn't a good listener because I've never gotten through a single day without hearing dialogue subtext. The first thing the writer can do to learn how to write dialogue subtext is to start listening for it in real-life conversations. The writer should even listen to his own words!

Don't tell me you've never heard it. Remember the last time you ran into an old friend and the friend asked if you lost weight. Isn't the friend saying they thought you were fat? Yes, they are! Sorry to burst your bubble, but they weren't making polite conversation. Start listening to what's NOT being said. What's not being said is the subtext!

Okay, you're still confused and lost. Here's another easy shortcut: Study comedians. Watch The Tonight Show with Jay Leno or a favorite sitcom. We all laugh when we get the meaning behind what they're saying, but these guys never say it directly. That's subtext! Comedy is built around subtext! Study it. Every time the comedian tells a joke, write down the meaning of the joke. Do this enough times and the writer will learn how to incorporate subtext into dialogue. I'm not trying to tell the writer to write only comedy. Just learn how to use the technique.

I bet some of you still don't get it. For some reason, subtext is illusive. Okay, here is an example:

A husband comes home to find his wife sitting on the couch stuffing her face with Doritos while watching Dr. Phil. He looks around the messy house and says:

HUSBAND
You know, honey, I mopped this morning.
(beat)
And last week.

WIFE
Thanks sweetie, appreciate it.

HUSBAND
Mopped last month too.

She gives him a 'so what' look and turns back to the TV.

Her dialogue and gestures are obvious – she doesn't care. But what does his subtext say? It says, "When the hell are you going to get off your lazy butt and mop the darn floor?" He never says this, but it's obvious what he's trying to say. That's subtext! Apply it to screenplay writing and the writer will look like a pro.

Dialogue Subtext Creates Emotion

Creating underlying meaning and have characters speak in a way that reveals what is not being said is the way to involve the audience in the story and most importantly, to create emotions. When someone is really saying they don't like us without saying it directly, it hurts! When the character hurts, the audience hurts. Audiences want to share emotions with the characters, especially the hero.

Dialogue subtext can also be used to enhance the genre's emotional core. If the script's a horror, does the dialogue evoke fear? If it's a comedy, is the dialogue filled with funny moments? If it's a romantic comedy, does the dialogue hint, via subtext, at love?

EVERY scene should evoke an emotion, which means – in my opinion – that every scene should contain subtext; either visual or via dialogue. Let me make this clear. I'm not just talking about the emotions experienced by the character. I'm also talking about the emotions experienced by the audience. Maybe the audience knows something the character doesn't know and when the character speaks the dialogue inadvertently becomes subtext that causes the audience suspense, loathing, ecstasy, fear, love, etc.

When you're watching a movie next time, really pay attention to the moments that hold you spellbound. How do they do this? I bet if you really pay attention the answer will be obvious; subtext!

Subtext Meaning Revealed

The writer finally starts to incorporate subtext into dialogue, then a story analyst writes notes that she didn't get what the character meant. Oh no, what happened? Isn't this the way to film-quality dialogue? Yes, but be careful. If the subtext is too vague, the audience won't get it. Just because you get a meaning doesn't mean the audience will.

Use the comedian's technique of using widely recognized subject matter when using subtext. In the example I gave above where the character Wade tells his friend Robert the fortune teller wasn't exactly what he had in mind for his birthday. It's widely known what a man would prefer to have for his birthday in place of a fortune teller, so there's no need to deliver the meaning by having Robert clarify what Wade's referring to.

However, if the meaning isn't obvious, then add it. Have the same or another character state the meaning. Be careful because this can destroy the emotion you've worked so hard to deliver to the audience. The only time I've ever delivered the meaning is when I was writing a script with a lot of local banter from a southwestern town. Many audience members won't get the southern wit and charm done via subtext without the meaning being delivered. Even so, I delivered it in subtle ways, often visually so I didn't spoil the emotional impact of writing dialogue with subtext.

Another way to master subtext is to learn to develop an ear for dialogue.

The Cliché Way to Subtext

Subtext is the illusive Bigfoot that causes aspiring writers to fail at become big game hunters (writers who've sold a script). I've devised a technique that uses clichés to teach writers subtext. I am not advocating you use clichés in your work. That's commercial suicide. Instead, use something you're familiar with, clichés, to teach yourself subtext! Let's take a look at how this works.

We all know what a cliché is. To sum it up, it's a common phrase with underlying meaning that's lost its originality due to overuse. For those of you who have asked me what's subtext; I bet you know the meaning of the following phrases:

1) The apple doesn't fall far from the tree
2) Don't count your chickens before they're hatched
3) Once in a blue moon
4) Have a lot on one's plate
5) Glutton for punishment

But wait a minute! You claim you don't know subtext, then how do you know the meaning of these phrases?

1) The apple doesn't fall far from the tree doesn't literally mean the apple only falls 1-2 feet from a tree. Its underlying meaning is a child who grows up very similar to his or her parents.

2) Don't count your chickens before they're hatched doesn't mean to stand in front of a chicken coop waiting for the chickens to hatch to count them. Its underlying meaning is don't put faith in something you don't yet have.

3) Once in a blue moon isn't a reference to vampires, werewolves or giant moons made out of blue cheese. Its underlying meaning is in reference to a rare event (like the rare blue moon).

4) Have a lot on one's plate isn't a reference to overeaters. Its underlying meaning is a person who has multiple things going at once that requires attention.

5) A glutton for punishment doesn't refer to overeaters who beat themselves with a stick at dinner time. Its underlying meaning is a person who seeks out burdensome or unpleasant tasks, things, people, situations, etc.

But I bet I didn't have to tell you the meanings. I bet you knew the meanings. See, you do know subtext and didn't realize it. I bet you can't get through a day without experiencing subtext. We've heard common phrases, like the ones above, so many times in our daily lives that we automatically know and understand their meanings.

Studying clichés and their meaning is a great way to understand subtext. However, you can't use clichés in a spec screenplay and hope to sell it. Let's say you have a scene where a guy thinks he won a $10K bingo and goes out and maxes out his credit cards. Later, he discovers it was a prank pulled by his buddy. The cliché 'Don't count your chickens before they're hatched' might apply to this scenario, but you can't use the cliché. Instead, work through phrases to use in the scene that provide an underlying meaning. For example, the buddy might simply say something like:

THE BUDDY
You should have waited.

It's a simple phrase, but in the context of the scene means the guy should have waited for confirmation and payment before going on a spending spree. We don't need the buddy to say everything because the mistake made is obvious. If the buddy did state everything, the dialogue would become too direct and repetitive.

Or the writer can setup a phrase that means 'Don't count your chickens before they're hatched'. The writer might have the buddy say 'Gotcha' when his prank is discovered. By setting up the "Gotcha" phrase early in the script, the writer establishes a scenario where the phrase's meaning is understood when he says it to the guy who went on a spending spree.

THE BUDDY
Gotcha!

Coming up with clever ways to deliver underlying meaning is actually fun! But what if the writer wants to do this same thing, only the writer wants to use visual subtext rather than dialogue subtext? When the guy shows up for

143

his bingo winnings, he gets baby chickens instead; literally a visual delivery of the underlying meaning.

Using clichés as a base to understanding, creating subtext and delivering its meaning can greatly enhance a writer's work. Take a look at every scene in a script. If it's lacking in visual or dialogue subtext, comes up with clever ways to create underlying dialogue and visual meaning without saying or showing things directly.

Once again, I must advise against actually using clichés in scripts. Why? Because producers want to see fresh, original work not overused crap. But at the same time, producers and audiences want to experience the story on an emotional level and the way to accomplish this is to involve the audience in the story. Subtext makes an audience feel like 'they get it' and when they understand the underlying meaning they feel emotionally involved. That's the power of subtext!

DEVELOP AN EAR FOR DIALOGUE

Industry professionals will often say a writer has an ear for dialogue. In other writer arenas this means the writer gets how people speak and can mimic it to seem realistic. In Hollywood, it means the writer can write film-quality, memorable – dramatized dialogue. After all, film characters do not speak like real-life people. The purpose of film dialogue is to entertain. However, the basis for that entertainment starts with real-life dialogue and this is where the writer can begin to learn how to have an ear for dialogue. Sorry folks, I don't believe having an ear for dialogue is a gift bestowed upon the few. I believe it's an acquired talent any writer can learn, but it'll take patience and persistence.

Here are a few exercises I'd like the writer to do. They can be painstaking, but fun and once completed, the writer will have an ear for dialogue.

EXERCISE #1 – Learning to Eliminate Filler Dialogue

In my opinion, this is the easiest way to develop an ear for dialogue. Most writers already know how to eliminate filler dialogue, but it's still a good exercise to do because filler dialogue in a screenplay can slow down the pacing, flatten the dialogue and frankly, it'll bore the audience to tears.

Here's what the writer needs to do: Go to Starbucks (or a local café or diner). Sit near the cash register and listen! Grab a cup of coffee, eat a slice of pie or enjoy a whole meal. Pretend to read a newspaper; I don't care as long as you're listening. When people interact with strangers (the cashier, waiters, etc.) they often use idle chit-chat (filler dialogue) because silence would be awkward. The # 1 filler chit-chat should be obvious; it's the weather. They'll talk about how the snow buried their car or left them stranded on I-60 overnight. They'll talk about the how rain never stops or how they hope it'll be sunny soon. If they don't talk about the weather, they'll pick another 'filler' topic. They might comment on the food or how they're stuffed like a Thanksgiving turkey. Or maybe they'll comment on the traffic. The common denominator is something everyone has in common; weather, food and traffic.

Sit there for two (2) hours! I know you think I'm nuts, but there's a method behind the madness. After two hours, I'm quite sure you'll hear enough filler dialogue that you'll want to scream and send me hate emails. The point is that the next time the writer sits down to write a screenplay, I guarantee the writer will think twice before writing a word of filler dialogue. Most importantly, the writer will be able to recognize when he/she is writing non-essential filler crap because the writer has done this exercise and developed an ear for filler dialogue -- and knows how to avoid it.

EXERCISE #2 – Stop Listening!

Go to a diner or café and order a meal. Go alone! Contrary to the title, this is a listening exercise. Sit with your back to others; maybe in a booth or at a table. I want the writer to eavesdrop on a conversation where the writer can't see who is speaking. I want the writer to stop listening to what's being said and start listening for what's NOT being said.

I once did this exercise during a busy morning at a Starbucks. Two men were sitting behind me discussing a presentation. From their conversation, it was apparent both had prepared the presentation, but only one man was going to give the presentation. Every time the man who wasn't giving the presentation mentioned how easy it would be to convince the listening party of the marketability of a product they were selling (I'm guessing they were salesmen), the other man would agree with comments like "Yeah, that's clear cut" and then he'd laugh ever-so-slightly and ever-so-nervously. His nervousness said what he wasn't saying; either he was anxious about giving the presentation or he wasn't convinced he could sell it to others.

Learning to identify what isn't being said along with what is being said, then applying this to writing can make it seem like the writer has an ear for dialogue. The writer can enhance a scene's dialogue by having what appears to be totally agreeable characters, but give one of them a nervous laugh and the audience will sense the underlying tension. This is what leads to compelling scenes and memorable dialogue moments.

145

EXERCISE #3 – The Secret Service Technique

Do you know why the U.S. Secret Service agents always wear sunglasses, even if it's snowing outside? Are they trying to look cool year round? No. They couldn't care less about how they look. They wear the sunglasses so others don't know what they're looking at. Give it a try. Put on dark sunglasses – ones where you can't see your eyes. Keep your head pointed straight ahead, but move your eyes to the right or left and watch what's happening. Anyone seeing you would think you're merely staring straight ahead when you're really watching the action to your left or right.

Okay, why am I giving the writer a lesson in Secret Service tactics? Because I want the writer to do something daring and bold so the writer can learn to have an ear for dialogue. I don't care if it is snowing where you live. Go to a local café, diner or coffee shop. Sit outside on the patio or inside. Wear dark sunglasses. Who cares what others think? Okay, you care. You shouldn't, but if you're that insecure tell folks you're an eccentric writer or tell a white lie and say you had your eyes dilated. Or wait until summer (coward!).

I want the writer to sit where others are in plain view to the writer's immediate right or immediate left. Pretend to be eating, drinking coffee or reading a book. Instead, you'll be staring straight at them! Just like a Secret Service agent. You're listening to what's being said, what's not being said and you're looking for gestures that say something totally different than the conversation.

I already told you in Exercise #2 how to listen for what's not being said. Now I want you to carefully watch the speaking people. Don't worry, they won't know you're watching them! Does one person agree with another, then frown or make a scowl? This gestures means they really don't agree – not entirely. Does one person keep checking his watch? Scratching his nose? Texting? Sipping coffee? All of these can be visual subtext that means something beyond the conversation. Can't you tell when a friend is in a hurry? Or when someone's upset? Sure you can, but how can you tell if they don't tell you? What specifically do they do or not do that gives it away?

It might seem easier to learn this technique by interacting with your own friends, but it isn't! Why? Because you have to interact too and this can be distracting. I want the writer in a position of observer only! Don't take notes! Don't write down everything they do. Just watch. If done enough times a few things will happen: 1) the coffee shop will think you're an international spy (LOL!) 2) seriously, the writer will learn to identify precisely what's said, what isn't said and the gestures that speak volumes beyond the conversation.

146

Then the next time the writer sits down to write, he/she will know how to create masterful, layered dialogue scenes.

EXERCISE #4 The *Liar, Liar* Technique

I've taught the writer how to listen for what's not being said, how to listen for what is being said and how to identify gestures that speaks volumes beyond the spoken conversation. Now it's time to take notes!

Go back to the café, diner or coffee shop. Well, you might want to pick a new place or the folks there could be tempted to call the cops. For this exercise, you'll be learning to do two important things to help develop an ear for dialogue:

1) Listen to a conversation and when the writer identifies what's not being said or sees a gesture that speaks beyond the spoken word – I want the writer to write down what the person actually wants to say! It's like in the movie "Liar, Liar" the hero couldn't tell a lie and had to speak what he was thinking! For example, if you see a woman cringe when her friend tells her she's returning to an abusive husband and the friend is supportive; the writer might make a note that says what the friend really wanted to say: "Are you out of your freaking mind?" By doing this exercise, the writer will learn what to write when it comes time for the screenplay. As mentioned at the beginning of this section, TV and film dialogue is dramatized. To create a conflict and a reversal, the writer would use the type of dialogue from his notes – what the friend actually wants to say – to dramatize the scene! Got it?

2) Listen to a conversation and identify the speaking types. There are three speaking types; Visual, Hearing and Feeling. Here are the differences:

Visual speaking people talk fast. They often finish other people's sentences and use phrases like "I see what you're saying" or "It looks good to me".

Hearing speaking people talk slower. They rarely interrupt and are often good listeners. They use phrases like "I hear what you're saying" or "It sounds good to me".

Feeling speaking people talk really slow – turtle speed. They take the time to get every word right and it's obvious they feel what they're saying. They use phrases like "I believe what you're saying" or "It feels good to me".

It's important to learn to identify the different speaking types in real-life. First, which one are you? I'm the visual speaking person. Many screenwriters are visual speaking people, while novelists are often hearing or feeling speaking people who can dwell into the deep recesses of their characters' minds.

After identifying your own speaking type, go back to the café and listen to multiple conversations at different tables. Go when it's busy! Identify the strangers' speaking types; the man sitting next to the window is a visual speaking person, the blonde with him is hearing, the waiter is feeling.

Why is this important to writing? It's vital for several reasons. The writer can pit these types against each other in the same scene. The visual speaking person might speak over the slower, feeling speaking person creating conflict, etc. Or the writer might want to start with a touchy-feely speaking person and turn him into a fast-talking stud. Lots of possibilities, but none work unless the writer can easily identify speaking types and understands how to apply them to his/her writing.

Now the writer knows why film dialogue sounds dramatized. It is dramatized and it's dramatized by the writer who has learned how to have an ear for dialogue!

COMMERCIALIZE A SCENE

Most screenwriters seem to understand a scene must:

- Move the story forward
- Contain conflict
- Start late, end early

Most also seem to understand how to set up and pay off plot elements via specific scenes. However, many overlook the most vital role of the scene; to provide emotional content. Two questions should be asked:

1) What is the emotional content of the scene?
2) What emotion am I trying to evoke in the reader?

Some might argue that a certain scene is merely being used to convey vital plot information. A scene can still convey information and hit an emotion. If it doesn't, IT IS NOT COMMERCIAL and should be axed or rewritten to contain emotional content. You're not writing an encyclopedia or a text book, you're writing a movie! This chapter will discuss how to create emotions via the visuals.

Use Action to Show Emotion

How does your character express anger, sadness, fear or any other emotion? Most screenwriters simply write "He's afraid" or "She feels sad," but this isn't screenwriting. Why? Because the writer needs to SHOW us he's afraid or she feels sad. Show, don't tell! How? Instead of writing "He's angry," have the character hurl a dish. Now we know he's angry because the action shows us. Show the heroine crying. Now we see she's sad.

I once told a screenwriter he needed to show us that his character was feeling sad after a relationship breakup instead of just writing "he feels sad." When the writer submitted the next draft he'd simply added a scene where the character tells his buddy how bad he's feeling. This isn't how it's done. Film's a visual medium. The writer has to show the emotion! Another reason is the actor needs to portray the emotion and he can't portray 'He's angry', but he can hurl a dish to show he's angry. Emotion is portrayed via action not words!

How Do You Show Sadness, Loss?

Use action. The character can cry, scream, shout or let us watch him tear up an old lover's photographs. In the movie *Hope Floats,* Sandra Bullock's character uses scissors to cut up everything in her house after a painful divorce from a cheating spouse. She doesn't have to tell us she's sad or angry – we can see it!

Finding visual ways to show emotion is the craft of screenwriting! Telling us is the mark of an amateur. Take your writing to the next level by going through your screenplays, pick out areas where you've told us how a character is feeling and come up with visual ways to show us. Here's another technique…

Use Contrast to Show Emotion

Contrast is nothing more than pitting opposites together, like conservative Republicans and liberal Democrats. For movies, we can use contrast to create and show emotion. Let's say you have a hero who just got dumped by his girlfriend. Don't have him run and tell his buddies. This doesn't work. It cheats the audience from experiencing the loss along with the character.

He's now a single, lonely guy so use contrast. What contrasts with a single, lonely guy? Loving, committed couples. Maybe he goes to a bar to meet his buddies to tell them what happened. Before the buddies arrive, the bar is holding a couple's contest to see who's been married the longest. Watching the hero interact in a room filled with couples will show us how he feels without the writer having to use a single word of dialogue.

Contrast can make an audience break down and cry! A woman's husband is killed in Afghanistan. She's pregnant and loses the baby. This alone is heartbreaking. But let's really tear the audience's heart apart by putting her in a situation with young families and their children. The visual contrast delivers an emotional blow.

Use Location to Show Emotion

What? How can a location evoke emotion? A funeral home might evoke sadness, but that's typical. A pro writer might take this to the next level by holding the funeral outside in the rain. There's nothing more depressing than a dark, rainy day in a cemetery. Notice how funerals in movies are usually held on a rainy day. This is no coincidence. The writer of the movie knew how to use the location to create emotion in the scene.

Remember the single, lonely guy? Forget the bar and his buddies. Just show him walking alone in the rain on a deserted street. That's all you need. Walking alone on a deserted street shows the character's emotional state and the rain reveals his sadness. Parks are often used in romantic comedies to show bright, happy people living and loving life to the fullest. Horrors often use old, creepy houses to evoke fear. A wild river might be used in an action/adventure to assure we have the ride of a lifetime. Take a good look at the locations you've chosen. Are they being used to show or create emotion? If not, why?

Use Reflection to Show Emotion

One of the ways psychiatrists get reluctant patients to talk about themselves is to ask what they think of a painting or other artwork in the room. The patient's opinion of the object is usually a reflection of his emotional state. For example, the patient might find a landscape painting with flowers 'lacking in substance' because he considers himself 'lacking in substance'. By the way, police detectives also use this technique to get suspects to talk about a crime.

For your screenplay, you don't have to wait until a shrink or a cop is in the room to use the reflection technique. If the single, lonely guy runs into his long-time, married forever friend have him shout at his friend that he's a moron for sticking with the same woman for years. His harsh words to the buddy are really a reflection of how he's currently feeling – he feels like a moron for sticking with the woman who just broke his heart. Notice that this is technically subtext! Hooray, we've added another way to layer in subtext to add depth to scenes!

Go through EVERY scene in your screenplay and make sure they contain an emotion. If not, edit the scene. Don't believe this is necessary? Do you know what producers do to scenes that lack emotion? They delete them!

SCENE BASICS

After learning how to layer a scene with emotion, it may seem trivial to review scene basics but it's the little things that make a script appear professional.

Action is Description

Whoever wrote the first screenplay rules or books did a great disservice to the screenwriter by using the word 'description'. Growing up we learned this term in reference to writing papers, thesis or novels. It often leads the writer to write unnecessary details and/or internally-driven paragraphs that don't translate to the screen and are useless in a visual medium.

I want you to remove the word description from your screenwriter vocabulary. From now on, I want you to think of the word ACTION! 99% of screenwriters write description like this:

INT. JOHN'S HOUSE – DAY

Newspapers stacked against a wall. Empty beer bottles strewn across a table. Dirty socks lie on a sofa.

-While this looks okay, is it? Well, it's okay if you're in the 99% category, but let's face it, A-list writers – and there are only a handful who make six/seven figure incomes – are NOT in the 99%, they are the 1%. Want to join them? Sure you do!

-Then stop writing typical description. It's no longer description - it's action! How do you make this necessary change to join the ranks of the pros? Simple – add an action factor, like a character. Let's see what happens when we rewrite this scene to include John:

INT. JOHN'S HOUSE – DAY

John walks past newspapers stacked against a wall. He moves empty beer bottles as he sits at a table, then pushes dirty socks from the sofa. He sighs, kicks up his feet and relaxes.

-Okay, we still described John's house, but this time we avoided doing so with typical description and instead used action! This is the way the pros do it because they know that done this way creates a moving picture in the mind of the reader, which assures they become engaged in the story and it can help make a sale!

-What if it's just an establishing shot with no characters? Then use a breeze, an animal, the mailman, a car or anything that provides movement to introduce us to the establishing location. Here's an example:

EXT. GOTHIC MANSION – DAY

A leaf tumbles in a gentle breeze. The leaf's caught up in a whirlwind and becomes entrapped in a vine-laden brick wall covered in blood.

-Needless to say, this is probably a dark, horror-type movie. I've set the tone, mood and atmosphere with an establishing shot that creates a moving picture.

Less is more in screenplays! By thinking of description as action, the writer will be forced to only write what's necessary to a scene. This should help create a light, lean and visually-appealing story. You want lots of write space on those pages!

Avoid Passive Words

A sure fire way to kill a moving picture is to overuse words like "is", "are" and words ending in "ing". Write in an active voice.

WRONG: John is running down the road.
RIGHT: John runs down the road.

-This might seem silly, but check your script for these words. Can those sentences be improved with a more active voice? If so, do it because it'll create a moving picture!

Looks Like Action

For fast-paced action scenes or sequences, I recommend using a pro format technique often referred to as stacking. By keeping sentences short and stacked against the left margin, the writer gives the feel of a fast-moving scene.

The car races!
Fast!
A bend ahead.
Two vehicles play chicken.
Headlights converge.
Closer and closer.

TRANSITIONS

The use of transitions is the #1 way to spot an amateur from a pro. Transitions are the way one scene ends and another one begins. If the writer failed to use a transition, then he's in the 99% category of wanna-be writers.

There are different types of transitions (see Format Chapter), but for this chapter I'll reference the visual-to-visual transition only as an example:

An American flag flies atop the aircraft carrier's uppermost deck.

EXT. COURTHOUSE – DAY

An American flag flaps against a pole.

-The flags mark a visual-to-visual transition between two scenes; an aircraft carrier and a courthouse. The visual transition doesn't have to consist of the same type of visual, like the flag.

A locomotive ROARS past.

EXT. CITY STREET – DAY

A car drives past.

Or perhaps a blue dress ends one scene and a blue sky opens the next scene. The goal is to use the visuals to create a smooth transition between the scenes. Remember in the movie *Forest Gump* when they're outside watching fireworks and the scene transitions to inside where they're watching fireworks on a TV. This is an example of a visual-to-visual transition. Next time you watch a movie, see how many transitions you can spot. I bet you'll see one at the end and beginning of most of the scenes in a movie. They also help a writer keep his story from being changed because producers and directors want stories with strong visual flow and removing a transitional scene can hurt this flow.

Tone, Mood & Atmosphere

Moving pictures aren't worth their weight if they don't establish and maintain a tone, mood and atmosphere throughout the story. The best example I can give is the movie *The Ring*. The movie uses dark overtures throughout the film. There are no bright, sunny days. This IS IN THE SCREENPLAY! It's a supernatural thriller and it opens with a dark day and an inciting incident and continues to maintain dark overtures throughout.

The key to a successful story is a consistent tone, mood and atmosphere throughout the scenes.

SHORTCUT TO SCENE CONFLICT

Conflict can often be misunderstood by the aspiring screenwriter. They mistake it for characters shouting at each other or believe it requires violence and don't understand why it's necessary because in a real-life situation the story's characters would get along.

Well, if you want real life stop writing screenplays and go live it. Screenplays are written for movies, which is fiction not real life! The way to sell fiction is via conflict. Even stories based on real events or real-life characters are dramatized (fictionalized) before they reach the big screen.

But wait a minute, you've written a heartwarming, Walton-style drama based on the good-old days when people got along, helped each other and conflict was unheard of. Are you serious? Mankind has historically gone to war in one part of the world or another roughly every decade since man first picked up a rock and learned he could use it to bash another man in the head. I doubt man has ever had a period where he lacked conflict!

I can't even get through a day or a week without conflict; whether it's judges who can't decide on scores for contest entrants, scheduling time with ever-so-busy visual effects people to finish a film, or that darn clerk at the grocery store who keeps short-changing me every time I buy a gallon of milk. Even small things can create conflict; the vacuum canister needs emptying or it won't run and the cat knocked over a bowl of Kit and Kaboodles. Or FedEx won't leave a package unless I sit waiting five hours to sign for it.

Life is conflict! How can you write a screenplay without it? If I read another story where life is oh-so grand, I'm going to puke! Life's a journey and frankly, I believe conflict is what makes life interesting. I'm not the only one who believes it; so do producers! More importantly, so do audiences!

Perhaps you need to go back and watch a few more reruns of the *Waltons* because every episode had conflict. Even characters helping other characters may have been doing so out of guilt (conflict), obligation (conflict), social necessity (conflict), acceptance (conflict), love (conflict), romantic interest (conflict), financial stalemate (conflict), family pressure (conflict), to hide something (conflict), etc.

Conflict can be subtle and doesn't require shouting or violence. It can be as simple as a character who glances away when speaking to another character, or a character who smirks after a comment, or a character says one thing and does another. Or a character who acts different alone than when he's around people.

Still struggling with conflict? Perhaps part of your story has conflict, but another part lacks it. Here's a SHORTCUT to assure no matter how Walton your story is, it will have conflict from page 1 to page 120.

Plot Irony Guarantees Conflict in Every Scene

Irony assures the main character runs into conflict at every turn, in every scene and every time he opens his mouth! If you don't know what plot irony is, go back to the Plot/Execution Chapter and read the section on Plot Irony.

Here are a few examples of plot irony:

A hero afraid to be alone is stranded on an island.
A hero afraid of commitment must marry in a month or forfeit a $10mil inheritance.
A hero who lives as a recluse is forced to move from his home.
A hero who lacks trust must trust someone else in order to survive a life or death situation.
A hero afraid of snakes is trapped on a plane with snakes.
A hero who's afraid of water must take out a killer shark.

Did you recognize some of the examples from movies? Notice how the plot irony surrounds the hero. Take what your hero's afraid of and create a plot that forces him to deal with it head on. This will create plot irony, which in turn will automatically create conflict in every scene.

Take a look at films past and present. Try to identify the irony. I guarantee it is there! Is it in your screenplay? If not, it won't sell! And worse is the fact I can guarantee that without plot irony the story will lack conflict somewhere. With plot irony the conflict never stops. Plot irony applies to all genres, all screenplays, every scene and every piece of dialogue.

It's the shortcut to guarantee conflict and the easiest way to guarantee a sale!

Visually Written Scenes Enhance Conflict

Learning to write visually is learning the craft of screenwriting. Here are two simple exercises to help the writer learn how to do this:

1) HEARD, BUT NOT SEEN

Write in script language (present tense). You may NOT use dialogue in the scene.

The subject: A person who can hear an event or object, but can not see it.

The scene: The character discovers something which he or she can hear, but can not see. Based on what is heard, the character reacts to the circumstance.

Then something happens that allows the character to see what's happening. Being able to see what's happening changes the character's perspective and we see him react to the new information.

2) SEEN, BUT NOT HEARD

Write in script language (present tense). You may NOT use dialogue in the scene.

The subject: A person who sees an event or object, but can not hear it.

The scene: The character discovers something which he or she can see, but cannot hear. Based on what is seen, the character reacts to the circumstance.

Then something happens and the character is able to hear what he's seeing. The new information creates a new perspective and we see the character's reaction to the new information.

-Most screenwriters will find #2 to be the hardest one to come up with. Here's an example of SEEN, BUT NOT HEARD from the TV show *Monk* on USA Network:

The scene: Monk's waiting in a living room to question a witness to his wife's homicide. The witness has unique statues in the room. Monk admires one; a big dog.

When he reaches to touch what he thinks is a statue, it barks at him! He jumps!

It's a hysterical scene fitting the defective detective and a great example of SEEN, BUT NOT HEARD and how the character's perception changes when the new element is presented.

Give it a try and see how many scenes you can come up with for each example. Use these techniques to create powerful visual scenes.

Reversals Create Scene Conflict

What if I told you that every single scene should change the course of the story? WHAT? Aren't these "changes" supposed to be left for big plot points like the end of Act I and Act II? I didn't say they had to be "big" changes. Having a character go out the back door when he was supposed to exit the front can create tremendous suspense and give the appearance that the story's changed course – even in a small way. These mini-twists can add tremendous depth and suspense to a story.

If a heroine tells her lover she loves him then slaps him, the audience will wonder where the relationship is headed. Will they stay together or break up? The story's direction seems to be changing due to this reversal and the audience will stick around to see what happens.

Think this is trivial? Producers have a standing rule to delete scenes that don't contain a dialogue or visual reversal. They do this because a scene without reversals will fail to keep an audience engaged in the conflict. Have you ever watched a movie and it was good, but it just didn't grab you? Ever wonder why? Go back and watch the movie again. I bet it's because the good story failed to include reversals and this left you feeling dissatisfied with the outcome. At the time, you didn't know why but now you do.

Eliminate the Technology

There is no conflict if the story isn't believable in terms of today's technology. Today's technologies can be used to enhance a story and create suspense, but can also stand in the way of creating conflict.

Movies that worked 10, 15, 20 years ago would fail today or require revisions due to the changes in technology. For example, *Die Hard* party goers could easily have used their cell phones to call for help rather than risking their lives to get to the nearest phone tucked away in an office.

Today's writer often has to deal with eliminating the technology to make a story believable. Otherwise the audience will wonder why the college kids being stalked by a serial killer can't call for help on their blackberries and why the couple lost in a snow storm can't use their GPS.

The easiest way to deal with technology so it doesn't cause a believability

158

issue with the story's plot is to eliminate it. Here are a few things that can happen to help eliminate technology from the plot:

-Dead cell phone battery
-No cell phone signal
-Broken cell phone
-Lost or misplaced cell phone
-Antagonist confiscates all techno devices
-Devices jammed by a known or unknown source
-Unpaid bill results in phone being shut off
-Minutes ran out
-Stormy weather interferes with signal
-GPS doesn't work
-GPS doesn't recognize location
-Dead GPS power source
-Forgot to bring the GPS

Getting rid of the technology can pertain to many different types of stories, but is mandatory for stories involving loss of free will, such as horrors or suspense movies where the characters are trapped in a place or situation.

Many of the ways to eliminate technology have already been used in movies, so try to be original. Add a twist. Perhaps one character had a workable cell phone all along. He never called for help because he's the 'real' antagonist. Perhaps the GPS has been reprogrammed or is controlled by the bad guy to take the hero where he wants him to go.

Have fun eliminating the technology and don't let it stand in the way of your story.

THE SOAP OPERA TECHNIQUE

The rule for scenes is 1-3 pages. Producers question longer scenes because they know something is wrong. Maybe the scene is too dialogue or visually heavy. Break it up and edit it down. Maybe the scene contains too much information in one, big chunk. Let's say that the writer must have the information in the script because it's vital to the story. That's fine, but break up the information by creating a number of suspenseful scenes that when put together reveal the information. If the information can only come from one source, then break up the long information scene with another scene and use what I call The "Soap Opera Technique" to create a compelling story. You can always come back to the scene later. So, what the heck is the soap opera technique?

I turned on the satellite one night and even with 500 channels, I couldn't find anything to watch. I clicked on the DVR. The only thing recorded was my sister's soap opera. Desperate to fill the hour void before *The Tonight Show,* I watched it. In the opening scene, WOMAN # 1 catches her BOYFRIEND in the arms of WOMAN #2. As soon as it happens, the scene cuts to another storyline. In the next scene, a MAN barges into a bar, hands a WOMAN a set of papers. He says he wants a divorce and she says, "We're not married!" Then the soap opera cut to a commercial.

In two scenes I was hooked. The soap opera held me in suspense. I had to stick around to see what happened to the woman who found her man in the arms of another woman. And I had to know why a man wanted a divorce from a woman who claimed they weren't married.

Poke fun at soap operas all you like, but these shows have been around for years. One of the longest established film characters is James Bond and soap operas were around when Bond was in diapers. How did they survive so long? In my opinion, it's because they're masters at holding the viewer in suspense by cutting a scene short. They're masters of the reversal. And they know how to use emotion to make anything possible.

Cut the Scene Short

One of the areas of screenwriting teaching I've disagreed with for years are books, seminars and gurus who teach every scene must have a beginning, middle and an end. NO IT DOES NOT! By skipping the beginning and leaving the end for later, the writer can use the power of the soap opera technique to create stories that hold an audience spellbound. Who says we have to see what happens when the woman catches her man with another woman. End the scene right there and leave the audience in suspense! Go to something else and come back to it! Cut the scene short by leaving the end hanging. I guarantee the audience will stick around to find out what happens.

The S.O. Reversal

The Soap Opera Reversal ends the scene before the end and does it with a reversal that guarantees the audience will stick around to see what happened. I gave an example above from the soap opera I watched where a man barges into a bar, hands a woman papers and says he wants a divorce, but she says they aren't married. Wow! What a reversal! Something completely unexpected happened. The audience never anticipated the woman would respond by saying they've never been married. It's a powerful dialogue reversal and by ending the scene right there and coming back to it later...or

160

maybe ending it with another scene…the writer creates tremendous suspense and has effectively used the Soap Opera Technique.

Emotions Make Anything Possible

Okay, I admit I got hooked on the soap opera. I record and watch it almost daily. One day I said to myself how can this character take back a man she tried to kill, marry him and be pregnant with his child? I know, it sounds melodramatic, but is it? Movies often make the unbelievable happen. We're asked to suspend our disbelief by writers who've setup scenarios that allow us to fall in love in a day, to scale the highest mountain in an hour and sail the sea to our most outlandish dreams. Obviously, the setup matters, but how do we really believe anything is possible? Look closely and the reason is obvious: it's the use of emotion. If the writer can make the audience feel love, then the audience will believe the heroine can take back a man she once tried to kill or fall in love with a man in one day. Same goes for any emotion. Create fear and even the most die hard hero can be made to shake in his boots.

LOCATION, LOCATION, LOCATION

Earlier we discussed how to use a location to create emotion. Locations are often overlooked by aspiring screenwriters as nothing more than a backdrop for characters. This might be true for TV, but locations are often as important in film as the characters. In *The Ruins* there wouldn't a story without the ancient site. The film *30 Days of Night* wouldn't be believable if it weren't for the Alaska setting. Locations are often what the entire story is about. We see this in films like *Phone Booth* & *Panic Room.*

With this said, writers should no longer take a location for granted. No More Boring Locations!

The Ring – Part I is a perfect example of how to utilize location to create memorable scenes. In this film there's a cabin, several houses, two apartments, a Ferrier boat, a doctor's office, a convenience store, a well, a ranch house, a psychiatric hospital, a library, a barn, a newspaper office, an island, etc. Pretty typical scenes we've seen in one film or another, but take a look at how the locations were handled to create creepy, suspenseful scenes.

First, notice there are no bright, sunny days in this film. The tone is dark and is maintained throughout the story, which gives each location an eerie feel. Note the library scene; this isn't a bright, public library. It's a dark, Gothic library.

Remember the scene where the characters enter the barn? By maintaining the tone, mood and atmosphere of the story, a simple barn now becomes a haven of mystery, intrigue, danger and suspense. This is done deliberately by creating an ominous atmosphere.

Some screenwriters believe this is the director's job or the set designer's job. Before the script sells there is no director or set designer attached- - there's only you, the screenwriter! This makes it your job to sell the story and if it's a scary movie like *The Ring*, then you'd better scare the crap out of the reader or all the locations in the world won't matter.

What if your location is ordinary - say the home of a husband and wife? Maybe their relationship is the issue. In the classic film *Sleeping With the Enemy* the couple live in a beautiful beach house and their relationship is definitely the core issue, but what stands out the most about the location isn't the house's ocean view, it's the fact that the husband controls every aspect of the house. Every can, container, and bottle in every cabinet is lined up and alphabetized. Every towel must be hung perfectly straight. This "control" creates a tone, mood and atmosphere of tension that gives us a memorable location - not just another beach house.

Use Tone, Mood and Atmosphere to Create a Memorable Location

Still not sure how this is done? What's the genre?

If it's a comedy find a way to add a comedic tone, mood and atmosphere to the location. In *Mrs. Doubtfire* the main location is a middle-class home in San Francisco, but look at how the location is presented in the opening scene. Remember the wild birthday party with the donkey? This is no longer a typical middle-class home; it's a fun house!

In the drama *Sweet November* the character lives in a typical San Francisco apartment. She has a TV, but instead of watching it, she grows plants in it. Here, the items within the location make it interesting. Notice that the lack of a TV lends itself to the story and sets the tone, mood and atmosphere for the location, which is maintained throughout the story.

Fantasy make-believe worlds are the easiest in which to create memorable locations. All I have to say here is *Lord of the Rings*. I think you get the picture.

Add an Establishing Shot

The first ten pages set the tone, mood and atmosphere of the entire story. Yet screenwriters don't realize that one of the easiest ways to set up the tone, mood and atmosphere of the entire script is with an establishing scene.

This is the opening shot where the credits roll. It doesn't have to be written in 1 to 3 pages to accommodate the credits. This is the director's job. Just write the main scene and the director will decide how long to let the credits roll.

How many movies have you seen where the opening shot is of a city skyline? This is done for two reason(s):

1) To set tone, mood and atmosphere. Notice how darker films show skylines under stormy conditions, while a romantic comedy might show birds chirping and the sun shining.

2) To give time to roll the opening credits. However, do not indicate CREDITS ROLL HERE. This is the director's job. Your job is to provide an establishing shot.

Just show an establishing shot that sets the tone, mood and atmosphere then move into the story. For example:

FADE IN:

EXT. NEW YORK CITY SKYLINE – DAY

Rain drenches the Empire State building. Lightning fills the sky.

-Note that this type of dark skyline shot would be appropriate for a film with dark undertones. This establishing shot would be inappropriate for a romantic comedy unless you're using the storm to help bring the two potential lovers together and it's going to be a "stormy" relationship.

Don't toss locations aside or take them for granted. Use them as a visual tool to commercialize the script.

Location Considerations

There are many reasons a script might be turned down. In today's economy, more and more producers are turning to stories with limited production costs to help ensure a profit. A primary consideration for a lower budgeted project can be the location. To appeal to producers seeking low-to-medium budgeted scripts, which are far easier for a first-time writer to sell, I'd advise writers to consider the following:

Limit # of Locations

A limited number of locations can significantly reduce the production cost. Why? The crew doesn't have to move lights, cameras, equipment, trailers, etc., across town or to another country. A common question writers ask is – Is a house considered one location if scenes involve the kitchen, bathroom and bedroom? Yes. It's one location with breakdown.

Try to stick with 1-5 locations. If your script does this, be sure to mention it when marketing the script because it's a definite bonus that could help sell the material.

Location Choice

A producer could turn down a script if the primary location would be difficult to access or replicate without significant production cost. Here are a few examples:

Water locations require special equipment for underwater filming or filming in or near the water, plus added insurance, special emergency personnel on set, stunt coordinators, and water gear, which is a very expensive endeavor.

Caves can be difficult to access, have treacherous footing, often can't secure equipment and the setting can be difficult to replicate without significant cost.

White House (or distinct landmarks) – Can't film there. No standing movie sets and the unique attributes of the location force a producer to build the sets at a huge cost.

Airport Terminals – Since 9-11, film crews can only film up to the check point of an airport terminal, not beyond. There are stages that have terminals, but at a cost of $10K or more a day, it's a cost most low-to-medium budgeted producers stay away from.

Bad Weather, Outdoor Locations

Try taking your video camera out in the rain. It's tough to hold with an umbrella, isn't it? Imagine taking movie cameras, lights, crews, dollies, etc., out in the rain, wind, snow or sleet. It's a significant cost.

SPFX Locations

Other worlds, fantasy worlds, alien worlds. These have to be created from top to bottom because they've never been seen before. I don't need to explain why this is expensive.

Period Piece Locations

What if tomorrow you had to change everything in your kitchen to the 1930's; every appliance, countertop, table, dishes, flooring, window coverings, etc? Imagine the cost.

Keeping location costs low can help make a first sale. Paying attention to how locations contribute to the tone, mood and atmosphere of scenes will set the writer apart from those who treat locations like nothing more than a back-drop.

CREATING VISUAL SUBTEXT

Earlier in this chapter we reviewed how to add emotion to scenes using contrast, reflection, action and even locations. All of those techniques add natural subtext to a scene by creating underlying meaning. In the chapter on Characters, we learned subtext gestures and how a character might say one thing, but his body language reveals another meaning (subtext).

The most important thing a writer can do to learn subtext is to start asking how everything in a scene can be used to create underlying meaning. First, what's the purpose of the scene? Let's say the scene is a setup for a murder mystery. We see a character using a straight-blade razor for a close shave. It seems like a daily routine for the character with nothing out of the ordinary, but the writer knows the razor will become a murder weapon. How can the writer add subtext to this scene?

Use Foreshadowing

Have the character cut his neck while shaving. Let us watch the blood splatter the bathroom mirror and soak his white t-shirt. By providing a slightly gruesome moment, the writer has foreshadowed a murder to come by using the visuals to provide underlying meaning; subtext. The audience will know that razor will serve an ominous purpose and they'll stick around to see what happens.

165

Use Flashback

It's rare that I recommend using FLASHBACKS, especially in Act II because they often are misused by a screenwriter, which results in the FLASHBACK stalling the story's forward momentum.

However, for the purpose of learning subtext techniques, let's discuss the FLASHBACK. The hero is a perfectionist. He must have a perfect life in a 'normal' world. He's trying too hard. Something is a miss. A FLASHBACK might show a scene where the character is running with an axe in his hand. Mr. Perfectionist's behavior just took on an underlying meaning. The audience may not know for sure what the underlying meaning is – is the character an axe murderer? Did he work as a lumber jack? Is he carrying the axe for self-defense? Is he chasing someone? The underlying meaning behind his actions creates scene suspense and the audience will wait around for the underlying meaning to be revealed. That leads us to the next subtext technique.

Withhold the Subtext Meaning

Under the dialogue section, I talked about delivering the subtext meaning in dialogue when the meaning isn't obvious. In scenes, the writer can set up subtext and let it ride until late in the story before revealing its meaning.

For example, a scene opens with a young woman tying an older man to a bed. It appears to be foreplay for kinky sex with leather bondage. The older man is smiling until the young woman beats him to a pulp with the leather straps. She leaves him bloody and near death. Her brutal action is subtext that shouts the fact that she has an underlying motive. Later in the story we discover she was viciously raped by her grandfather. The underlying meaning behind her actions (subtext) isn't revealed until late in the story. Done this way, the writer has used scene subtext to create a setup and a payoff.

Use Location Contrast

Previously, we've discussed locations in depth and contrast, but let's combine the two to show how they can be used to create subtext. The easiest example is from the film *The Shawshank Redemption*. During the prison scenes, the location is grey, dreary and dangerous. At the end there are actually two scenes I'll use as examples of location contrast:

1) When the hero escapes the prison via a sewage-filled pipe. He exits the filth to find himself standing in the pouring rain. He raises his arms and feels the freedom. This might be a night scene, but it's in stark contrast to the prison's confinement; it's visual subtext that shouts "I'm free". Even the sewage pipe provides subtext – he has to crawl through shit, just like he had to go through shit – to escape.

2) Secondly, the end scene on the beach where his friend meets up with him. During the movie, all we see are dank prison walls; a virtual dungeon. In the end scene, we're exposed to the bright, sunlit beach with its calming blue waters. It's like night and day when compared to the prison. The contrast between the two locations is obvious; one symbolizes confinement, the other freedom.

Use Objects to Create Underlying Meaning

The previous chapters we discussed character gestures, but what if a character who taps his finger on the table with one hand while holding a letter opener in the other hand? A strange combination with the tapping finger and the letter opener (object): strange enough to cause the audience to start seeking the underlying meaning behind the letter opener and the character's odd behavior.

In other words, the writer can use objects to create a question in the reader's mind. A question that promises the meaning will be revealed by the end of the story. This can be used with any scene and for any genre to create underlying meaning that can be revealed in the scene or later.

Animal Subtext

In previous chapters, I advocate watching for subtext in your daily life, mostly in other peoples' dialogue and behavior. There's another way to study subtext; via the family pet. Do you have a pet; a dog, a cat, a bird, a hamster or perhaps a horse? Pets don't speak, so how do you know when they're hungry, thirsty, hurt, fearful, hot, cold, etc.?

Since the pet can't tell us, they show us! Same goes for screenplays – don't tell us, show us and watch the underlying meaning translate to subtext.

Dogs bark a warning. Cats purr to show affection. Dogs whimper to be let out to go potty. Cats scratch to get attention at feeding time. Birds sing a happy song or curse a learned word. Birds flutter their wings in fear. Horses whinny for attention. Horses buck when they sense danger.

All of these 'actions' tell us something without saying a word. Next time you're tempted to tell us something in a screenplay via dialogue, stop! Instead, think of an action or reaction you can use to show us!

So far, you've learned how to create dialogue subtext, express emotions via subtext, create character subtext, use locations to create subtext and you've learned how to recognize subtext in everyday life from family, friends, strangers, co-workers and even your pet. The more you practice recognizing subtext, making note of it and incorporating it into your writing, the closer you are to a screenplay sale!

THE HERO'S SCENES

The hero might seem like the character most writers nail, but usually he's the character most writers fail to deliver. It's usually because the writer's identifying too closely with the hero and hasn't separated himself enough to cause the hero real trouble. As I've said in previous chapters, the hero isn't your friend. The writer's job is to emotionally destroy this character, then rebuild him into a new character.

One of the ways to do this is to pay special attention to the hero's involvement in individual scenes; the hero's scenes. It's easy for the hero to get lost in the overall story, but when the writer takes a close look at individual scenes, the writer can spot hero deficiencies and fix problems.

Hero's Scene Introduction

Did the writer give the hero a worthy entrance? Was he introduced in a unique and memorable way? A-list actors want a grand entrance. No boring entrances. Even if the story is a family drama, it's the writer's job to come up with an interesting way to introduce the hero.

The hero's description should include; physical appearance, age, job and a dominant personality trait. When a hero's first introduced is the only time a writer can add extra information that doesn't necessarily translate to the film at that precise moment, like a personality trait. This trait is vital because it tells an actor how to portray the role.

Hero's First/Last Appearance Scenes

The hero should get the first scene or as close to the first scene as possible and if possible, he should be introduced first. From the moment the audience takes a seat, they're looking for the hero. Don't create confusion by introducing others first. If the writer does introduce other characters first, just be sure the hero has a grand entrance that overshadows the prior introductions and makes it clear this character is the lead.

The hero should get the last scene. Giving the last scene to a supporting role is story suicide. An A-list actor isn't going to be upstaged by a secondary character. He'll want the final moment and he should have it!

Hero's Internal Conflict Scene Introduction

Introduce the hero's internal conflict when we first meet him. It's the easiest way to assure the writer hasn't overlooked this important factor. Pros do this routinely, but amateurs fail to reveal an internal conflict until Act II or never! Use the introductory scene to introduce the hero and his internal conflict then worry about introducing the external conflict.

Hero's Scenes in Act II

The hero should get the majority of scenes in Act II. I've actually read scripts where the hero was present in 9 out of 10 scenes in Act I, then disappeared until the end of Act II, only to reappear in time to save the day. The purpose of Act II is to use the external conflict to force the hero to change. This means that EVERY scene in Act II should contribute to the hero's arc, even if the hero isn't in a particular scene. To do so will mean the hero has to be present, which means he should be in a majority of scenes in Act II. Scenes where the hero isn't present should still contribute somehow to driving the hero toward his goal. For example, we might see what the antagonist is planning and we'll know the hero has to rise to the occasion if he's going to outwit the clever antagonist.

Hero's Birthday Party Scene

Guess what, he doesn't get one! The purpose of a story isn't to give the hero a party where he gets everything he wants. The purpose is to create scenes that challenge the hero's flaw and force him to change! Don't throw him a party scene; throw him a 'get the hell out of town' scene. Challenge him with every scene and he should never get what he wants. If he does get it, then it should be in a different way than he planned.

Hero's Scene Emotions

Does every scene toy with the hero's emotions? Do we feel suspense, joy, sadness or anger when we watch this character? If not, the writer hasn't developed scenes based on emotions he knows will affect the hero. Push his buttons! Check every scene! Does it evoke some kind of emotion from the

169

hero and/or the audience? It should. Don't tell me crap like "This scene is for information purposes only, so it doesn't need an emotional core." or "I can't have my hero being overly emotional in every scene". If you're saying things like this, then you're not a screenwriter because writers know every scene must have conflict and even a quiet drive in the country can evoke emotions if handled effectively.

By the way, information only scenes – really? Are we watching Wikipedia or a movie? Learn to integrate information into highly charged, emotional scenes rather than just tossing the information at the audience like you're handing out leaflets.

Hero's Scenes & Genre

The hero's scenes (and all scenes) should stay true to the genre. If the hero's in the midst of a horror being chased by a demon, don't take it easy on him by putting him up at the comedy Hilton for the night. Keep him in the midst of the genre by developing every scene based on the tone, mood and atmosphere of the genre.

Hero's Scenes: Beginning, Middle and End

One of the worst pieces of advice I've seen in screenwriting books is to make sure every scene has a beginning, middle and an end. Imagine the writer's about to reveal a killer by pulling back his cloak, then at the last second the scene ends. Oh, but wait, according to Hollywood gurus we need to see who the killer is to provide an ending. What crap! It's far better to get into the scene in the middle and end before the scene reveals too much information. This creates tremendous suspense and drives the hero's story forward. Soap operas have been around for 30+ years by using this technique in every single scene! Try it and watch your work suddenly get the attention it deserves.

Hero's Scene Integration

Does the writer bore us to death by describing the wallpaper or does he know that description means action! Does the writer integrate action with description to assure the hero becomes part of the scene rather than another ashtray in the room? Instead of writing a general description of a room, have the hero enter, walk past the hideous wallpaper, knock over dirty ashtrays and flop onto the oversized couch. The writer just described the room using action! This is vital in writing for a visual medium because it involves the reader in the story and it creates moving pictures. It also helps the writer avoid overwriting unnecessary description. If you can't help but write about the wallpaper, then you're a novelist not a screenwriter.

Hero's Reversal Scenes

Every scene should contain a reversal. The reversal can be provided via dialogue, visuals or a combination of both. Some writers use several types of reversals in every single scene. I guarantee the reader won't know what's going to happen to the hero next if the writer provides appropriate reversals, which will keep the reader (audience) in suspense regardless of the genre. The only exception to the 'reversals rule' is an opening, establishing shot. If you have information only scenes, go back and add conflict, reversals or find a way to dump the encyclopedia style of writing and learn to write for the visual medium known as film.

Recently, the trend with pros has been to add multiple reversals to scenes. I think this is the pros way of competing in today's tough, economically-driven marketplace. A writer should consider this when writing scenes. Is there a way to add a visual and a dialogue reversal? Or maybe two dialogue reversals? Or two visual reversals?

Hero's Nemesis Scenes

Like it or not the antagonist's plan is what drives the story! Without his plan, deliberate or not, the hero would have no reason to change. This means the nemesis should be in the hero's face, especially in Act II's scenes because this evokes change and forces the hero to become a new man in order to beat the bad guy! The antagonist's initial scenes should reveal him to be more powerful than the hero! That's right – I said MORE POWERFUL! If he's less powerful than it's obvious the hero can beat him. If he's more powerful, virtually unstoppable, then the hero will have to change to take him out! Check every scene involving the antagonist – is his plan king? Is he more powerful? Is he in the hero's face in Act II? Does he go head-to-head with the hero in a final showdown?

Hero's Dialogue Scenes

I probably shouldn't have to say this, but the hero should get the best lines in every scene he appears in! If you don't understand this…save yourself a lot of time and money by staying at your day job. The hero should also get the last line!

Hero's Secret Scene

This is the scene where the hero's all by himself (or thinks he's by himself) and we see how he acts, which reveals his true emotions, true intent, true self, etc. For example, a Boy Scout type character might break up the furniture when he's alone, thus revealing he has a temper. Or a tough-ass cop might break down and cry in private. Assuring the hero always gets this scene will provide the audience with insider information and make them feel closer to the hero.

Okay, I've gone through the hero's scenes. Now it's your turn to use it as a checklist and go back through every scene in your screenplay and see how it stands up to the hero's scenes.

ACT II'S SCENES

Screenwriting 101 classes, books, seminars and workshops say the same thing about Act II's scenes: the scenes should contain conflict and move the story forward. Both are accurate, but the area few cover is the arc. For commercial purposes, every scene in Act II should contribute to the hero's arc.

The reason so many screenwriters get stuck with 60 blank pages staring at them in Act II is because they haven't fully developed the hero's internal conflict or don't understand how Act II contributes to the hero's arc.

I've chosen a simple example from the movie *Jurassic Park*. The hero is setup as a man who doesn't want the responsibility of kids. We learn this when he's first introduced (Act I). He thinks they're smelly, expensive and he'd rather spend time digging up animals that have been dead for 65 million years. This is the internal conflict he needs to overcome.

So, what happens in Act II? He gets stuck rescuing two kids from man-eating dinosaurs! Every scene in Act II contributes to him changing his mind about kids. What about the scenes with other characters when the hero isn't present? If you take a close look at these scenes, they help forward the external conflict and therefore contribute to the hero's internal conflict resolution! If the scene doesn't move the external conflict forward, it'll often reflect the hero's internal issues. For example, there's a scene in the movie where the park's founder is eating ice cream and talking with the hero's girlfriend. At this point in the story, the hero and the kids are missing and the dinosaurs are on the loose. The park's founder speaks of his passion for what he created, love for his grand kids, etc. All of these things 'reflect' the hero's internal conflict.

The great thing about developing all of Act II's scenes based on the hero's arc is that they often hold strong emotional value. It's what makes the audience identify with the hero and it's what makes the audience have an emotional connection with the hero!

Take a look at every scene in Act II. The scene may contain vital information, it may have conflict and probably does a good job at moving the story forward, but does it contribute to the hero's arc? It should!

Still unsure how to do this? Then ask the following question, "How does the external conflict force the hero to change?" In *Jurassic Park*, protecting two kids from man-eating dinosaurs forces the hero to realize kids aren't so bad.

Presenting an external conflict that forces the hero to change an internal problem will result in the hero's arc! Screenwriters who consistently develop scenes for Act II based on the hero's internal conflict (arc) rarely find themselves staring at 60 blank pages because they're busy developing scenarios that'll push the hero and force him to change! It's what makes screenwriting challenging, yet fun! And it'll make those empty 60 blank pages fill up fast.

SCENE DIAGNOSIS

Writing scenes means more than providing information and conflict. If a scene can be removed without hurting the story, then it doesn't belong in the script. Every scene should be vital. Here's a diagnosis to help a screenwriter determine if scenes in a script are lacking.

Here are the things the screenwriter should already know:

Every Scene Must Have

Conflict
Move the story forward
Hold good pacing
Contain a dialogue or visual reversal
Contain dialogue or visual subtext
Integrated action/description
*Only exception is establishing shots
Majority of scenes should contain emotional stakes

Here are the things that are often lacking in scenes:

MAINTAIN TONE, MOOD & ATMOSPHERE
A knife-wielding killer shouldn't show up in a RomCom.

MOVES THE STORY FORWARD
If the scene can be removed without hurting the story, then the scene doesn't move the story forward. Every scene should be vital to the story and contribute to moving it forward. Edit, remove it or a producer will.

HOLD GOOD PACING
Each Act has specific pacing requirements. In Act I, a writer can take his time with longer scenes, more description, character introductions, etc., during the setup phase. In Act II, the writer should be building to a climax. In Act III, the writer should be creating scenes that are shorter and faster to give a feel that the story is wrapping up.

KEEP CHARACTERS CONSISTENT
Bob should not be Bob on one page and Bobby on the next page. Keep names in description consistent and in dialogue cue indicators. Other characters can call Bob whatever they want, but the screenwriter should stick to Bob.

PROPER FORMAT
Beyond understanding the basics, be sure the format enhances the visual style.
No directing!

NO CLICHES
It should be obvious to avoid clichés in dialogue.
Try to avoid them in description too. I can't tell you how many times I've read the phrase "like a deer in the headlights". Originality counts!

DISTINGUISH CHARACTERS
Without the dialogue cue indicators, can we tell who's speaking? We should.

CONTAINS EMOTIONAL STAKES
Every scene should evoke an emotion or remove it! If a scene's only purpose is to convey information, then it requires more development. The scene should make the reader laugh, cry, get angry, feel frustrated, experience suspense, be upset, happy, etc. If not, ask, "What emotion am I trying to convey in this scene?" The more scenes that contain emotion in the story the better. This doesn't mean you have to show people crying every minute. It can be as simple as a question in the reader's mind and leaving it unanswered until later in the story, which creates suspense throughout the scenes.

CONFLICT

Conveying information or letting us in on an interesting event or situation isn't enough. There must be conflict! It can be subtle, in-your-face or help build to a larger confrontation. Conflict doesn't have to mean characters are screaming at each other. A character who taps his finger and rolls his eyes while listening to another character speak can create tremendous conflict without speaking a single word.

CONTAIN SUBTEXT

Every scene should contain visual and/or dialogue subtext or delete the scene. If you don't, a producer will. See sections in this book on how to create subtext.

REVERSALS

This is when something unexpected happens. Often spec scripts fail because the screenwriter only added a twist when it came time to spin the story at Plot Point I, Plot Point II or at the very end. Well, guess what - - a reversal (mini-twist) should be in every single scene! This keeps material fresh and keeps the reader (audience) guessing.

LIMIT DESCRIPTION

Keep description to 4-6 lines.
Visual writing doesn't require novel-length description.
Integrate action with description. Only write description that involves action.
This should help prevent the temptation to describe the wallpaper.

INTEGRATED ACTION/DESCRIPTION

Is the description written as part of the action or just written as description? The reason writers are too heavy on description – I've seen writers describe an entire room down to the wallpaper - is because they're not thinking of description as action. To create visual pictures the two should be integrated to create a visual flow. See sections in this book outlining how to achieve this vital component of screenwriting.

LIMIT DIALOGUE

Keep dialogue to 4-6 lines.
This isn't always going to happen, but it does create a stronger visual style of writing if the dialogue is faster paced.

GOOD PACING

Act III's scenes are where I've seen the biggest problem. Act III wraps up the story, so the scenes should be shorter and faster to give a sense that the story's drawing to a close.

TRANSITIONS
Use scene transitions to create a visual style and look like a pro. I've never read a pro script that didn't use this technique. It should be used to end and start every new scene in the script. A bonus is that using transitions makes it difficult for a producer or director to remove a scene without disrupting the flow created by the transition.

PROPER SCENE LENGTH
Keep majority of scenes 1-3 pages. Even Spielberg doesn't shoot 5 minute long scenes.
Check the entire script. Any scenes running beyond 3 pages, edit.

INTERCUT PROPERLY
If INTERCUTS between phone conversations or fast-moving scenes aren't done properly, it'll lead to visual confusion. The trick is to establish BOTH scenes visually before intercutting.

RECOGNIZE HERO'S REALM
Keep dreams, fantasies and flashbacks reserved for the hero.

ACT II EQUALS ARC
Every scene in Act II must contribute to the hero's arc.
Whether the hero's in the scene or not, the scene should move him toward change.

THE TEASER

I'd refrain from calling "The Teaser" the inciting incident. Why? Because I've read thousands of screenplays with inciting incidents that weren't teasers and I've read thousands of screenplays that had an opening teaser without an inciting incident. What's the difference? I'd say the difference is how the story's information is revealed, how much of it is revealed and when it's revealed.

An inciting incident sets up the story by establishing tone, mood, atmosphere and genre. While a teaser does this too, the teaser tends to leave out vital information. The teaser provides just enough tantalizing information to make the reader (or audience) want to watch to see what happens. Another difference is story page location. An inciting incident might take place on page 3, 9, 10, but a teaser opens the story on page 1. Another difference is the page length of each. An inciting incident can take pages to develop, but a teaser is limited to 1-3 pages. The teaser is providing a 'taste' of what's to come. Finally, an inciting incident may or may not create suspense, but a teaser always creates suspense.

A teaser can be used to help engage an audience in an otherwise drawn-out drama. For example, in the film *Lolita* rather than taking us through pages (minutes) upon pages of establishing a relationship between the characters, which could lead to boredom, the writer opens with a tidbit (a teaser) from an end scene. In the scene, the hero's being chased by police. He has a gun and is covered in blood. That's all we see, then the story starts. The teaser provides just enough information for the audience to sit through the next hour or so of drama to get back to the point where we find out how the hero ended up being chased by police.

It can often be difficult to tell a horror from a drama unless it opens with a teaser, which is why many do. In *The Ruins*, we see a character trapped in a tomb with creepy vines and strange noises. The character cries for help, we hear screams then the story opens and continues through many minutes of establishing drama-type relationships, etc. All of this takes place so we can get back to the creepy tomb. The teaser established the horror and gave us a taste of what's to come.

A film with non-stop action can be as overwhelming to watch as a drawn-out drama. Many writers decide to open an action script with an action teaser, like a car chase or the hero parachuting out of plane or bungee jumping from a helicopter, etc., then the story proceeds to the dull drawn-out relationships only to return to the action. If the writer had opened with the relationships and brought the action in later it would be difficult to categorize the script under the action genre.

I've often read screenplays that I didn't get the genre until late in the story. Perhaps the reason the town's people are acting funny is due to an alien invasion. How would I know this story is really a science fiction instead of a drama? If it takes longer than 10 pages for the reader to know the genre, then the writer hasn't done his job. But wait – the writer doesn't want to give away the big 'alien' reveal. Fine, then open with a sci-fi teaser that gives just a taste of what's to come...perhaps we see strange lights in the sky and a spacecraft crashes, then the story proceeds with the weird town's people. Don't wait until your story's half over to reveal the genre, use a teaser!

Avoid Slow Openings

A clue that your screenplay could use a teaser can be found in the first ten pages. Does the story have a slow opening? Do we know the genre in the first ten pages? Do we know the hero's internal and external conflicts? Do the first ten pages create suspense, regardless of the genre? If you answered no to any of these questions, your story could benefit from a teaser.

As mentioned above, the trick to a teaser is keeping it short. It should be no more than 1 to 3 pages in length; the shorter the better. Provide as little information as possible. In *The Ruins*, we have no idea who the character is, how she came to be trapped in the tomb or anything. In *Lolita*, we have no idea why the police are chasing the hero, why he has a gun or anything. The teaser should provide just enough information to create suspense. The suspense will become a driving force that will keep the audience glued to their seats, even if the next 70 pages (minutes) are dull. I promise if you have a strong teaser the audience will stick around to find out what happens.

The Teaser Must Have a Big Payoff

Don't show a bloody knife in the opening minute then we learn later it was nothing more than ketchup on a kitchen knife while someone was making a sandwich. The teaser requires a huge, plot-changing event as the payoff!

If using a teaser from a scene that happens later in the story, like in *Lolita* where we see the hero being chased by police, be sure to repeat the entire scene and finish it. Just because the audience saw what happened in the teaser doesn't mean you should start that scene from where it left off earlier. You must repeat the entire scene as if the teaser never took place.

Create Visual-Only Teasers

Screenwriters often mess up the teaser by making it too long or by including too much information. This is often the result of adding too much dialogue or any dialogue to the teaser. Once the writer starts adding dialogue, it's easy to slip into the 'too much information' mode, which defeats the purpose of the teaser. One trick to help avoid this pitfall is to create visual teasers only; no dialogue. We only see the police chasing the hero in *Lolita* – there's no dialogue in this opening teaser. While we hear the character screaming in *The Ruins* there's no dialogue to hint at what's happening. Seeing only visuals literally impairs the audience's hearing senses leaving them with unanswered questions, which creates suspense. I believe it's fair to say a writer can carry a fairly dull story on the back of an opening teaser that's so darn compelling the audience can't wait to see what happens. I'm not advocating writing dull stories, but I think you get the picture of the importance of using a teaser to enhance your story.

I'm not going to mention the title of a film I once saw that was boring as hell, but what I will tell you is that the writer opened by showing the heroine finding an old box with a skeleton key in it. This teaser so intrigued me that I sat through the next two hours of an utterly dull story waiting to see what that

178

key unlocked. It unlocked nothing and was merely being used metaphorically. A bad call on the writer's part! A teaser requires a huge, plot-related payoff, but I admit the teaser kept me watching.

Use a Repeat Teaser

A teaser is usually 1-5 pages long, preferably closer to 3 pages and is used to entice the audience into the story. An example is an opening page where we see a dead body. This immediately engrosses the reader in the story by creating suspense and asking, "Who killed the victim and why?" Assuming it's a homicide. The teaser also sets the tone, mood and atmosphere for the entire story. A teaser isn't necessary in a script, but can be an effective technique to grab the reader. There are two kinds of repeat teasers: 1) Long to short 2) Short to long

LONG TO SHORT
This teaser shows a lot of detail, but leaves out one vital piece of information that's revealed late in the story. For example, we see a murder take place in detail, but never see the killer's face. The killer's revealed later when the scene repeats and the killer's identity is revealed. The trick to making this type of repeat teaser work is when the scene repeats, make it shorter. Provide just enough information so the reader understands that the teaser's repeating then reveal the killer's identity.

SHORT TO LONG
This teaser leaves out the details and shows the end result. Later in the story, the details are revealed. Using the killer scenario, this type of teaser wouldn't show the murder. It would only reveal a dead body. Later, we'd see how the person ended up being killed and by whom. The trick to making this type of repeat teaser work is when the scene repeats, to make it longer than the teaser and fill-in the details.

End with a Teaser

One of the things producers love is a story they can turn into a profitable sequel. A story can be conclusive and leave a hero for the next sequel, but sometimes stories leave us with a teaser. This is usually done in horror or suspense thrillers, but I'm sure a clever writer could figure out a way to make it work in any genre. An example from a suspense thriller would be from the hit movie *Silence of the Lambs* where the heroine learns the cannibalistic Hannibal is still alive, then we see him on an island resort following his next prey. This certainly promises Part II and ends with a teaser. Horrors almost always end with a teaser. It's actually a requirement of horror (read 'How to Write a Horror' section of this book) that the threat remains in the end. This is actually a mini-teaser that promises the killer, ghost, evil, vampire, zombie, werewolf or witch will be back to scare us another day.

CHAPTER SEVEN: FORMAT - THE KEY TO PRO SCREENWRITING

WHY FORMAT COUNTS

The easiest way for a producer to weed out the amateurs is to flip through a script to see if the format is correct AND to see if the format is being used to enhance the story. Amateurs take format for granted. To them it's nothing more than a nuisance; they slap it on the page without giving thought to how format can contribute to the story or how it can distinguish their individual style and voice. Pros know better. They know how to use format to enhance the plot/execution, characters, dialogue and scenes. And they know how to use it to create a style and voice that will distinguish them as master screenwriters.

Mastering format isn't optional if an aspiring screenwriter wants to become a paid professional. It's mandatory! But it can be confusing. Even when the writer understands how the basics work, the writer may not understand how to take formatting to the next level to use it to create style and voice. And even further to create suspense, fear, comedy, love and many other visual and dialogue experiences. Yes, format can do more than tell us whether we're INT. or EXT.!

It's time to show you how to properly format and take it to the next level. Let's start by gathering up every source you've used to learn formatting from; books, magazines, produced and unproduced scripts. Go to the nearest trash can and throw them away! By the time you read a book on the market, the format has probably changed – Yes, formats change in Hollywood. By reading scripts, you're hoping the other writer got it right. Well, he must have because it's a produced script, right? Remember what I said earlier? Established writers can get away with breaking the rules, so there's no guarantee the format they are using is the current industry format! Don't worry if what you're about to read will be outdated soon because I'm going to reveal how to assure you're ALWAYS using the most current format!

FORMAT 101: COMMON PITFALLS

Proper format has been argued more than any other area of screenwriting. One writer thinks something is correct while another thinks it's wrong. One guru says format it this way, another says something else. Who's right? Who's wrong? Format can make your head spin!

Formats Change

Formats are determined by producers. These changes are quickly evident to those working in the biz on a daily basis, but can take time to trickle down to the aspiring screenwriter. By the time the changes reach the writer they might have been discontinued or even changed again. But don't worry because I'm going to reveal how to keep track of producer changes.

Ten years ago it was standard to put (CONTINUED) at the top and bottom of every single page in a screenplay. This is no longer done. This format style has gone out-of-style. Using it today will make your script look outdated and will rank you an amateur!

Here are a few Format Styles that are currently out-of-style:

✓ CUT TO:, DISSOLVE TO:, FLASH TO:, etc.
  Any directorial transition between scenes is out-of-style. Most producers don't seem to mind whether a screenwriter still uses these or not, but almost all agents and managers frown upon their use.

✓ (CONT'D) or (cont'd) when a character speaks twice, back-to-back in a scene.
  This used to be pretty standard, but lately it's considered to be obvious the same character is speaking again and the (cont'd) is no longer perceived as necessary.

✓ The "we" or "us" references in description.
  The last thing you want to do is remind the reader that they're reading a screenplay. You want them to become part of the story. This reference removes the reader from the story. It's also considered a 'directorial' reference, meaning it should only be used by directors and is therefore out-of-style.

✓ FADE IN: or FADE OUT: being used in the body of the script.
  FADE IN: should only be used at the beginning of a script. Nowhere else.
  FADE OUT: should only be used at the end of a script. Nowhere else.
  If you have dissolves between scenes use FADE TO BLACK then write the next primary slug indicator to indicate a Fade In.

✓ Camera fades to, ANGLE ON...etc.
This is equivalent to reminding the reader that they're reading a script because it removes them from the story and is therefore out-of-style. Any use of camera terminology is considered directorial and is not acceptable in a spec script.

Will your script be tossed into the slush pile if you've used one of these out-of-style techniques? No, but being aware of what's acceptable format and what isn't will make you look more like a pro and you won't have to worry that your script will look outdated. Also, remember that in today's economy producers are making fewer films. The aspiring screenwriter doesn't want to give the producer any reason NOT to purchase the script. Think about this a minute. If you're a producer with millions of dollars at your disposal and two good scripts are in front of you, are you going to pick the writer who's a master at formatting or the guy who slopped it over? If you think the producer will pick the script based solely on the story, you're badly mistaken. The producer has to work with this writer for months, even years to come and he'll want the writer who's proven he's the pro. Therefore, the winning script is the writer who knows format!

Format Mistakes

Being out-of-style can hurt a writer's chance at a sale, but there are other common mistakes to avoid. Here are a few of the most common mistakes I see again and again:

✓ EXT. TRUCK – DAY
The exterior of a vehicle is NOT A LOCATION. Slug to the larger primary slug indicator. If the truck is on a road write:
EXT. ROAD – DAY
-However, the inside of a vehicle IS A LOCATION. For example,
INT. TRUCK (MOVING) – DAY
-Note the (MOVING). It's common to state the status of a vehicle at the time of the scene because there's a huge difference between a vehicle that's moving and one that's (PARKED) or (AIRBORNE).
-See more examples under Vehicles as Locations

✓ Know when and how to use (O.S.), (O.C.), (V.O.) and (FILTERED)
I see this mistake in many screenplays. The character will be talking on the phone and the other party's dialogue is marked as (O.S.), yet (O.S.) means the character is in the scene!

Here is the proper way to handle these:

- ✓ Off Stage or Off Camera (O.S.) or (O.C.) = the character is in the scene, but just off stage or off camera and we can only hear them and not see them.

- ✓ Voice Over (V.O.) = character's voice is being heard over the film like a narrator. This format, however, is also acceptable for phone conversations.

- ✓ Filtered (FILTERED) = character's voice is being heard through a device like a phone, walkie-talkie, radio, TV, etc. It's also okay to write (ON PHONE), (ON TV), (ON RADIO) instead of (FILTERED).

  All of these format styles are placed to the immediate right of the character cue indicator. See more examples under Phone Conversations and Understanding Dialogue Cue Indicators.

- ✓ In screenplays background is written as b.g.

- ✓ In screenplays foreground is written as f.g.

- ✓ Only CAP character's name upon initial introduction.

- ✓ Dialogue that's interrupted vs. dialogue that trails off. Interrupted dialogue is followed by a double dash (- -) Dialogue that trails off is followed by triple dots (…)

Vehicles as Locations

Writing scenes that take place inside and outside of a vehicle can be confusing. Should it be written as an INT. or EXT. primary slug indicator? What if the character's voice is heard from outside of the vehicle, is it (O.S.) or (V.O.)? What if the location is on the deck of a boat? How do you write scenes where the vehicle is parked and then moving?

-Always indicate the status of a vehicle at the time of the scene because there's a huge difference in a scene when a vehicle is moving and when a vehicle is parked. If a car is moving down a highway, it's slugged as follows:

INT. CAR (MOVING) – DAY

If the car is parked in a parking lot, it's slugged as follows:

INT. CAR (PARKED) – DAY

-If the vehicle is first parked, then moving (or vice verse) write the slug in the order of the action:

INT. CAR (PARKED/MOVING) – DAY

-What if the scene switches between INT. and EXT. of the vehicle? This is where many get confused. The answer is: It depends on the shot.

-For example, if the scene switches from the interior of a vehicle to an exterior of a highway with a wide enough shot to show the highway, signs, etc, then it's slugged as:

EXT. HIGHWAY – DAY

However, if the shot is CLOSE ON the vehicle where we don't really see much of the highway, then it's slugged as:

EXT. CAR (MOVING) – DAY

Note: With an EXT. CAR shot be sure the reader knows where the location is if it hasn't already been indicated.

-What if the shot is EXT. CAR – DAY, but we can hear the car's occupants speaking? Is it (O.S.) or (V.O.)?

Either one is probably acceptable, but most producers would agree that EXT. CAR or EXT. HIGHWAY with the vehicle in the shot and the voices being heard is a separate scene and (O.S.) wouldn't apply. It's best to use (V.O.) since the character's voices are being heard over the film.

-What if the location is on the deck of a boat?

Most producers agree that an interior shot ONLY applies to a location with four enclosed walls, so the deck of a boat wouldn't be INT. BOAT DECK. Instead, it'd be slugged as:

EXT. BOAT DECK

Note: If this is, however, a wider shot where we can see the ocean, lake, etc., then use the rule above and slug as follows:

EXT. OCEAN – DAY

When used properly primary slug indicators can become strong visual aids to help the story come alive on the paper.

Phone Conversations

There are two areas of phone conversation formatting where I repeatedly see errors: 1) The use of the proper dialogue cue indicator extension 2) Failure to establish both locations prior to Intercut.

First, there are technically three different extensions you can use: (V.O.), (FILTERED) or (ON PHONE). Here's how they look:

HENRY (V.O.)
Hi Jane, how are you doing?

HENRY (FILTERED)
Hi Jane, how are you doing?

HENRY (ON PHONE)
Hi Jane, how are you doing?

(FILTERED) is the "in vogue" one to use, meaning it's the most recent format accepted. However, (V.O.) is so popular that it's also widely accepted. Be careful using (ON "THE" PHONE) because the reader might think they're able to see and hear the character in the scene, rather than just hearing their voice over the phone. A quick note in regards to (ON "THE PHONE"), if it's written as...

HENRY
(on phone)
Hi Jane, how are you doing?

...then it's a character/actor cue and it means we see the character speaking on the phone.

HENRY (ON PHONE)
Hi Jane, how are you doing?

-Here the voice is being heard through the phone.

Here are the proper definitions of the extensions:

185

(FILTERED) – Character's voice is being heard through a device, like a phone.
(V.O.) – Character's voice is being heard over the film, like a narrator. However, voice over is widely used for phone conversations and is acceptable.
(ON "THE PHONE") – Character's voice is being heard through a phone.

(O.S.) is NOT appropriate for phone conversations because off stage (or off camera) implies the character is in the scene and we can only hear him, but can't see him. If a character is talking on the phone in another room and we can't see him, then it's (O.S.)! Otherwise, use the proper format(s) listed above.

A note about extensions: Be sure to use the same extension consistently throughout the script. If you used (V.O.) for one phone conversation, don't use (FILTERED) for another one later in the script. Consistency is the mark of a pro. Pick one and stick with it.

Secondly, if a phone conversation cuts back and forth between two locations then YOU MUST establish both locations then indicate INTERCUT and just write the dialogue. Here's an example.

INT. HENRY'S APARTMENT – NIGHT

Henry watches TV, talks on the phone.

HENRY
Hey Jane, how are you?

INT. JANE'S HOUSE – NIGHT

Jane washes dishes, holds the phone against her ear.

JANE
Great! How's the new job?

HENRY (V.O.)
It sucks, but it pays the bills.

INTERCUT

JANE
I hear ya.

186

HENRY
How's your nightmare day job going?

JANE
The same.

-This is the proper way to INTERCUT a phone conversation. Another alternative is to leave out the INTERCUT and use primary slug indicators to cut back and forth. It takes up more page space, but it's acceptable.

Use of Caps

There's controversy on when to use CAPS in a spec screenplay and when not to use them. Here's my two cents:

Use CAPS to introduce the characters! All characters! This helps the Casting Director who can skim through the script and pick out roles to fill. Capping a character's name also tells the reader a new character is being introduced. This is the ONLY time a character's name should be in CAPS with the exception of the secondary slug indicator to call for a specific shot.

CAP sound effects! Here's where the big controversy comes in. Many screenplay gurus will tell you not to do this. I wonder how many of them have worked on a movie set? Well, sound effect guys, like the Casting Director, rely on these effects being in CAPS so they can easily identify them in the script. I believe the reason it's advocated not to use them is because many screenwriters don't understand what justifies the effect. Use CAP when it's an extreme noise that would not necessarily be heard on set; like a GUNSHOT, EXPLOSION, etc.

CAP extremely important details. For example, if a red pen on the table is a clue in a murder mystery, either CAP it as follows:

She sees a RED PEN lying on the table.

Or use a CLOSE UP as follows:

CLOSE UP on a red pen lying on the table.

Or use a second slug indicator and call for a separate shot:

She sees a...

187

…lying on the table.

Use CAPS sparingly and only when absolutely necessary.

Fade In & Fade Out

The only place in a screenplay that FADE IN should appear is on page one! The only place in a screenplay that FADE OUT should appear is on the final page of the script!

I've often seen screenwriters use FADE IN and FADE OUT as a scene transition. This is incorrect formatting. The scene's description and/or action should visually reference the transition without the improper use of FADE IN and FADE OUT.

Here's another good reason not to use FADE OUT before its time: A screenwriter submitted a requested horror script to a production company. The producer called the screenwriter and said they liked the premise, but were confused by how it ended. Apparently, around page 90, the screenwriter used the words FADE OUT. The FADE OUT happened to appear at the bottom of the page of the .pdf file (Adobe Acrobat) and the reader thought the story had ended! The screenwriter explained to the producer that there was still more to the story, but the producer wasn't impressed that the screenwriter didn't understand proper formatting.

Also, don't write THE END after or before FADE OUT. The words FADE OUT used in a screenplay means THE END. Save THE END for novels, not screenplays. Also, a producer might think the writer really aspires to be a novelist because novelists use THE END.

Screenplays should end in FADE OUT. It's right-justified and is followed with a period.

FADE OUT.

If you're considering not using FADE IN at all, this is a mistake. FADE IN identifies the script to a reader as material written specifically for the big screen. Without FADE IN, the reader might confuse the material for a radio, stage play, MOW, etc.

Consistency

Extreme Screenwriting has noted over the years that professional screenwriters have one thing in common, regardless of the genre they write or if they write for TV or Film and that one thing is consistency!

This tip is to help aspiring screenwriters look like the pros. Here's a list of items that pros do consistently:

-Keep character names consistent! Just because the story's characters call William by Bill or Junior or Billy doesn't mean the screenwriter should do it. Pros will pick one name, like William and call the character this name in the description and dialogue throughout the script!

-Pick either (O.S.) or (O.C.) and keep consistent. Off stage (O.S.) and Off camera (O.C.) mean the same thing, but pros will pick one and stick with it throughout the script.

-Pick either (FILTERED) or (V.O.) and keep consistent. Pros know that it's acceptable to use either (FILTERED) or (V.O.) for phone conversations. The trick is to pick one format usage and use it for all phone conversations in the script.

-Keep font consistent! Pros know that the title page with script's title and contact information should be the same font as the rest of the script, Courier 12! The title should NOT be a larger font!

-Don't use BOLD anywhere in the script. A recent trend has been to BOLD the primary slug indicator.

-Keep title page information consistent! Don't have your name, phone # and email on one script, then just your name and email on another. Pros put all their contact information on every script! If the screenwriter has an agent, the agent's contact information goes on the script, not yours!

-Pages look consistently balanced! There are no T-Pages or all-dialogue pages in a pro's script! A T-Page is a page that has only one line of description and all dialogue, literally making the page look like the letter "T". Pros know that a marketable script is balanced! See how to under the section Avoid T-Pages and All-Dialogue Pages.

-Description and dialogue consistently sound different. Pros know that if there's a clever reference to a visual and/or action in the description that a character shouldn't say it in the dialogue. For example, if the description says

'He struts in like a proud peacock' – a character in that scene shouldn't say, "Why do you strut in here like a proud peacock?"

-Keep primary slug indicators consistent! Pros know to keep the slugs consistent and complete. Don't write INT. HOUSE, then write INT. HOUSE – DAY. Always write INT. HOUSE – DAY. Pros know better than to assume a reader will know it's the same day or that it's DAY!

-Keep visual flow consistent. Pros know how to manipulate the visual look of their material. For example, pros often write short, pithy sentences that are close to the left margin when creating action scenes. This gives the illusion that the scene's moving fast. For more dramatic or slower scenes, pros use regular description paragraphs.

-Keep use of numbers consistent in dialogue. Pros know to either use the actual number (1, 2, 3…) or write out the number (one, two, three…) in dialogue. The trick is to keep the usage consistent. If you write out the word in one section of dialogue, then do so throughout the script. Note: Most professional proofreaders will advise screenwriters to write out the numbers in dialogue because this clarifies proper pronunciation to the actor.

There are many more consistency items that could be listed, but this will get you started. The tip is to get in the habit of keeping everything about your script, story, characters, plot, format, etc., consistent! A heightened level of consistency helps the screenwriter rise above the level of amateur and makes the screenwriter look like a pro!

The 4-Line Rule

When is description and/or dialogue too lengthy? The rule is no more than 4-lines of description or 4-lines of dialogue.

How does this work if the screenwriter has a non-stop action scene with no dialogue and all description? The answer is simple: break up the action into manageable blocks of no more than 4-line paragraphs. In fact, if the scene involves action, it's advisable to use even shorter description lines that are deliberately broken up to give the visual feel of moving 'fast' on the page. Keep the lines short so the description tends to grip the left margin. This makes for a fast read!

Even if the scene is a dramatic moment, keep the description broken into manageable paragraphs of no more than four lines total. Another tip is to only write description that's incorporated with the action to avoid writing details that are unnecessary.

190

What if the character is required to give a political speech that's bound to run over 4 lines? Then simply break up the lengthy dialogue with action/description. What are we seeing as the character speaks? Is he fidgeting? Is the audience rolling their eyes, shuffling in their seats or leaving? By breaking up the lengthy dialogue, the screenwriter keeps the visual flow moving. Never forget that film's a visual medium and this means paying close attention to the visual details and knowing when to use them to break up lengthy dialogue.

A word of caution regarding lengthy dialogue; if the information provided in the dialogue can be conveyed visually, it's in the writer's best interest to do so. Try to use visuals first and dialogue secondary to convey information to an audience.

A script should be roughly 60% description and 40% dialogue. Keeping within the 4-line rule will help maintain a balanced appearance to the overall script.

Spacing Issues

COVER PAGE
Title is centered on the page (mid-way down the page) with written by below it (single or double spaced) and writer's name below written by (single or double spaced). Writer's contact information is located in the bottom, right of the page and is single spaced. Be sure to include an email, but don't include copyright or WGA registration information (this is provided with a release form upon request to read a script). Don't list what draft it is or date the material.

SCRIPT PAGES
No page # on page 1. Page numbers start on page 2. They're located in the upper right hand corner and are followed by a period. Double space after FADE IN:. Double space after each primary slug indicator. Triple spacing anywhere in the screenplay is considered a page cheat and tells the reader the script is probably too short and requires more development.

SCENE DESCRIPTION
Keep blocks to no more than 4 lines of description/action. It's okay to single space and stack description lines to give the pacing of a fast-moving action scene. For example:

Tim dodges the knife.
Sidesteps the assailant.
Grabs the weapon.

The way description is written and spaced can create a visual flow if properly done. Heavy passages with limited spacing will read like a novel and won't be considered lean enough to qualify for the visual medium known as film. Extra Note: Fast-moving scenes can be broken up into double spaced lines to give the feel of the action taking place:

Tim dodges the knife.

Sidesteps the assailant.

Grabs the weapon.

DIALOGUE
All single spaced. The trick with dialogue is to avoid the use of a wryly and overuse of words in CAPS and exclamation points, etc.

FADE OUT
Single space after the final description or dialogue, then write FADE OUT. It's right justified and followed by a period.

Scene Numbers

Scene numbers run down the sides of a script next to the primary slug indicator. I've recently had scripts submitted for coverage with the scene numbers included. If a screenwriter submits a script to a production company with scene numbers, it probably won't be read.

Why? Because scene numbers indicate the script has been optioned, is being prepared for pre-production or is close to principal photography (filming). Why would a producer be interested in a script that has other legalities attached with another producer due to an option or otherwise?

If the script is being presented as a spec script (written without upfront compensation), then it should NOT have scene numbers. The scene numbers can prevent the script from receiving serious attention. Secondly, it makes the screenwriter look like an amateur because a pro would know that scene numbers aren't added until after the script's been optioned or sold and it's done for production purposes.

When submitting a spec script, it should look like a spec script without scene numbers.

Montage or Series of Shots

A Montage or a Series of Shots? If the writer is showing a passage of time or there's a central theme use MONTAGE. For example, if the writer wants to show a character's gradual age transition from boy to man, then use a MONTAGE to show the time passage. A Montage is usually written with more description than a Series of Shots and hints at DISSOLVES and other transitory techniques. It's often accompanied by music.

A SERIES OF SHOTS is a quick 'glimpse' of an event or moment. It doesn't show a time transition and is written with limited, if any description. Rather it indicates the location and the 'shot' or just the 'shot. It helps provide a bridge to quickly cut between scenes. Anything else is probably a MONTAGE.

The Establishing Shot

A function of the establishing shot is to setup a location where the story will take place or a portion of the story. Most writers don't go beyond this when considering the establishing shot, but they should. Why? Because the establishing shot can be a vital component in revealing genre and setting the story's tone, mood and atmosphere.

I've often seen screenwriters write the establishing shot as follows:

EXT. HOSPITAL – DAY (ESTABLISHING)

INT. HOSPITAL – DAY

Joe enters the ICU.

-This might seem okay because everyone knows what a hospital looks like, but it fails on many levels. First, it doesn't provide any visuals whatsoever. Film's a visual medium. Are there ambulances parked outside? Are people rushing in wounded? Is an old woman waiting by the curb in a wheelchair?

Secondly, it doesn't show the reader what the genre is. This establishing shot to open a story doesn't reveal if the story's a comedy, horror, action/adventure, suspense thriller, etc.

The screenwriter's job is to create moving pictures and to keep the reader engrossed in the genre. This establishing shot doesn't accomplish anything. But what if the writer wrote the following:

EXT. HOSPITAL – DAY (ESTABLISHING)

Dark, ominous clouds choke the sky. Bolt lightning, followed by a CRACK of thunder.
Joe uses his coat to shield his head as rain pours.

A shadowy figure ducks behind a vehicle in the parking lot, watches Joe.

-This establishing shot clearly sets up a potential suspense thriller or maybe a horror because it establishes a dark tone, mood and atmosphere and presents a threat. It also involves the reader in the visuals of the story.

Establishing shots in the beginning of a story are vital to establishing tone, mood, atmosphere and genre. Establishing shots can also appear at other points in the story where a new, important location comes into play. I'd advise the writer to make sure that any time an establishing shot is used that it keeps the story's visual flow going by maintaining the tone, mood, atmosphere and the genre.

Flashbacks

Flashbacks can destroy an aspiring screenwriter's chance at a first sale. Why? Not because they're wrong to use, but because they're improperly used. First, writing a story out of chronological order is okay. It's a difficult skill to masterfully pull off. I'd advise aspiring screenwriters to stick with stories told in chronological order.

Here's what to avoid:

BACKSTORY INFORMATION
It's tempting to use a flashback to fill in back-story information. It's an easy and quick way to get the necessary information into the script. A problem often occurs because during the flashback the main plot has stopped while the information is being provided. Imagine being in an airplane and the pilot announces he's stopping the plane mid-air to refuel. Sound crazy? He'll crash the plane. That's what happens to the plot, its forward momentum stalls and can easily crash the entire story.

Another problem with using a flashback to fill in back-story information occurs when the information could have been covered in the main plot. If we need to know Uncle Joe's cousin was a convicted felon, do we need to see him in prison ten years ago? Can't Aunt May tell us? Can't we see a prison tattoo and get it?

194

If a screenwriter's considering using a flashback for back-story information, first try to figure out if there's a way to convey the information either visually or via dialogue in the current story. If so, do it and steer clear of the flashback. Or make sure the back-story information pushes the plot forward.

POV FLASHBACK

The screenwriter uses the flashback properly, but uses flashbacks for every character in the story. Wrong! Since a story revolves around a hero, then using a flashback for secondary characters breaks the hero's hold on the story. Plus, it can literally cause a hero identification problem since the audience will be confused as to why they're seeing a flashback from a supporting character.

Flashbacks should be reserved for the hero! Fantasies and dreams should also be reserved for the hero.

THE RIGHT WAY

When should you use a flashback? My advice is simple; use it to convey back-story information that misleads the audience. For example, if Mindy appears to be the victim in a partial flashback, then later is revealed as the killer, then the flashback has been used as part of the forward momentum to create suspense and mislead the audience.

Another way to properly use a flashback is to put the audience in a superior position. For example, if John tells his mother he never slept with Carol, but we see a flashback where he did, then the audience knows John's lying. It puts the audience in a superior position because they're privy to information that certain characters in the story don't know.

A flashback can be used to convey back-story information, but only if there is no way to layer the information into the present-day story line.

WHERE IT OCCURS

Where a flashback occurs can also hurt a script. While I advocate using this technique sparingly, the worst place to use it – in my opinion – is in Act II. Why? Because Act II is supposed to be about the hero confronting his flaw. Can he do this if the writer spends this valuable screen time in the past? Find ways to bring his past flaw into the present without resorting to the use of a flashback.

In Act III, a flashback can destroy the possibility of a viable resolution. In Act I could work to setup valuable information, but again it stalls the start of the story.

The use of a flashback is up to the screenwriter, but it should be given careful consideration. Also, be aware that many story analysts consider it a cheat because it's an easy out as opposed to finding more creative ways to convey the information in the confines of the main plot.

Grammar and Typos
Does Grammar Really Matter?

Of course it does. The catch is to understand how "film grammar" works. It's different than standard prose. Standard prose is the way novels are written, not screenplays.

The goal in screenplays is to write visually and to involve the reader on an emotional level with the story. This means taking the reader outside the character's internal thoughts to a visual realm where all emotions are revealed externally.

A note about grammar: Far too many screenwriters spend far too much time concerned about this area when 99% of you have a pretty good grasp on it. Relax. Write in an active voice and eliminate the need to worry about grammar.

Can't Film a Typo – Does it Really Matter?

Here's the answer: If you plan to write a script no one will ever see - typos do not matter. If you're expecting someone to pay you for your material then typos do matter!

Would you pay six figures for a script with typos? Why would anyone? There are plenty of screenwriters out there willing to take the time to look professional and the money should go to them, not to the lazy screenwriter who didn't take the time to give the material a polished look.

A Word About Typos

I'm a big advocate for using editors to make sure a script looks polished by finding those "few" overlooked typos. However, I've seen many scripts where the typos number in the dozens!

When I mention it to the screenwriter they usually respond with, "I'm not worried about typos, only content. I'll have an editor look at it later."

This is fine, but here's a question for you to ponder:

"What if your script sells and you're called to the lot to make last minute changes to several scenes totaling 15 pages?" There won't be an editor in sight and if you consistently have a large # of typos they're sure to pop up here and you'll look very unprofessional.

Use the editor to polish your scripts, but try harder to eliminate typos. Consider it part of the process, just like writing effective dialogue, scenes or plot. It's all part of being a professional screenwriter.

Don't forget to use words like THE....

For the record, I've decided to include the most common typos I see:

It's and its
-It's a rainy day.
-She removes its collar.

Your and you're
-Your hair looks nice.
-You're the winner.

To, too and two
-I'm going to the store.
-There are too many books to read.
-Two people stand in line.

Break and brake
-The glass falls and breaks.
-The car brakes give out.

Peak and peek
-He climbs to the mountain peak.
-He peeks through the window.

They're, their and there
-The girls had their hair done.
-They're going to the movies.
-There are two independent films playing today.

Steel and Steal
-The skyscraper is made of steel.
-A burglar steals a rare painting.

Then and Than
-They went to the movies then went shopping. (Then means "next")
-The box weighs more than he expected. (Than means "comparison")

OK
It's spelled "okay" in screenplays.

I'm sure there are plenty more, but I'll spare you the English lesson. Typos stand out like sore thumbs to a Hollywood reader - eliminate them like you would a cockroach because finding one in a script is just as appalling as finding a cockroach stuffed between the pages. If this visual imagery doesn't inspire you to get rid of the typos then all I can say is "good luck."

COMMON PITFALLS

The #1 pitfall I see in screenplays is a lack of a fundamental understanding of how a script is written. I don't mean the obvious stuff like "show don't tell." I mean how it's literally written = active, visual voice.

What is an active, visual voice? It's the voice of the screenwriter because it has the ability to draw a reader into the story to the point where they're no longer just reading the script, they've actually become a part of the story.

The easiest way to do this is to follow this simple rule:

Limit the use of the words "is", "are"
and words ending in "ing"

This might be part of common prose, but you aren't writing a novel, you're writing a screenplay! Let's look at some examples and see why this is so important. I'll use simple examples...

WRONG: Joe is running.
RIGHT: Joe runs.

WRONG: Carrie is walking down the street.
RIGHT: Carrie strides down the street.

WRONG: The men are playing poker.
RIGHT: The men engage in poker.

WRONG:
Carrie is walking down the street. She sees her neighbors are leaving for work. She waves as she's walking past.

198

RIGHT:
Carrie strides down the street. She spots her neighbors as their car backs out of a driveway. She waves "goodbye."

This is English 101 stuff, but I see it every single week. Keep the "is," "are" and "ing" words to a minimum to maintain an active voice that'll involve the reader on an emotional level with your story.

The #2 pitfall I see is writing description that's not incorporated into the action!

This usually results in the screenwriter overwriting a scene's description. If you hone a scene down to description that's only part of the action then you'll incorporate the two into a cohesive and professionally written piece.

Here's an example:

WRONG:

INT. JOE'S HOUSE – DAY

Old newspapers strewn everywhere. Dirty dishes stacked on a coffee table. JOE, 20's, enters. He walks over to the couch, flops down.

RIGHT:

INT. JOE'S HOUSE – DAY

JOE, 20's, enters. He steps over a stack of old newspapers. Makes his way past a coffee table stacked with dirty dishes and flops down on a couch.

-By incorporating the description with the action two things are accomplished:

> Involves the reader with the visuals = emotional involvement.
> Limits the description to the visually significant portion of the scene.

If you've ever been told your material lacks "depth" or isn't emotionally involving it's probably due to one of the pitfalls listed above.

This technique will quickly eliminate excessive description that's not essential to the story.

199

The #3 pitfall I see is writing too little!

We've all seen, heard or read that less is more, but this has been greatly misinterpreted by screenwriters. Many write so tersely that they've completely eliminated the reader's emotional involvement in the story. By doing so they've completely eliminated their chance for a first sale.

For example, if the screenwriter were writing a scene that takes place on Halloween night the terse writer would write.ß

EXT. STREET – NIGHT

A full moon. Pumpkins. Costumed kids. Jack-o-lanterns.

I get the picture, but where's the emotional involvement in this scene? I feel like I'm reading a grocery list.

Less is more
means to write only what's part of the action
and is relevant to involve the reader in the story.

It doesn't mean to write a grocery list. Let's look at this scene again.

EXT. STREET – NIGHT

A full moon illuminates costumed characters as they make their way past pumpkin-filled yards and ghostly jack-o-lanterns.

-This is slightly longer = one line longer, but it involves the reader on an emotional level. It's the screenwriter's job to involve the reader on an emotional level. Unfortunately, the terse style is unlikely to accomplish this goal.

#4 Show, don't tell.

All writers have heard this before. In screenplays, more than any other type of writing, it's especially important to understand the visual power behind this style of writing and how it works to write a story for the big screen.

If a character gets angry, don't just write "he's mad". Try to show it. Have him throw something across the room. Show us how mad he is!

If a character is feeling lonely, then put him in a room filled with loving couples and let the contrast show us how lonely he feels, but never tell us how lonely he is; show us.

If a character is sad the writer can use a visual backdrop to express the sadness. How many funeral scenes have you seen in a movie where it's raining? Plenty. This is because the dark mood created by the rain expresses the sadness of the character without having to be told the character feels sad.

These are just a few examples of how to show don't tell.

Avoid T-Pages & All-Dialogue Pages

There should be few, if any, all-dialogue or T-Pages in a spec screenplay. A T-page is a page with all dialogue and only one line of description, making the page look like the letter "T".

More than two of these pages can quickly make the script look like the screenplay isn't visual enough for the big screen because it's dialogue heavy.

The easiest way to fix these is to simply add more description or action, but be careful. Make sure the description/action is relevant to the story.

Secondly, check to see if any of the dialogue's information can be presented via the visuals. Here's an example:

David wants to tell Cindy he loves her. He can simply say it:

DAVID
I love you, Cindy.

Or this dialogue can be deleted and replaced with a visual.

David hands Cindy a dozen roses with a ring wrapped around the stem.

Always go for the visual delivery first, dialogue secondary. This also helps to keep the dialogue from sounding too direct. Be sure to flip through your screenplays and fix any T-Pages or all-dialogue pages.

The Stage/Page Rule

If there's an action scene with two soldiers fist-fighting and the description indicates 'Zeus knows he has an army in the bushes', then the writer has violated the stage/page rule. The writer MUST show the army, not tell us about it. Remember, the audience won't see the script.

If the description indicates a character smells something burning, then the writer has violated the stage/page rule UNLESS the writer shows the character sniffing the air or we see the fire or someone comments on the smell. Remember, the audience can't smell what's on the screen. Just write: Sam sniffs the air, cringes. Fire rises from a greasy skillet on the stove.

If the description tells us the character was once shy back in high school and hasn't gotten over it, then the writer has violated the stage/page rule. The audience will never see the script and will have no idea the character was once shy. If the writer wants to show us the character is shy, then it must be done via the visuals. In other words, we must see it play out. Maybe the character blushes, turns away or fumbles with his words.

The easiest way to avoid violating the stage/page rule is to think of description as action, rather than as description. Rather than thinking of ways to describe things, think of ways they're incorporated into the action. This will keep the focus on the stage and the writer won't violate the stage/page rule.

UNDERSTANDING SCENE TRANSITIONS

One of the easiest ways to tell a pro from a wanna-be is how they handle scene transitions. What's a scene transition? It's how one scene ends and another one begins. The most common way is to simply write the next scene, but is this how the pros do it?

Not usually and for good reason.

The tighter the scene transitions, the more difficult it'll be for someone in Hollywood to change or remove a scene later. Isn't your goal to keep as much of your original story intact as possible? This is one technique that isn't foolproof, but will help you in this area and will make you look professional at the same time.

What are these transitions and how do they work?

Scene transitions can be any combination of the following:

- Sound to Sound
- Dialogue to Dialogue
- Visual to Visual

- Dialogue to Visual
- Sound to Visual

Here's how these work:

Sound to Sound
A sound from one scene is either carried over to the next scene or an identical sound is heard.

Example: A scene ends with a phone ringing and the next scene opens with a phone ringing.

Dialogue to Dialogue
A character says something and in the next scene the very first character to speak says the exact same thing or a conclusion of what the first character said.

Example: A male character in one scene says, "I love her because…"
Then in the very next scene a female character finishes the line with, "because he's the greatest guy ever."

Visual to Visual
Scene ends with a visual that carries over in one form or another to another scene.

Example: In the film "Forest Gump" Forest and Jenny are outside watching fireworks. The scene ends with the fireworks then we see a CLOSE UP of a TV with fireworks and the scene has transitioned from outside to inside where they're watching the fireworks.

Dialogue to Visual
One character says something and it's followed in the next scene by the visual.

Example: One character expresses anxiety about a bomb going off and in the opening of the next scene we see the explosion.

Sound to Visual
We hear a sound at the end of a scene and at the beginning of the next scene we visually see where the sound is coming from.

Example: We hear a scraping noise in a house scene then in the opening of the next scene we see a teacher scraping her nails across a blackboard.

These are a few common techniques to transition scenes so they look professional and commercially prepared. Another is to use a technique I'll refer to as "overlapping."

The Overlapping Transition

Here's how overlapping works:

We see the exterior (establishing) shot of a building and we hear someone talking then we're suddenly inside the building where we see the individual talking. This isn't strictly a directorial decision. Screenwriters use it consistently as a way to visualize their stories to keep the reader involved and show a master level of writing.

Here's how it would look:

EXT. COURT HOUSE – DAY

Lawyers and defendants enter.

> JOE (V.O.)
> I intend to prove Mary Jones is guilty…

INT. COURT HOUSE – DAY

Joe strides before the jury.

> JOE
> ….of first degree murder.

This isn't just a great way to transition scenes, it also keeps the visual flow going!

The great thing about the commercial techniques presented above is they force a screenwriter to write TIGHT and LEAN without giving up any of the good stuff!

The Location Transition

By 'location', I'm not referring to where the story takes place. I'm referring to where the story begins and where it ends.

A location transition brings a story full circle by literally ending the story where it began. For example, if the story began with the hero locked in a jail cell, it might end with him walking out of the jail. If the story opens in a sleazy bar, it could be brought full circle by ending in a sleazy bar.

The establishing shot can also be used as a location transition. If the story opens with a shot of the Brooklyn Bridge, perhaps we see the hero leaving NY via the Brooklyn Bridge in the end scene.

Sometimes writers use location transition contrast to bring the story full circle. What the heck is this? Let's say the story begins with a rainy funeral scene, it might end with a bright, sunny wedding. Both are events where people gather, but they are in stark contrast to one another. This 'contrast' becomes a location transition that brings the story full circle. Other examples of location transition contrast might be opening with a desert, ending with ocean (dry to water) or sky to earth or a homeless man (in opening scene) to a man in a business suit (end scene).

Sometimes writers literally use an object as a location transition. Perhaps the first thing we see in a movie is a close-up of a spinning globe and the story ends with a close-up of a spinning globe.

Take a look at the beginning and end of your screenplay. Does it have a location transition? If not, can it have one? Is there a way to use an aspect of the opening scene, like the location, an object, etc., to transition it with the end to bring the story full circle? If so, do it!

Why is this so important? Because it provides closure for the audience by giving them the sense that the story has come full circle. Obviously, they won't realize why they get this sense of closure, but the screenwriter will know it's done deliberately. The pros know how to do it and I want you to look like a pro!

The Reverse Transition

Learning to use transitions as a bridge between scenes will set you apart from the amateurs since 100% of pros use it and less than 2% of aspiring writers use it. The easiest way to learn transitions is to start looking for them in movies. Every time a new scene begins you should be able to identify the type of transition used.

Let's expand upon the transition by a specific type of transition I refer to as a reverse transition. I also refer to it as a character transition. It's where a character, usually the hero, says one thing then the next scene opens with him doing the exact opposite. By the way, this also provides a built-in reversal (twist) – another vital selling point in any screenplay.

Here are two examples:

In the comedy "Anger Management" the hero and his girlfriend are taking a break from dating. The hero's trying to act like it doesn't matter that his girlfriend's out with another man. He says he doesn't care that she's at a local restaurant with the man, then as the next scene opens we see him escorting a date into the restaurant. He says one thing, but does the exact opposite in the next scene.

In the horror "Lake Placid", the heroine is an in-door girl who works in a NY museum. She refuses her boss's offer to go to the wilderness to work on a case and adamantly says there's no way she's going to Maine. The scene ends and the next scene opens where we see her in a Cessna flying over the Maine wilderness.

Note: In order for this type of transition to work, the reversal must happen IMMEDIATELY! As soon as the character says he won't do something, the scene ends and the next scene opens with him doing what he said he wouldn't. A tight transition is mandatory to make this work.

This type of reverse transition also works for a character who insists he will do something, then open the next scene where he's blocked from doing it. I hope I've lit a fire under your butt and you're hot to start adding clever transitions to your work so you'll look like a pro.

The Next Day Transition

The writer finishes a scene INT. HOUSE – DAY and the next scene is in the same house only it's the next day. 99% of writers will write: INT. HOUSE – NEXT DAY. This seems reasonable and looks right, but the audience will never see the script. How do they know it's the NEXT DAY?

This is where the format error takes place.

Without a proper transition and/or description (action) reference(s), the audience could easily assume it's still the same day.

Go ahead and write INT. HOUSE - NEXT DAY in the primary slug indicator, but clarify it by using visuals and or dialogue. For example, show a shop or restaurant turning a closed sign to open. Or show something repetitive that indicates it's a new day. By 'repetitive', I mean something an audience recognizing as happening daily, like mail delivery or the paper boy tossing a paper onto a lawn (this one shows it's morning), or use something as simple as a clock. Other visuals to use to show it's a new day could be a change of the character's clothing or dialogue where the characters exchange 'good morning' greetings.

My favorite is repeating an establishing shot in between the two scenes. For example, when the scene ends, go to EXT. HOUSE – DAY and show the sun setting behind the house, then go to EXT. HOUSE – DAY and show the sun rising. Let us hear the birds chirp and see the paperboy, then go to INT. HOUSE- NEXT DAY....well, technically – if you do it this way, there's no need to write NEXT DAY!

Regardless of the choice, the important thing to remember is how the audience is experiencing the scenes. Be sure to include proper transitions, visual and/or dialogue to clarify it is indeed the NEXT DAY.

Finally, make sure to use a transition between EVERY scene. This will make it difficult for a producer or director to cut scenes because he won't want to mess up the flow.

The Time Jump Transition

Most of us are familiar with seeing a character pick up the phone to make a call – the scene ends – and in the next scene we see another character answering a phone. This is a transition. There are many different types and combinations; visual, dialogue, sound, etc. Let's say we see a terrorist planting a bomb (visual) and as the next scene opens we hear it explode (sound); this would be a visual-to-sound transition.

But are there other ways to use transitions? Yes. Sometimes a writer might want to jump ahead in time a few hours, a few days, weeks or years. Or the writer might want to go back in time. In these instances, I'd advise the writer to use a time transition jump.

For instance, we hear a character telling another character that he's getting married next week, then the next scene opens at the wedding. This is a dialogue-to-visual, time jump transition. We've moved across time to one week later at the wedding.

Using this type of transition is a good way to handle FLASHBACKS. It's wise to use FLASHBACKS sparingly, but if the writer does decide to use them, a time jump transition can help smooth the way to and from the past. Perhaps a tourist accidentally finds an ancient relic while exploring a tomb. In the next scene, the writer might open the FLASHBACK with a king holding the relic the tourist just found. This is a visual-to-visual, time jump transition. The same technique can be used again to go from the past to the present.

I recommend writers use transitions at the end/beginning of every single scene. Why? It keeps the visual flow going and engages the reader in the story. Secondly, it makes it difficult for a producer to cut scenes without messing up the visual flow. It's a good way to help ensure the story remains intact; the way you wrote it!

The Sequel Transition

In today's economy, a producer is more likely to purchase a screenplay with sequel potential than one without sequel potential. What if I told you that you can purchase a car and get two additional cars paid for? Or two additional houses? Or two additional diamonds? Or you can just have one of each. Wouldn't you take the 3-package deal? A producer who purchases a screenplay that becomes a sequel usually only pays for the first script and if the finished film is a success, he can franchise the story into one or two sequels (maybe more!). Since sequels are usually paid for by the distributor, for example, a studio, the producer has not only saved money, but he's made a boat-load of it! Okay, I think I've made the point of why a producer would be more interested in a screenplay with sequel potential, but just saying you think your screenplay has sequel potential isn't enough. The 'sequel potential' should be in the script's ending in what I refer to as the Sequel Transition.

This is tricky, so pay attention! First, I'm not advocating leaving a story unresolved. That's fool's play! The trick to making a Sequel Transition work is mere seconds of screen time. That's right – I said seconds. What do I mean? Something is going to happen right at the end – something that takes only seconds of screen time – that will propel the story into a sequel, BUT – and that's a big BUT – leaves the current plot fully resolved!

The horror genre provides the best examples of the use of what I've come to call the Sequel Transition. In fact, it's mandatory that a horror ends with the threat remaining, BUT where the monster is defeated. Look at the classic film "Halloween". In the end, Michael Myers is shot by the psychiatrist and falls through a second-story window to the ground. He appears to be dead. Jamie Lee Curtis's character asks the question, "Was that the boogie man?" The shrink turns to her and says, "As a matter of fact, it was." When he turns back to the window, Michael Myers is gone! We see the empty ground for a split second and the movie ends! Michael Myers has been defeated, but he lives to return another day.

This is a classic example of a Sequel Transition. First, it allows for a completed plot because Michael Myers has been defeated. Secondly, it allows for sequel potential because Michael Myers is still out there. He could return at any moment. Finally, the sequel transition happens in seconds when we see he's gone!

Here are a few more examples from horror so you get an idea of how to create a Sequel Transition, which is the shortest of all the transitions because it takes mere seconds. In the classic film "Carrie", an arm (Carrie's arm) grabs the girl from the grave. Carrie's dead, but she still seems to have the supernatural ability to return. In the classic film "Hocus Pocus", the witches are dead, but we see their evil spell book's eye blink at us. The witches have been defeated, but can their spell book could bring them back. Notice how we only see these 'Sequel Transitions' for a second or two, then the story abruptly ends! And yes, the story must immediately end after the Sequel Transition!

Okay, this is great, but how does this work for other genres? Use the model above! Do NOT deviate from it. For example, if the story is a Romantic Drama and we see the happy couple hugging at the end, maybe the female love interest sees an old flame in the distance and the story ends abruptly! The problem with this is that most writers will be tempted to have her speak to the old flame. NO, just end the story. What about a Suspense Thriller? If you're dealing with a serial killer and he's been caught, then have a copy cat killer show up on the scene, then end the story abruptly! In a comedy, maybe the hero who's overcome a fear of swimming, then discovers he's inherited a plane, but OH NO…we find out he's afraid of heights, then the story ends abruptly! The first story was a comedy dealing with a hero's fear swimming. We'll get to rejoin this same hero in Part II to see if he can overcome his fear of heights.

As you can see, this technique can be applied to any genre and it's a good way to get a producer to purchase the screenplay because sequel potential means money in the back for the producer and for you (see Extra Tip).

Extra Tip: If you add a Sequel Transition and the screenplay sells, make sure you write into the Literary Deal Memorandum that you get first dibs on writing the sequel. This could be future money in the bank and imagine if you've sold a few of these. That $100K sale could end up banking you half a million by the time you write the sequels. Isn't that few seconds of extra screen time worth the extra money? You bet it is!

UNDERSTANDING PRIMARY & SECONDARY SLUG INDICATORS

Many screenwriting teachers advocate writing in all master shots. This means writing the screenplay with only primary slug indicators, like INT. HOUSE – DAY. While others advocate using secondary slug indicators to show visual movement within a scene or to emphasize how a scene is being filmed without adding directorial references like CUT TO:. These secondary slug indicators reveal shots within a primary location, such as the BEDROOM in a house.

Here's how both styles look on paper:

Master Shots:

INT. HOUSE- DAY

Susan enters through the front door.

INT. BEDROOM – DAY

Susan stumbles into the bedroom, collapses drunk on the bed.

Secondary Slugs:

INT. HOUSE – DAY

Susan enters through the door and stumbles into the

BEDROOM

where she collapses drunk in the bed.

The screenwriter should use the style best suited for the story. For example, if a story has locations with lots of movement within a single location, then secondary slugs can help keep the movement flowing and even add to the visual texture of the story, while locations with minimal movement can be handled with all primary slug indicators. Even a combination of the two based on the visual movement within a location can work effectively.

Some writers may also choose to write in all primary slug indicators except for action scenes where they'll break up the scenes with secondary slug indicators and literally make the pages look like they're moving faster to give a visual feel for the action taking place on the pages.

After the Primary Slug

Screenwriters know the primary slug indicator tells the reader the location, whether it's day or night and where the scene takes place. For example:

INT. HOUSE – DAY

Most writers get this right. On occasion it is written incorrectly. An incorrect primary slug indicator is one that runs longer than one line, adds description to the slug or information that doesn't translate to the screen, like precise times. Here's an example of an incorrect primary slug indicator:

INT/EXT. BIG, BROWN & UGLY MEDIEVAL CASTLE IN HEART OF ENGLAND – 10A.M. MORNING

Using both INT/EXT is wrong! Why? Because the production crew needs to know where they are filming and often exterior shots are filmed at a different location than the interior. For example, the audience might see the exterior of a castle, but the interior was shot on a sound stage. That's TWO locations, not ONE!

Further, writing an exact time of day is ridiculous! Unless the writer shows a clock or something specific, the audience can only see that it's daytime or night time. They have no idea what time it is! Writers should remember that the audience won't see the script.

SAME LOCATION – DIFFERENT SLUG
I also need to mention that when a writer decides to call a location INT. MATT'S HOUSE – DAY, then the location should remain the same throughout the script. I've read scripts where I thought there were three different houses only to realize late in the story that it was just one location. If Matt lives on First Street, don't refer to his house as INT. MATT'S HOUSE – DAY on one page, then later refer to the location as INT. FIRST STREET HOUSE – DAY. The reader and production crew will assume it's two different locations!

Okay, let's get past the incorrect primary slug indicator and talk about what comes immediately after this important slug. If I asked ten screenwriters what comes after this slug they'd all say description. They're almost right. What comes after the primary slug indicator is action driven description. This prevents the screenwriter from turning into a novelist and describing everything from the wallpaper to the color of the carpet. We've hit upon this already, but let's take a closer look. Here are right and wrong examples:

WRONG

The living room's crammed with newspapers, trash, dirty ashtrays, rodent droppings and fast food containers. Dusty cobwebs obscure a clear view of the exterior. It's a hoarder's paradise. A cat scurries from a hiding place near the couch and claws the arm of a chair before darting into another room.

ALEX, 40's, enters. He's as gruff looking as the room itself; unshaven with a stained t-shirt and crusty, brown underwear.

-This is wrong because the writer didn't incorporate action with the description, which resulted in overwritten description.

RIGHT

ALEX, 40's, an unshaven, stained t-shirt slob in brown-laced underwear enters. He stomps over a stack of newspapers, kicks his way past dirty ashtrays and plops down on a rodent-infested couch.

 A cat SCREECHES, runs over his lap and escapes into a nearby room.

-Written the RIGHT way involves the reader (audience) in the story and creates a visual flow. Notice I left out the cobwebbed window. It just didn't seem necessary to the purpose of this scene. Also note that I even had the cat get in on the action.

NO DESCRIPTION
While I'm harping on the right way to write description, I often see primary slug indicators that are followed by no description at all. This provides no visuals for the reader. I have no idea what I'm seeing! ALWAYS add description after the primary slug indicator, even if the scene is continuing from a previous scene. Treat each primary slug indicator as its own, new scene.

THE PRONOUN MISTAKE
When a writer opens a new scene with He, She or They, the reader is left to guess who the writer is talking about. I once read an entire 3-page sequence thinking the 'He' was the story's hero only to discover it was the antagonist! NEVER open a scene with a pronoun, even if it's continuing from the previous scene. DO NOT ASSUME the reader knows who He, She or They are.

212

WRONG

INT. HOUSE – DAY

He walks in and picks up the gun.

RIGHT

INT. HOUSE – DAY

Alex walks in and picks up the gun.

TWO SLUGS IN A ROW
Only ducks should be in a row! This is sloppy, lazy writing that provides no visual style whatsoever because the writer didn't bother to add visuals.

WRONG

EXT. HOUSE – DAY

INT. HOUSE – DAY

John enters and picks up the gun.

RIGHT

EXT. HOUSE – DAY

John races to the door.

INT. HOUSE – DAY

John enters and picks up the gun.

-I don't care if I've seen this house fifty times in the story. If the writer's showing it again, then something must be happening in conjunction with the house....so show it after BOTH slugs.

START WITH ACTION
Incorporating action with description is important because it creates visual flow and prevents the writer from over-describing a location. But a problem arises in screenwriting that writers have learned from writing classes and reading books; the problem is writing an introductory sentence (to a paragraph) or in a novel, writing an introductory, description paragraph.

213

We're so darn used to doing this that we naturally want to do so in screenwriting. That's why it's so important to learn screenwriting because it's a specific trade. In screenwriting it's best NOT to write an intro sentence or an intro description paragraph. Instead, the best way is to either incorporate action with description or even better....

....start with action! Forget the damn wallpapers, go straight to the character(s) and show us what he/she is doing. Keep us on his or her viewpoint and leave out the introductory crap. If you can't write this way, then maybe you're a novelist because you aren't a screenwriter.

STRAIGHT TO DIALOGUE
Another mistake I often see is a primary slug indicator followed by dialogue. For example:

INT. HOUSE – DAY

MATT
Where's the money, Joe?

JOE
It's not here.

-This is wrong! The writer provided no visuals whatsoever. The reader has no idea what's being seen. Is Matt standing, sitting, holding a gun or smoking a cigarette? Is Joe near the door, at a table, etc.? Also, the reader has no idea who is in the room until they speak. This wrong format tells the reader that the writer isn't suited to write for the visual medium known as film because the writer can't even form a simple picture in the reader's mind by remembering to always include visual action/description at the beginning of every scene. This includes continuing scenes! Don't leave the reader guessing as to the setting just because the characters moved from EXT. to INT. It's the writer's job to set the stage!

The primary slug indicator is very important and what comes after it is just as important!

Sluglines & Description

Most screenwriters know that the primary slug indicator should not contain description. Here's an example of the wrong way to write a primary slug indicator:

EXT. JUNKY, DIRTY HOUSE - DAY

The easiest way to fix this is to keep description where it belongs, in the description and out of the primary slug indicator as follows:

EXT. HOUSE – DAY

A junky, dirty place.

This is Formatting 101, but the area most screenwriters mess up when it comes to primary slug indicators and description is repeating the obvious.

Here's an example of the wrong way:

INT. COUNTRY STORE – DAY

Inside the country store, Cassandra sets a basket on the counter.

-The primary slug indicator already tells the reader that we're inside the country store, so there's no need to repeat this information in the description.

Here's the correct way to write it:

INT. COUNTRY STORE – DAY

Cassandra sets a basket on the counter.

-This keeps the visual flow going without repeating information already known.

If a screenwriter finds that their primary slug indicators are running over one line, it's probably due to an improperly formatted primary slug that includes unnecessary description.

It's okay to distinguish one location from another such as:

INT. JOHN'S HOUSE – DAY
INT. MARY'S HOUSE- DAY

The screenwriter gets into trouble when they start adding adjectives to the primary slug indicator:

INT. JOHN'S DUMPY HOUSE – DAY
INT. MARY'S NEAT HOUSE – DAY

Save the description for the description. Keep the primary slug indicators clear, concise and don't repeat information between the slug line and the description.

Scene Shifts

When writing a scene that begins inside and shifts to the outside, it's tempting to continue the description without using a new primary slug indicator. This is incorrect formatting!

Any shift from inside to outside or vice versa, requires a new primary slug indicator! Here's an example:

WRONG WAY

INT. JOE'S HOUSE – DAY

Joe follows Wendy to the front porch. They argue. Wendy gets in her car, leaves. Joe storms back into the house and slams the door.

CORRECT WAY

INT. JOE'S HOUSE – DAY
Joe follows Wendy.

EXT. JOE'S HOUSE – DAY

Joe & Wendy argue on the porch.

Wendy gets in her car, leaves.

Joe storms back inside and slams the door.

The same rule applies to shifts in time. If a scene takes place inside a house at night and then it's morning; a new primary slug indicator is required. Here are examples:

WRONG WAY

INT. JOE'S HOUSE – NIGHT

Joe reads a book, falls asleep.

His alarm clock RINGS. He gets up, heads to the bathroom.

RIGHT WAY

INT. JOE'S HOUSE – NIGHT

Joe reads a book, falls asleep.

INT. JOE'S HOUSE – DAY

Joe's alarm clock RINGS. He gets up, heads to the bathroom.

Additional Note: Don't overuse terms like MORNING, EVENING, etc. in the primary slug indicators. An audience can't tell the difference between DAY AND MORNING OR EVENING unless the writer provides a visual or dialogue to indicate a specific time. To the audience it's just DAY.

UNDERSTANDING DIALOGUE CUE INDICATORS

To understand Dialogue Cue Indicators it's imperative to know their definitions:

(V.O.)
The voice over is traditionally used when the character is speaking over the film like a narrator. However, it is acceptable to use it for phone conversations.

(O.S.) or (O.C.)
Off stage or off camera is used when the characters can be heard, but not seen because he's off stage.

(FILTERED)
Filtered is used to indicate a character's voice is being heard through an electronic device such as a phone, walkie-talkie, TV, etc.

(ON TV), (ON PHONE)
This type of dialogue cue indicator can be used instead of (FILTERED) or (V.O.)

The trick is to pick one and stick with it consistently throughout the script. For example, if the writer decides to use (V.O.) for all phone conversations in Act I, then don't switch to (FILTERED) in Act II. Consistency is the mark of a pro!

What if a character is in a different room in a house than the scene is being shot in, yet we can hear him talking?
-This is either (O.S.) or (O.C.) depending on the screenwriter's choice. Remember, if you pick (O.S.), the writer must use only (O.S.) for the rest of the story.

What if the character is traveling in a vehicle, but the scene is shot outside the moving vehicle, yet we can hear the character talking?
-This is (V.O.) because the character is in the scene inside a moving vehicle, but his voice is being heard over the film, similar to how we'd hear a narrator speak.

What if a scene is close up on an item in the location where we can only hear the characters speaking, but can't see the characters?
-This is (O.S.) or (O.C.) because the characters are in the scene, but we can only hear the characters.

Dialogue Formatting

Here are the basics to looking like a pro:

Keep dialogue cue indicators consistent. If a character's name is KEVIN SMITH, don't refer to him as KEVIN in one dialogue cue indicator, then SMITH in the next. This can easily cause reader confusion.

KEVIN
(into phone)
It's me, Kevin.

LATER

SMITH
(into phone)
Hi, it's me, Kevin.

Pick one and stick with it! Is he KEVIN or SMITH? Whichever you pick, the same name should be used in the description. Don't refer to the character as KEVIN in the dialogue and SMITH in the description. Let other characters make the multiple references. It's the screenwriter's job to remain consistent.

DON'T OVERUSE exclamations points, underlying or bold. Use sparingly and only when absolutely necessary for dramatic effect.

218

Learn to write dialogue format the way actors interpret it.
Dialogue followed by a double dash tells the actor that the dialogue is
interrupted.

KEVIN
(into phone)
Hi, it's - -

Dialogue that's followed by three dots tells the actor that the dialogue trails
off.

KEVIN
(into phone)
Hi, it's...

With this in mind, don't tell us what just happened in the next dialogue cue
indicator or the formatting is wrong:

KEVIN
(into phone)
Hi, it's - -

JOHN (O.S.)
(interrupts)
Kevin, I'm here.

Just write:

KEVIN
(into phone)
Hi, it's - -

JOHN (O.S.)
Kevin, I'm here.

PHONE CONVERSATIONS
Before Intercutting between two locations, be sure to establish BOTH the
locations. Otherwise, the reader has no idea what the scene looks like –
they're reading blind.

INT. KEVIN'S PLACE – NIGHT

Kevin chomps on a sandwich, picks up the phone and dials.

INT. JOHN'S PLACE – NIGHT

John plops down on the couch, answers the phone.

INTERCUT

DON'T WRITE description into the dialogue:

KEVIN
(stands up, walks across the room,
picks up the phone)
Hi, it's Kevin.

Correct way:

Kevin stands, walks across the room and picks up the phone.

KEVIN
Hi, it's Kevin.

Leave action in the description where it belongs. You can use sparingly in
the dialogue wryly, but it's best to keep to the description as much as
possible.

LIMIT DIALOGUE PRONOUNS
If the majority of dialogue in a scene starts with a pronoun the dialogue will
sound flat when performed by actors. Actors know this and often change
these lines. As screenwriters, we don't want actors changing our lines – why?
Because they often do so without referencing how it'll affect the rest of the
story – they're too focused on the immediate scene and its delivery.

Check every scene in your script. Eliminate pronouns.

KEVIN
I'm here.

JOHN
Me too.

KEVIN
I had a bad day.

JOHN
I know what you mean.

KEVIN
I can't get a break. My boss is a jerk.

JOHN
My boss is too.

Revised scene:

KEVIN
I'm here.

JOHN
Come on in.

KEVIN
Bad day, how 'bout you?

JOHN
Yeah, me too.

KEVIN
Boss is a jerk.

JOHN
I hear ya.

-In the revised scene, I've limited the overuse of dialogue so it sounds film-worthy when performed by actors.

Using (O.S.) to Create Style

What is (O.S.)? It means Off Stage. Sometimes written as (O.C.) for Off Camera. Either one is acceptable. It is used in dialogue or written as o.s. in description. For dialogue it means the character's voice is heard in the scene, but the character isn't seen because he or she is off stage. The character is present, just out of sight.

Don't confuse this with a (V.O.) voice over where the character's voice is heard over the film like a narrator. They are two different formats used for different reasons.

Pro writers know how to use (O.S.) to create style. Being unable to see the character's facial expression when something is said can lead to mystery, intrigue, wonder, suspense, anticipation or even setup a reversal.

It can also be used to create fear. Fear of the unknown can be powerful. If the audience can hear someone, but can't see what's happening to the character, it can build intrigue, suspense, wonder, awe and terror. Or it can be used to create misinterpretation and reversals. Perhaps the character is screaming "Help, help!", then the scene shifts where we see the character is really in a live play being performed before an audience. He wasn't in need of help at all.

Let's also take a look at o.s., which also means off stage but is used in description. In this case someone or something is off stage. Again, this can be used to create emotions, to create misinterpretation and reversals. If we hear a dog barking we might perceive pending danger, then we see the dog was on a TV.

Stop using (O.S.) and o.s. like a punctuation mark and come up with ways to use it to create a writing style that shows a producer you understand how to write for the visual medium. If you fancy yourself a drama writer, a horror writer, a romantic comedy writer or any other specific type of writer, then you should be able to come up with ways to use (O.S.) and o.s. to enhance the style you're creating.

INTRODUCING CHARACTERS

There are a few formatting rules to be aware of when introducing characters, especially in regards to the story's main roles:

-Only CAP the character's name upon initial introduction. When a reader sees a name in CAPS (JOHN, SARAH, DAVID), it's assumed that the screenwriter is introducing a new character. If the character appeared earlier in the story it will cause reader confusion. Capping names applies to ALL characters in the script, even the DOORMAN.

-Add a personality trait when first introducing the main characters. This is the ONLY time a screenwriter can get away with doing this! It's acceptable to introduce a personality trait and even expected. Why? Because it tells the actor how to portray the role. The trick to this is to keep it simple. Here are a few examples:

SYLVIA (30s) is a she-bitch in heat on the prowl for soul-mate number five.

JOHN (40s) is going on 12 mixed with his hippie long hair and tweed pants; he's a walking bong straight out of Woodstock.

-Don't forget the obvious description of age and basic appearance. For some reason, screenwriters often leave this out. I had one writer tell me it's because he didn't want to narrow down the possibilities of who could play the role. This sounds like a valid argument, but worrying about who will play the role is beyond the screenwriter's scope. The film "Flight Plan" starring Jodie Foster was originally written as a male lead. The writer wants to paint a vivid picture of the story at the reading stage. Let casting directors and producers decide if the red-headed, freckled lead should be turned into a tall, dark and handsome role.

-Try to avoid similar names. Too many names starting with the same letter can cause confusion, even to the screenwriter. I once read a script with a James, John and Joe. The writer didn't notice the screenwriting program he was using kept auto-inserting James' name since it's the first alphabetically. Many of the intended dialogue for John and Joe was going to James and this created character and dialogue confusion throughout the script. It can also make it easy to confusion the characters.

THE GENRE FORMAT

First, I'd like to say for the record that screenwriters with multi-genre scripts give me a headache! 9.9 out of 10 have subjects and worse, formats, that are all over the place! It feels like I've fallen into the rabbit hole – if you know what I mean!

I'm here to tell you that your screenplay's genre is a determining factor in how to handle the format. Bet they didn't mention that in the formatting book you purchased for $19.99. Heck, they didn't even mention it in the 'how-to' screenwriting book you purchased for $29.99.

Let's look at the first genre determination. It's page length based on accepted formats; Dramas run the longest up to 120 pages, Horrors average 90-105 pages, RomComs run around 105-110 pages as do comedies, Action/Adventures run around 110-115 pages, Sci-Fi around 100-105, etc. The more action your script has the shorter you'll need the length to be because action takes up more screen time than paper time and doesn't fit the one page equals one minute of screen time rule. Opposite is true for dialogue-driven stories. Actors can rattle off two pages for every minute of screen time. This is why Hollywood advocates a 60-40% rule with stories being 60% visuals, 40% dialogue. In addition, any script falling under 90-

pages won't be given serious consideration. Same goes for scripts coming in over 120 pages – forget it!

Genre determines format style. A drama may contain heavier description paragraphs compared to a fast-paced action with broken up description. Comedies may have quick, one-word paragraphs that hit a visual punch-line, while RomComs might play with pretty words to set a romantic feel. A horror might ask a descriptive question – "Did he hear something?" during a scary moment, while a Sci-Fi might slam us with an unexpected visual – like a UFO flying overhead.

Genre determines dialogue format. By now you should be getting how this works, but here goes. Dramas tend to have weighty dialogue that often runs more than 4-6 lines with characters who talk out their emotions, give speeches and lengthy monologues. Comedies rely on quick punchlines to deliver the message. RomComs rely on broken sentences where characters can't find the words to tell each other how much they're in love. Action/Adventures like big heroic dialogue that relies on memorable moments that plays on words like "Live to fight another day".

Genre determines the characters' format. Horrors have characters the format allows us to kill, including the hero (the only genre that allows this!), while the evil one can get away! RomComs require single people struggling to find love. Comedies require characters teetering on tragedy, which creates comedy. All stories in all genres should end with the hero getting the last visual or last piece of dialogue!

Genre determines plot-ending format! This is the most common mistake I see. In horrors, the threat must remain or the script won't sell in this genre! RomComs notoriously require a chase scene at the end to sell. Comedies must end with a punchline or comedy visual.

Genre determines the plot itself! Horrors require a loss of free will for the characters' fear to work. RomComs must make it appear the characters will never get together to create suspense. Comedies must have a basis of tragedy to work.

What happens when the writer mixes the genres is confusion because the rules become muddled. This might not seem like a big deal, but it is to a producer who will need to sell the material to a specific audience. What is the easiest way to guarantee a story has an audience? You got it, the genre! A precise genre guarantees a built-in audience. Don't you follow genres? Sure you do. While I'll pay money to see a good horror flick at the theater, I wait for the DVD to see the RomComs. Last time I asked my friend if she wanted to go see a horror, her response was, "No, let's see a comedy". She didn't say, "No, let's see a comedy, drama, sci-fi, horror flick".

Genre is a marketing king! Understanding how the genres work and applying the genre rules to your screenplay will lead to one destination; a sale! See "How to" Chapters for how to write for specific genres.

USING FORMAT TO CREATE EMOTIONS

And you thought creating emotion was a function of the plot or characters. That's how amateurs think! Keep reading and I'll turn you into a pro!

As writers know or should know, every scene must evoke some type of emotion, whether it's fear, laughter, anxiety, suspense, etc. What you might not know is how to use format to help you create fear, laughter, anxiety or suspense.

Let's say the writer wants to scare the audience with a slasher scene where a bad guy with a big knife kills a pretty girl. Just writing the scene in straightforward visuals might be enough. But what if the pretty girl hears the knife's blade against a closed door o.s. (off stage)? Or what if she hears breathing o.s.? The proper use of off stage in reference to what the pretty girl is seeing and hearing can create tremendous fear.

Only revealing what's taking place in the f.g. (foreground) or b.g. (background) of a scene can create suspense, foreboding, mystery, etc. Using CLOSE ON can help a writer hide the identity of a killer by only revealing a gun, but not who's holding it. This creates suspense, which on an emotional level is known as anxiety. It's guaranteed to keep an audience watching.

The way format is handled can help provide visual twists that can evoke a number of emotions. One of my favorite scenes from the TV show "Monk" is when he's investigating a museum. He sees what he thinks is a statue of a German Shepherd, but when he touches it, the statue growls. It's a real dog! Written with secondary slug indicators, the writer can use the format to heighten this scene's twist and create a 'shock' emotion.

Monk approaches the statue. He touches it.

THE STATUE

....growls!

MONK

225

....jumps back...

RETURN TO SCENE

...as the German Shepherd trots to the other side of the room. Takes up post.

-A writer wouldn't write every scene like this, but would use the secondary slug indicators as a format technique to create a specific visual in the reader's mind to help add flare to the twist. The writer is literally manipulating the visuals via format to create the emotional experience!

Voice Over (V.O.) is when the character speaks over the film like a narrator. Think of films like "Forrest Gump". It can create extreme emotions because it allows the audience inside the character's mind, but should be used sparingly. Why? Because film's a visual medium and most films rely on the visual to deliver the emotion, not the dialogue.

However, there is another format technique involving (V.O.) the writer can use that creates ambience in how scenes transition from one place to another. Listen closely and you'll notice this technique used in films and TV. It's when you start to hear the character speak before one scene ends, then a new scene opens and the character continues to speak.

Here's an example:

EXT. COURTHOUSE – DAY

People flow in and out of the revolving door entrance.

LAWYER (V.O.)
...If the glove don't fit....

INT. COURTHOUSE – DAY

Lawyer speaks to a jury.

LAWYER
...you must acquit.

-As I mentioned above, this creates flow and makes an audience feel intricately involved in the story. If the audience feels like they're part of the story, they'll experience the story on an emotional level.

226

In dialogue, format can be used to reveal the character's emotional state. Using three dots (...) tells us a character's dialogue trails off, while a double dash (- -) means the character was interrupted.

SUSIE
I don't know if I can marry...

-Obviously, Susie's torn as to accept a proposal or not. A strong emotional moment created by her dialogue trailing off (...).

ANDREW
Why'd you say - -?

SAM
Shut up, I'll say what I want!

-Obviously, this is a heated, angry moment. The double dash (--) reveals that Sam has cut Andrew off mid-sentence. The format has been used to create an angry, tense moment.

By the way, triple dots and double dashes aren't just for dialogue. You can use them in description too. Perhaps one visual dissolves into another. Instead of incorrectly writing DISSOLVE TO, the writer can use triple dots to show the visuals trail off...

The Blue Ridge Mountains fade into the backdrop...

Or a visual might be interrupted with a double dash (- -).

The door swings open and in walks - -

-Here the writer interrupts the visuals and withholds revealing who entered from the audience until later in the story. This creates suspense.

There are many different ways to use format to create emotion. If used properly, format can vastly improve a writer's ability to deliver emotion on paper. The writer should consider format as carefully as he considers plot, characters, scenes and dialogue.

Most importantly, the writer will be a step ahead of the amateurs because amateurs think format is a necessary evil and slap it on the page like it was nothing more than a page number. But you know better because you've moved beyond the ranks of the amateurs by using format to create emotions.

Learning proper screenplay format is vital to being recognized as a professional screenwriter. So why do I continue to see sloppy formatting, improper formatting and often a complete lack of understanding the purpose of formatting in terms of creating a visual style? I'm not sure why, but here's what I do know: If I hire a plumber he better know how to fix a sink. If I call a fireman he better know how to put out a fire!

Format is part of a screenwriter's trade just like sinks and fire hoses are a part of plumber and firemen's trades. It's mandatory to know how format works and why it's vital to getting the job done. Without it the screenwriter looks like an amateur – heck, let's face it. The screenwriter who hasn't taken the time to learn format and truly understand how it can be used to enhance visual style is an amateur!

Screenwriters get paid what lawyers get paid; big bucks! They don't make big bucks if they haven't mastered their trade.

Format is more than just letting the reader know if a scene takes place inside (INT) or outside (EXT). Pro screenwriters know how to use format to create or enhance the tone, mood, atmosphere, flow, pacing, etc.

Here are a few examples:

Let's say the scene is fast-paced, like a car chase. It's okay to write it in normal descriptive, paragraph style, but writing in single-lines that are stacked close to the edge of the left margin creates a visual flow for the reader that literally makes it seem like the scene's moving fast. Take a look:

The car veers, misses a pedestrian. A second car closes in. The two race at top speeds. People scatter from crowded crosswalks. Breaks SQUEAL. Horns HONK. Speeds reach up to 80 – 100 miles an hour.

Here's another way to write this using visually-enhanced format style:

The car veers, misses a pedestrian.
A second car closes in.

The two race at top speeds.

People scatter from crowded crosswalks.

Breaks SQUEAL. Horns HONK.

Speeds reach up to 80 – 100 miles an hour.

Note: This style should only be used to create a sense that the scene is moving fast and to enhance the pacing. It should never be used to cheat the page count by expanding the script.

Another note regarding pacing: At the end of a screenplay, the scenes should become shorter and faster (regardless of genre) to create a sense that the story is wrapping up. This is an important format technique that is often overlooked by aspiring screenwriters.

SLUGS
In formatting there are several kinds of slug indicators; primary slugs, secondary slugs, dialogue cues and descriptive dialogue cues.

PRIMARY SLUGS
This one is the easiest. It's either INT. or EXT. The trick is to refrain from adding description to the location's primary slug. Put the fancy description where it belongs; in the description. Note: This slug should NEVER be more than one (1) line long or the writer is overwriting.

SECONDARY SLUGS
This slug is often misused or misunderstood. A secondary slug calls for a SHOT within the primary slug (location). For example, if the writer wants to draw attention to a specific – highly important item – he can use a secondary slug.

John stares at the pool of blood, notices a

LOCKET

open-faced with a photo of a couple.

BACK TO SCENE

John reaches to pick it up.

-The locket had better solve the crime scene or be imperative to the story before the writer calls for a SHOT using a secondary slug indicator. Also note that the scene now requires BACK TO SCENE to clarify that we're no longer looking solely at the locket, but have returned to a wider view of John.

-Do you see how this creates a picture in the reader's mind? See why proper format is so important and how it can be used to create a picture in the reader's mind?

Secondary slug indicators can also be used to move between rooms in a single location without having to use a new primary slug indicator every time the scene shifts from a house's KITCHEN to its BEDROOM or BATHROOM. However, once the scene shifts to an entirely new location or outside, the writer MUST use a new slug! Continuing to use a secondary slug when the scene has clearly shifted locations is a common mistake I often see.

DIALOGUE SLUGS
Another misunderstood format style – Here are the rules:

If the slug is next to the character's name, then it's an indicator as to how the dialogue is being heard:

JOHN (V.O.)

-In this case, John's dialogue is being heard over the film via a voice over. (FILTERED) John's dialogue would be heard via a device, like a phone, TV, etc. Note: It's acceptable to use (V.O.) for phone conversations. (O.S.) or (O.C.) means we can hear the character speaking, but can't see him. He is in the scene just off stage. Note: If a writer decided to use (O.S.), it should used consistently throughout the screenplay and should not be interchanged with (O.C.). Keep usage of all slugs consistent!

If the slug is beneath the character's name (often referred to as a wryly), then it's an indicator as to how the actor should deliver the line.

JOHN
(angry)

-This one should be used sparingly because actors don't like to be told how to deliver dialogue. Use it when the delivery changes the meaning of the scene or the meaning wouldn't be understood without it.

-It's also okay to add brief description via this slug, but again it should be part of how the character's delivering the dialogue.

JOHN
(reaches for phone)
No, I didn't speak with her yet.

-If used as description the slug should never be more than a few brief words and should never be more than one line long.

TECHNOLOGY FORMAT

Modern technology is everywhere. I can't imagine any of us can get through a day without watching TV, logging on to the Internet, checking for phone text messages, etc. It's part of the modern lifestyle.

It's so much a part of our world, that most scripts will probably have some sort of technology in the story line. We might see something on a computer screen, a phone display screen or on TV. If it's vital information, we'll want the audience to see it too.

First, the writer needs to realize that the technology is not a scene.

INT. COMPUTER SCREEN – DAY

This is wrong! The computer screen isn't a location. This needs to be written in what's called a master shot. Where is the computer? Let's say it's in Harold's bedroom, then write:

INT. HAROLD'S BEDROOM – DAY

Set the scene by adding description, then write a secondary slug indicator for the computer. A secondary slug indicator is a shot within a master scene. Basically, it means we're going to a CLOSE UP of something vitally important to the story. But we don't want to use the words CLOSE UP. Here's an example of how this would look:

INT. HAROLD'S BEDROOM – DAY

Harold sits at a desk staring at a computer screen. He starts to sob.

ON COMPUTER SCREEN

A picture of Harold's girlfriend with another man.

BACK TO SCENE

Harold turns off the computer, exits the room.

Notice I wrote BACK TO SCENE. I've shown the audience the vital information on the computer screen; Harold's cheating girlfriend, but now I want to return to the room so we can continue the story with Harold. For a moment we're ON COMPUTER SCREEN, then we're BACK TO SCENE.

This is the correct way to handle technology in a scene. The writer can do this as many times as necessary in the scene to reveal vital information being provided via technology. The key to remember is the information must be vitally important to the story or there's no need to use the ON TV, ON COMPUTER SCREEN, ON PHONE DISPLAY, etc.

Also, don't feel like you have to show the information being displayed by the technology every single time. Maybe we see Harold in front of the computer and watch him sob, but we don't learn why until later. Knowing when and how to reveal information is part of the challenge of creating suspense in a story. But if the story calls for the information to be revealed, you now know how to do it properly.

REPETITION FORMAT

Often when providing coverage I have to tell writers not to repeat information that has already been revealed via the visuals or dialogue. I then receive email follow-up questions that go something like this: "But how will the other characters know the information unless it's told to them?"

I believe TV is to blame for the confusion when it comes to repeating information. Unlike films, TV is a talking-heads medium where it's acceptable to repeat information. Detective shows have made repetition an art by summing up a case at the end of the show; literally repeating everything we've learned in summation style, then announcing the suspect. Because we watch more TV than movies on a daily basis, we're used to this. Then the writer sits down to write a screenplay. He has an arson situation where investigators reveal their findings to one character. This character in turn meets up with other characters in a different scene and repeats everything he just learned about the arson case. This works in TV, but NOT in film. In film, one of two things should happen: 1) either the character sums it up by saying something like, "It's arson" or 2) the writer gets into the scene late – right after the character has already conveyed the vital information to the other characters, thus avoiding repetition.

Why is repetition accepted in TV, but not film? It's this simple: When a story's playing out on a 50-foot screen and information is repeated it kills the impact of the scene and can make the entire story seem contrived. Why? Because film's a visual medium, not a talking-heads medium. Whereas, in

TV it's acceptable for repetition because we're not as committed to the visual process.

Next time you watch TV listen for the repetition. I guarantee it's there. Then go to the movies and watch how the story cleverly avoids repetition, which keeps the visuals moving forward.

THE FAMILIAR REVERSAL

A writer can't use clichés in their scripts because the underlying meaning is so overused that it becomes stale and producers want fresh material. But what does a writer do when a situation is familiar? Like the cliché, the writer can't resort to the familiar because it can seem overused. But wait a minute, shouldn't we write what we know? Yes and No. Write what you know, but give the familiar a reversal.

A million times I've seen opening scenes where a character's alarm clock rings, he gets out of bed, goes to the bathroom, brushes his teeth and gets in the shower. This is too familiar and frankly it's boring to watch. It's too familiar; too overused. My advice to shake things up is to take a look at the genre and use the genre to determine an appropriate reversal.

For example, let's say the story is a comedy. Let's take another look at the boring opening scene with comedy applied. The alarm clock rings and the character gets out of bed. He's still groggy and instead of peeing in the toilet, he pees in a briefcase he left sitting on the toilet seat. He then proceeds to brush his teeth with Preparation H instead of toothpaste. He gets in the shower and we hear him scream....instead of a water shower, it's a raw sewage shower from a faulty pipe, yuck!

What if the genre is suspense thriller? Let's take another look at the boring opening scene with suspense thriller applied. The alarm clock rings and the character gets out of bed. While he uses the toilet, we see a shadowy figure watching him through a window. He brushes his teeth and notices a bloody handprint high up on the mirror. His eyes follow a blood trail to the shower where he finds his dead wife!

Okay, I think you get the point! If you don't, stop reading now and go back to your day job. Let me sum up the 'familiar reversal'; take a familiar situation and add reversals based on the genre. Why? Because you want to keep the reader guessing and the way to accomplish this task is to use a familiar reversal.

It's the little things that can make or break a screenplay. Format being #1. Here are a few tricks to help the writer maintain a quality level of formatting worthy of a big pay day:

(O.S.) and (O.C.) written into description isn't written like it is in a dialogue cue indicator.

WRONG:

(O.S.) we hear an owl HOOT.

WRONG:

O.S. we hear an owl HOOT.

RIGHT:
O.s. we hear an owl HOOT.

RIGHT:
An owl HOOTS o.s.

Note: Can also be written as o.c.

BACKGROUND
Yes, the writer can write out the word background in description as follows:

We see an owl in a tree in the background.

Correct format for screenplays is:

We see an owl in a tree in the b.g.

Note: Background is reduced for formatting purposes.

MOS
This is an old, but still widely accepted format that many aren't familiar with. If you're watching a movie and you can see characters speaking, but can't hear what they're saying – they're voices are muted out, then it's MOS.

MOS means without sound. We're seeing the characters speaking, but there's no sound.

John and Sandra speak at a table MOS.

Note: Do not write WITHOUT SOUND...that's improper format. Use MOS and look like a pro.

WRYLIES
Actors hate these because they don't want the screenwriter trying to direct them and prefer to suffer through their own translation of the material. Well, that's great, but if they deliver a line that was supposed to be funny in a dramatic intent, they can literally change the meaning of a scene, possibly an entire story.

A wryly appears below a character cue indicator and it tells the actor how to deliver a line:

JOHN
(angrily)
I said shut up!

The best way to avoid an actor ignoring the wryly because he/she doesn't want to be directed by the screenwriter (who's about as important as the coffee boy in Hollywood, just better paid), then forget the wryly and write the way you want the line delivered in the dialogue:

Angry:

JOHN
I said shut up!

Technically, the writer is still telling the actor how to deliver the line, but written into description it doesn't come across so directly. The actor won't even notice you've just directed him!

Note: Do NOT write wrylies next to the character's name:

JOHN (angry)
I said shut up!

Note: If you can't write it in the description, then it goes BELOW the character's name. Information next to the name.

The little things continued...

1) Write out #'s in dialogue. Don't assume the actor will say the numbers as the writer intended. For example:

JOHN
I need 12 eggs.

The actor could interpret this and say "I need a dozen eggs", but the writer needs the number twelve said for story purposes. Should be written as:

JOHN
I need twelve eggs.

-Writing out #'s in dialogue includes, dates, years, etc. This rule does NOT apply to description, only to spoken words.

2) Keep Slugs to One Line – Put Excess in Description

Primary Slug Indicators that run over one line look sloppy on the page. They also indicate the writer has overwritten and if he/she has overwritten here, he's probably overwritten in other areas too. Keep slugs to one line:

WRONG:
EXT. SMALL HOUSE NEAR WOODS AND POND – DAN'S CREEK, PHILADEPHIA, PA – DAY

CORRECT
EXT. HOUSE – DAY

A small house sits near woods and a pond. A roadside sign reads: Dan's Creek – Philadelphia, PA

-Remember the audience won't see the slug so they'll never know this vital information unless the writer adds it visually into the story where it belongs.

3) Don't start a new scene with a Pronoun:

WRONG:
INT. HOUSE – DAY

She enters flushed and out of breath.

RIGHT:
INT. HOUSE- DAY

Susan enters flushed and out of breath.

4) Don't start a scene with only Dialogue.

Film's a visual medium. If the scene opens with characters speaking, then what am I seeing? Done this way causes the story to lack visuals. Imagine sitting in the theater and a new scene begins with a black, blank screen where you can hear characters speaking, but you can't see them. That's exactly what happens in the reader's mind when the writer opens a scene with only dialogue. ALWAYS set the scene's visuals into motion.

WRONG:
INT. HOUSE – DAY

JOHN
Adam has the goods, let's roll.

WESTLEY
Let's wait, man. I want my take now.

SUE
He'll bring it, promise.

EDDIE
I'm with West…we split the dough now.

-What the hell are we seeing here? NOTHING!

RIGHT:
INT. HOUSE – DAY

John enters, tosses an empty duffel bag on the table. Sue, Westley and Eddie stare at him, dumbfounded.

JOHN
Adam has the goods, let's roll.

He turns back to the door, when Westley remarks:

WESTLEY
Let's wait, man. I want my take now.

Sue lights a cigarette, blows smoke Westley's way.

SUE
He'll bring it, promise.

Eddie raises an eyebrow, suspicious.

EDDIE
I'm with West...we split the dough now.

-As you can see, the added visuals provide a moving picture of the scene and this is how it should be done!

5) Don't use CONT'D when a character speaks twice in a row.

This is an old, outdated format. All it does it distract the reader. The only time this is advisable is when the dialogue continues to another page. Also, if a character continues to speak in a new scene, treat it like a new scene – meaning there should NOT be a CONT'D because he's speaking for the first time in the new scene.

WRONG:

JOHN
He's here with the dough.

Everyone turns to the door. John greets the mobster:

JOHN (CONT'D)
Welcome, Don Jose.

RIGHT:
JOHN
He's here with the dough.

Everyone turns to the door. John greets the mobster:

JOHN
Welcome, Don Jose.

WRONG:
INT. HOUSE – DAY

John enters to address the cronies:

JOHN
The Don's waiting outside.

They move to the door.

EXT. HOUSE – DAY

John exits, introduces the cronies:

JOHN (CONT'D)
Don Jose, this is….

RIGHT:

INT. HOUSE – DAY

John enters to address the cronies:

JOHN
The Don's waiting outside.

They move to the door.

EXT. HOUSE – DAY

John exits, introduces the cronies:

JOHN
Don Jose, this is….

Knowing what they mean and using them properly in format can enhance the professional quality of your script.

ACTORS & FORMAT

Every once in a while I take a peek at some of the boards on various websites and I often see the argument against the techno side of screenwriting, as if it's some hideous monster that hinders creativity and any real artist should avoid it like the plague. Well, I'm hear to tell the anti-techno folks that learning one's craft is was sets the professionals apart from the amateurs.

Actors are a case in point. How an actor interprets the format in a scene can shift his interpretation of the scene, the character he's playing, the other roles and even the delivery of his performance! Still think the techno stuff isn't important?

Let's take a look at how the actor interprets a script:

The Double Dash (--) used in dialogue tells the actor that the dialogue is interrupted by another character or by something that happens in the scene. Here's an example:

JIM
This is the way he --

SUSAN
What? Don't tell me what --

JIM
I'll tell you whatever I want!

If a Double Dash (--) appears in the scene's description, the actors knows to break up the action and/or visual movement!

Triple dots (…) in dialogue tells the actor that the dialogue trails off. Here's an example:

JIM
This is the way he…

Triple dots (…) in the scene's description tells the actor that the action and/or visual movement slows.

If the actor sees that all of his dialogue is (O.S.) Off Stage, he knows he has to be present for the scene, but doesn't have to go through wardrobe or makeup because he doesn't appear on camera.

If an actor sees o.s. in the description, he knows that the action and/or description is taking place off stage and while the audience can't see it, he'll have to create a reaction that allows them to experience it via his performance.

If an actor sees (V.O.) in a scene, then he knows that this will require him to go to a sound stage at a later date and provide the dialogue for this scene. Note: Some indie director's do voice overs during a scene to avoid the sound stage cost, but 99% of the time, a voice over is done on a sound stage.

If an actor notices most of his dialogue is improperly formatted because all of it starts with a pronoun (I, He, She, We), then he'll most likely edit it because actors know that if too much of a scene's dialogue starts with pronouns that it'll sound flat on the film.

A wryly tells an actor how to deliver a line. Here's an example:

JOHN
(angry)
She's out of here!

Actors don't like to be told how to deliver their lines and prefer to interpret the character based on the character's personality, the story and the scene. Use sparingly!

If a character's initial introduction isn't properly formatted to include a personality trait, an actor could interpret the character incorrectly and a horror could turn into a comedy. Adding a personality trait is only acceptable upon a character's initial introduction, but keep it brief. Here's an example:

KEITH (20s), brazen and immature with dark-brown hair, muscular build...

These are only a few areas of format and how they're interpreted by the actor, but I believe the examples provided give a clear picture of why learning one's craft is so vital.

Don't assume any errors would be fixed before an actor reads the script! That's just plain lazy and if you're not interested in learning the techno stuff and how it's vital to the creative interpretation of your work, then find another medium to write for and stay away from screenwriting because professional screenwriters know format!

But wait a minute! You've tried to learn formatting and have read 10 books, but they all say something different. Who's right and who's wrong?

First, the reason they're different is because formatting changes! These changes are made yearly by producers and unless you work in the industry, you'll never be able to keep up with them.

How to Keep Up with Format Changes

I promised to reveal how to keep up with format changes so you always look like a pro and won't have to second guess if your format is correct or not.

Fade In Magazine sells a Spec Format Guide (more like a nifty pamphlet) that's updated yearly with the current industry standards. Buy it once a year and you'll always look like a pro! It's available via their website under the Publication section! It's that simple.

The great thing about formatting is that the more you learn to use it, the more you'll come up with ways to use it creatively to enhance visual movement, style, voice, characterizations, etc. Stop thinking of it as techno garb and start seeing it for what it really is: a way to enhance the creativity of your script, its visual movement, style, voice, characterizations, dialogue interpretation, etc.

SCREENPLAY LENGTH

The obvious rule regarding page length is anything over 120 pages is too long and under 90 pages is too short, regardless of the genre. Get the page length wrong and the writer risks not being taken seriously in Hollywood.

Different genres have acceptable page length. Knowing the range of these page lengths is important but be aware that the numbers listed here are subject to change based on current trends in the industry. If you follow the biz closely, you'll know when these changes take place. In the meantime, let's take a look at the current ranges for page lengths based on genres:

DRAMA: 115-120 pages
This is the only genre where hitting 120 pages is acceptable. This category also includes Crime Drama and Film Noir.

SUSPENSE THRILLER: 105-115 pages
This page length applies to all the thrillers; action thriller, supernatural thriller, etc.

COMEDY: 105-110 pages
The closer to 105 pages the better.

ROMANTIC COMEDY: 100-105 pages
RomComs should come in slightly shorter than a feature-length comedy. Unlike comedies, RomCom tend to have a chase scene at the end that moves fast. This accounts for the difference in the page count.

ACTION: 90-105 pages
An action sequence with a non-stop blow 'em up stuff might be a page long in the script, but it'll hit around 3 minutes of actual screen time. Because of

this, it's best to keep action scripts in the lower page range. Be careful: don't go below 90 pages or the script will look too short.

ACTION/ADVENTURE: 100-115 pages
Unlike action, the action/adventure relies more heavily on exotic backdrops mixed with dialogue, so the writer can get away with a longer page count.

ANIMATION: 115-120 pages
In an animation, the writer is the director. That means the writer will be adding camera angles and other directorial references that will length the script. Most spec writers won't add camera angles, even if the genre is animation. I'd recommend steering clear of angles.

HORROR: 90-110 pages
Psychological horror can be slightly longer at 110-115 pages, but if it relies heavily on visual effects, then go with the lower page count.

What if the script is a combination of genres? What if it's an action/comedy? Ask yourself, if the movie were in a video store, what shelf would it be on, the action shelf or the comedy shelf? Which genre takes up the most screen time, the action or the comedy? One will probably stand out as the primary genre. Go with the page length for this genre.

What if the script is under 90 pages? Then something's most likely wrong. A short script means the hero wasn't given enough conflict to overcome or the antagonist has disappeared for a majority of the story when he should have been going head-to-head with the protagonist.

Here's what short Acts mean:

Act I – Not enough setups to validate the rest of the story.
Act II – Hero wasn't given enough conflict to overcome.
Act III – The hero's arc is weak. He hasn't changed enough to take on a full resolution.

Exception to the page lengths noted above: I'd say the exception is independent films, which are often reliant on a small to medium budget to get made. This often requires a shorter page length for the script regardless of genre.

POV 101

For those who don't know, POV stands for point of view. When writing a novel the writer decides between a singular point of view (first person) or multiple view points (second-third person) to tell the story. Once the writer chooses one viewpoint style, he has to stick with it. But what about screenplays? Is there a POV guideline? Whose POV is the story told through? Is there a POV in a film? Is it the hero's POV? Is it the antagonist's POV?

In my opinion, it's none of the above! I'm sure some writers will disagree and argue that it should be the hero's POV or even a multiple character POV. Wrong! I'm not saying this isn't the hero's story because it is, but....

...the screenplay should be written from the Audience's POV! How the audience is experiencing the story is how the script should be written. For example, the audience might see or hear something the hero isn't privy to. Or the audience might be in on a secret and will wait around until the secret's revealed. What's being seen or heard by the audience is what should be on the page.

Understanding a screenplay is written from the audience's POV is very important. Why? Because writing a screenplay from this POV gives the audience a 'superior position', which in turn makes them feel more connected and emotionally involved with the story and its characters. It also works well to create suspense, especially if the audience knows information the hero doesn't know.

Finally, it's important because the writer needs to involve the reader (story analyst or producer) in the story to the point that they forget they're reading a script and become immersed in the plot. The easiest way to do this is to write the story from the audience's POV.

HERO'S INTERNAL CONFLICT FORMAT

Many writers struggle with the hero's internal conflict. It's illusive, like a ghost in a haunted house. Go to your script right now and look at the hero's introduction description and the hero's introduction scene. Does the hero's introduction description include his (or her) internal conflict? Does the hero's introduction scene include his (or her) internal conflict?

If not, stop right there! Don't write another word. The screenplay already has a problem. The easiest way to fix this problem and to assure the writer has included an internal conflict for the hero is to make sure it's formatted in two places; the hero's introduction description and the hero's introduction scene.

Here's an example of a RIGHT/WRONG hero introduction:

WRONG:
Jack's a 30's mechanic with brown hair and a pot belly.

RIGHT
Jack's a 30's arrogant jackass mechanic with brown hair and a pot belly.

-By adding the fact that he's an 'arrogant jackass', the writer has included an internal conflict for the hero to overcome. It's okay to add a personality trait to the hero's introduction description because it tells an actor how to portray the role, but it also reveals the hero's internal conflict. Don't get carried away by over-describing the hero's internal conflict, just sum it up with a few descriptive words.

-The RIGHT introduction description reveals a hero with an internal conflict related to the fact that he's an 'arrogant jackass'. But the audience won't see the script, so the writer needs to visually setup the internal conflict. Use the hero's introduction scene to show us he's an 'arrogant jackass'.

WRONG
Jack enters a mechanic's shop. Another MECHANIC, 30's, works on a vehicle.

JACK
Did you finish Mrs. Jones' car, she's waiting?

MECHANIC
Another thirty minutes.

JACK
No problem, I'll let her know.

Jack exits.

RIGHT
Jack huffs into the mechanic's shop. Another MECHANIC, 30's, works on a vehicle. He cringes when he spots Jack.

JACK
Hey, bud, you finish the old lady's car?
I could've had it done an hour ago.

MECHANIC
I need another - -

JACK

What, hour? Are you kidding me?
I could've had three cars locked and loaded.
We ain't makin' no money at this speed.

MECHANIC

I'll let her know.

Jack huffs toward the exit.

JACK

Nah, don't bother. I'll let her know I'm taking
over the job. (under his breath) Want somethin' done
right, gotta do it yourself.

Jack exits.
-By showing the audience Jack's arrogance, the writer has revealed his
internal conflict.

-Use the screenplay's format to remind you to include the internal conflict
when the hero's first introduced and in the hero's first scene (or one of the
opening scenes in Act I).

TEN RARELY USED TECHNIQUES

For those who'd like to explore more ways to use format to create style,
visuals, subtext, etc., then here are ten rarely used techniques the writer can
incorporate into a script:

1) Triple dots (…). These are commonly used in dialogue when the
character's speech trails off. It's rarely used in description, but when it is
used it means the same as DISSOLVE TO:. Since writers aren't supposed to
use DISSOLVE TO: because it's a directorial reference, a writer can simply
end the description/action with triple dots to indicate the scene dissolves (or
trails off).

2) Double dash (- -). These are commonly used when dialogue is interrupted
by another character or by something taking place in a scene. It's rarely used
in description, but it means the same thing; the action/description has been
abruptly halted. Maybe an explosion takes place or a shocking revelation. It
can be used any place in the description/action, but is most often used at the
end. Do not overuse.

3) MOS means 'without sound'. It's the oldest formatting technique around and I believe it's one of the first ever used in screenwriting. Using this means we can see the characters speaking, but we can't hear them. I rarely see it used by aspiring writers, but it's a common technique among pros. Here's how it looks:

The ladies gossip MOS at a table.

4) o.s. (small letters). It means off stage and is commonly used in dialogue and written as (O.S.) in caps. It's rarely used in description, but means the same thing. Something is happening off stage. No matter where it's located in the description, it's still lower case, unless it's at the start of a sentence. Here are examples:

O.s. the sound of thunder.

She hears muffled voices o.s.

5) f.g. means foreground. Writers commonly use b.g. (background), but it's rare to see the use of foreground (f.g.) in description, but if properly used can bring attention to something without improper use of camera angles.

6) Secondary Slug Indicators. It's common to see primary slug indicators. In fact, all writers use these, but the secondary slugs are rarely used or often used improperly. A secondary slug is a breakdown or shot within a primary slug indicator. For example, if the writer wants a character to walk from room to room in a house, he can write out every single primary slug indicator or just use a secondary slug:

INT. HOUSE – DAY

John hustles with a bag of money from the living room into the

KITCHEN

where he hides it in the stove.

-Or the secondary slug can be used to bring attention to something. Used this way means we're breaking away from the wide scene to a closer shot of something or someone.

INT. HOUSE – DAY

Bill, Dave and John count the money and put it into a bag.

JOHN

exits with the bag.

-Written this way, the scene's visuals move off a wide of the three men to a close up of John. The secondary slug has created a visual flow that reveals how the writer wants the story told without the writer trying to direct the film with camera angles.

-Use sparingly to bring emphasis to something or to handle breakdown within a location.
Do not use as follows:

JOHN exits with the bag.

-A CAPPED name in a sentence like this means a new character is being introduced. Writers often think they're bringing attention to the character, when all they're doing is causing confusion. What they meant to do was use a secondary slug indicator and I just showed the writer how to use it properly.

7) Transitions. I've written entire articles about transitions. A transition is how one scene ends and another one begins. By keeping the flow going between scenes the writer creates style, atmosphere, pacing, etc. The easiest example is when a character dials a phone in one scene, then the scene ends and as the next scene opens we hear a phone ringing and someone picks it up. This is a sound to sound transition. The writer can use visuals, sounds or a combination to create transitions. In one scene we can hear an explosion, then open the next scene where we see the explosion or the aftermath. Pros use transitions between EVERY single scene to create flow. It also makes it difficult for a producer to delete a scene because he'd be messing up the cinematic cohesion of the material.

8) (FILTERED) means a sound is being heard through a device like a phone, walkie-talkie, radio, etc. Writers commonly use (V.O.) for phone conversations, which is acceptable, but can cause the novice writer confusion and make them reluctant to venture into the (FILTERED) world. (V.O.) technically means the voice is being heard over the film like a narrator, but it's been so widely used for phone conversations that it's accepted. However, (FILTERED) is technically more accurate since a phone voice would be heard via a device. The writer can use either one, but only ONE format style in a script. Don't start off using (FILTERED) for one phone conversation,

248

then switch to (V.O.) in another scene. This ranks the writer an amateur. Pros tend to be consistent.

9) (O.C.) means off camera and it means the same thing as (O.S.) off stage. Most gurus and producers steer writers away from using (O.C.) because it makes it seem acceptable that if a writer can use off camera than he can use camera angles in a script. Wrong! The writer can use either (O.C.) or (O.S.) in dialogue, but must chose one or the other. Don't use both in a script. Consistency is key.

10) Stacked description. Pro writers know how to create flow and pacing that matches a scene. For example, if the scene's a fast-paced car chase, the pro writer might decide to stack the description on the left-hand margin. This makes for a fast-paced read that draws the reader into the action and involves the reader visually with the story. Here's an example:

The car CAREENS around a corner.
HITS a pole.
BOUNCES off.
HITS another car.
Before it SLAMS into a police cruiser!

These sentences can be clumped together like above or each line can be separated by a space!

These Ten Rarely Used Techniques can add a new look and feel to a writer's work and make them stand out as a pro!

Is the Script Market Ready? The Flip Through Test

How can a writer be sure a screenplay will pass the 'test'? Having a screenplay evaluated by a professional story analyst is recommended. But I have a word of caution where 'coverage' is concerned. I think studio-style coverage can be valuable, but here's the problem I have with it. First, studio-style coverage presents a logline and synopsis, which is information already known by the writer. Secondly, it breaks down the plot, characters, dialogue and scenes, but provides vague references to problem areas. I've read coverage with comments like, 'the plot doesn't work' or 'the dialogue is on the nose' or 'the scenes fall flat'. In my opinion, for coverage to be effective, a writer needs to know why the plot doesn't work. The writer needs to know how the dialogue is 'on-the-nose' and which 'scenes fall flat'?

Extreme Screenwriting takes studio-coverage to another level by providing page-specific notes that pinpoint precise problem areas and how to fix them. In addition, Extreme Screenwriting provides a comprehensive checklist to determine exactly where the script has issues. I created the checklist based on actual reasons I've seen producers give a screenplay a PASS. If a writer can hit a YES to every point on the checklist, then the writer stands a good chance at a potential sale. If the writer doesn't know what a specific point means, then the writer needs to study this book in its entirety!

Here is the commercial checklist used by Extreme Screenwriting. A screenplay should receive a YES to EVERY point on the checklist or the writer needs to go back to the drawing board:

PLOT/EXECUTION:
- The plot/execution is unique (ordinary with a twist)
- If it's an ordinary story, does it have a twist that applies to the entire plot
- First ten pages grab the reader
- First ten pages introduces the hero
- First ten pages introduce the internal conflict
- First ten pages introduce the external conflict
- First ten pages establishes genre
- First thirty pages sets up the story
- Plot Point I spins the story in a new direction
- Plot Point II spins the story in a new direction
- Acts are well-balanced, no short or long Acts
- External conflict presented in Act I

- Internal conflict presented in Act I
- Protagonist/Antagonist identified in Act I
- If plot-driven, is script balanced 60% plot, 40% dialogue
- If character-driven, is script balanced 60% dialogue, 40% plot
- No apparent plot holes
- Plot setups have payoffs
- Plot is cohesive
- Plot is believable (based on setups)
- Plot revolves around one central conflict
- Plot has rising tension
- Plot contains irony
- Plot creates huge stakes, especially for the lead role
- Plot's external conflict forces the protagonist to change
- Plot fits the gene (Ex: Comedy, does it make you laugh?)
- Plot maintains the genre
- Plot has an underlying theme

CHARACTERS:
- Protagonist is easy to distinguish from other characters
- Protagonist has a memorable introduction
- Protagonist provided a physical and personality trait upon introduction
- Protagonist internal conflict presented when introduced
- Story revolves around an important event for protagonist (life-altering)
- Protagonist's worse-case scenario happens
- Protagonist forced to take action (reluctant hero)
- Empathy created for protagonist (if anti-hero, do we at least understand motives)
- Reader involved on an 'emotional' level with protagonist
- Reader identifies with the protagonist
- Protagonist has emotional stakes in the story's outcome
- Antagonist's plan is clear
- Antagonist initially appears to be stronger, more clever than the protagonist
- External conflict forces the protagonist to change
- Internal conflict forced to the surface in Act II
- Protagonist motives/actions believable (based on setups)
- Protagonist resolves the central conflict (in Act III)
- Protagonist arc complete
- Secondary characters three-dimensional

DIALOGUE:
- If dialogue cues were removed, is it obvious who's talking
- Dialogue reveals distinct personality traits
- Dialogue fresh/original, cliché free
- Dialogue contains conflict
- Dialogue contains subtext (underlying meaning)
- Dialogue presents reversals (twists)
- Dialogue makes use of metaphors
- The script's title is used in the dialogue
- Hero gets the last line
- Dialogue suits the genre
- Dialogue contains repeat tie-in line to show change in hero
- Protagonist gets the 'good lines', not secondary characters

SCENES:
- Story location(s) is unique or presented in a unique fashion
- Scenes maintain tone, mood and atmosphere of the story
- Scenes maintain the established genre
- Act I scenes properly setup Act II, Act III
- Act II scenes move hero toward arc
- Act III scenes resolve conflict
- Scenes get in late, get out early
- Scene transitions used
- Majority of scenes 1-3 pages long
- Scenes are a combination of description/action/dialogue (no all-dialogue pages)
- Scenes move story forward
- Every scene contains a dialogue or visual reversal
- Scenes contain conflict, not just information
- Scenes are handled via descriptive action, not just description
- Scenes integrate action with description
- Scenes use contrast to convey emotions
- Scenes contain metaphor and subtext to create visual images
- Scenes contain emotional stakes
- Scenes hold good pacing (shorter in the end)
- Scenes written in proper format

COMMERCIAL VIABILITY:
- The idea alone will sell the story
- First ten pages would grab a story analyst
- Idea/plot has enough twists compared to similar produced material

252

- Script's title fits the story/genre
- Plot falls into a specific genre with similar produced films
- Plot has a market, such as motion picture, cable, straight-to-video
- Plot can be summed up in one visual image (like a movie poster)
- Lead character roles will attract A-list talent
- Dialogue will attract A-list talent
- Majority of scenes could be used in a movie trailer

LOGLINE & TITLE EVALUATION:

- Does logline focus on the external (visual) conflict
- Does logline create a visual image of the story
- Does logline reveal the genre
- Does the title present a visual of the story
- Does the title suit the genre
- Does the title grab the reader

The Flip Through Test

Did you know that a story analyst can flip through a hardcopy screenplay and be able to tell if the story works or not merely by looking at how the pages are laid out – without having read a single word? For example, if I flip through a script and I see huge 20-line blocks of endless description, then I know it's overwritten. Or if I see endless pages of nothing but dialogue, then I know the script relies too heavily on dialogue and isn't visual enough to reach the big screen.

Is Act III's scenes shorter and have faster pacing than the rest of the script? If Act II's scenes run 3-4 pages, does Act III's scenes run 1-2 pages? They should.

Are there any T-pages or all-dialogue pages? A T-page is a page with all-dialogue and only one line of description literally making the page look like the letter "T". More than two of these means the script's too dialogue heavy. Same goes for all-dialogue pages. There should be few, if any in a screenplay. Film's a visual medium!

Is the description written in blocks of 4-6 lines? If blocks run longer, then break them up into manageable chunks so the script doesn't appear to be overwritten. Resolve this issue by only writing description that's incorporated with action; start thinking of description as action.

Is dialogue consistently over 6 lines long for every single character? This doesn't work. Short, pithy sentences with an occasional long-winded character would probably work better.

The format is all over the place. One page uses (O.C.) and the next page uses (O.S.). Both mean the same thing, but a lack of consistency can quickly reveal an amateur.

Is there a page cheat? Does the writer have a 90-page script where they've triple spaced before every new primary slug indicator? If so, the script's too short to produce.

A short script means something is missing and the story doesn't work. A long script means the writer hasn't studied screenplay writing or they'd know less is more!

No FADE IN or FADE OUT. I don't care what so-called gurus are saying, use these two! FADE IN tells the reader the story is meant for the big screen. Without FADE IN, the reader is guessing as to the intended audience. Is it the silver screen, TV, stage or radio? FADE OUT means THE END. Don't use both. THE END is for novels. Screenplays end with FADE OUT! Don't use it prematurely or the reader will think the story has ended! Only use these two at the beginning and end of the script!

There is no number 1 on the first page. The page numbers begin on page 2. Why? Because FADE IN means the beginning or page 1 – which is another reason it's so darn important to write FADE IN!

Directorial or camera directions. There is only one time it's okay to play director. It's when you're going to be the director. If you're planning to sell the script so someone else can direct it, then this makes you the screenwriter! Do not use 'we' references or CUT TO:, etc.

Only CAP character names upon initial introduction. CAPPING a character's name repeatedly in the story will cause the reader to believe you're introducing a new character.

Keep character names consistent. If he's WILLIAM to the writer, don't list him as BILL in the dialogue cue indicator and BILLY in the description. The other characters can call him whatever they want, but the writer should keep the name consistent.

Don't use names that are too much alike. Barbara, Betty, Betsy, Bobby, Branson,....Carol, Conrad, Conway, Cochran,....get the picture? It's too easy to mix up the characters. Plus, if the writer uses Final Draft, the neat feature that automatically pops the name into the dialogue cue indicator could easily put in the wrong name due to the similarities – I've seen this happen a lot!

A sure fire way to see if the writer has a winning script is to flip to the end. Does the hero get the last line or the last visual? If not, the writer hasn't studied screenplays or his story won't make it to the big screen. The big screen is the hero's canvas!

The page 1 test. By reading only page 1, can the reader tell the genre? Well, the writer technically has 10 pages to setup the genre, but most pros do it on page 1 with word 1.

Genre suitable length. If the writer indicated the script's a horror and it's 120 pages, it's too long. Genres have acceptable page lengths. The only genre where it's acceptable to have a 120 page script is Drama!

Other items that can easily be determined by flipping through a script:
1) Budget – multiple locations, big EXPLOSIONS, lots of characters, bad weather, costumes, period pieces. All of these equal one thing, a big budget.

2) Market – A dialogue-heavy script won't make it to the big screen, but might be suitable for TV or cable. A big action sequence script is too big budget for TV or cable and will have to go big screen. Somewhere in-between could be a straight-to-DVD hit.

Bet you didn't know I could tell if your script works without reading a single word! Well, I can and so can every gate keeper in the biz. This might scare you, but I've actually seen production company readers go through entire stacks of scripts in a single day. How? Because they flip through the scripts to find the ones they know don't work and toss them aside as a PASS. Still think format isn't important? I guarantee it's as important to your career as teeth are to a dentist's career! But wait a minute, don't production companies do coverage on scripts? Only production companies with studio-level deals are required to provide coverage on scripts, per their union agreement with WGA. Smaller companies do NOT have to do coverage! That means you get one shot at it, so don't screw it up with crummy format. Make sure your script passes the flip-through test.

REVIEWS: KNOW WHEN TO MAKE CHANGES & WHEN NOT TO

A screenwriter contacted me asking for an expedited review because a producer had requested his script. Why would a screenwriter who wants to be considered a professional market a script before it's been reviewed? <u>This is career suicide.</u>

When a screenwriter finishes a script it's like a hot potato; they can't wait to get it out of their hands. Some will argue their script is a timely idea and can't wait because it's a hit movie in the making. If it's so great it can wait forever and someone will still buy it, so slow down. Why?

#1 Because you're the screenwriter and frankly you're too close to the material. You need outside opinions.

#2 You're only going to get one shot at this – don't blow it by sending something out that's not ready.

What happens if you ask for an expedited review and the review comes back recommending a page-one rewrite? You're screwed because a producer isn't going to remember you three months down the road when you've completed the re-write.

DO NOT SEND OUT MATERIAL UNTIL IT'S BEEN THROUGH A REVIEW PROCESS

First, let's look at <u>common mistakes</u> in regards to reviews so you'll know how to get the best possible reviews. Here are the mistakes:

- Having someone unfamiliar with screenplays review the material.

   -If you have to tell someone what INT. or EXT. means before they read your script, then they have no business reading the script.

   -Have a spouse or relative read the script. After all, the screenwriter believes his/her spouse will be honest with them. If you want honesty from your spouse, wait until they divorce you.

- Using competitive websites to get reviews.

   -I'm very supportive of websites like Zoetrope and Trigger Street. They provide a community for writers to share frustrations and information about the industry. However, when you have a situation where screenwriters are in competition with one another for placements with the site's production company, you should be wary of the review. It could sway towards being overly critical.

-If you have hooked up with other screenwriters on these types of websites whose critiques you trust, then go for it. Just be aware of the status quo.

- Getting only one (1) review and making every single change then proceeding to market.

    -I don't care if the reviewer is an Academy Award winning screenwriter you need more than one opinion to get an overview of the material and to make the right decisions about what to change and what not to change.

- Paying to have studio-style coverage done. I provide screenplay coverage to over two-dozen production companies and have no idea why a screenwriter thinks this could possibly be helpful to them on a spec level. Why?

    -Because it's too vague. Studio-style coverage provides a logline and synopsis of the material. This is information you already know. Second, if it references a problem it's usually written something like:

    > "The plot structure fails."
    > "The dialogue is too on-the-nose."
    > "Characters read flat."
    > "Story's confusing."

    -These are vague references given to a studio or production company as an overview of the material. Exactly why did the plot structure fail? On what page does it fail? Or does it fail throughout the script? Is all the dialogue too on-the-nose or just a particular character? What dialogue on what page would be an example? Are all the characters reading flat? Why are they flat? What's confusing about the story?

    -None of these questions will be answered in studio-style coverage.

    -Look for services that offer "script notes" for more in-depth coverage.

- Getting too many reviews.

    -Some screenwriters go overboard and get 10-15 reviews and make every single change. Most of the reviews aren't worth their weight in professional gold and besides, making every change recommended isn't a wise approach to the review process and shows a lack of confidence in your own material.

-Other screenwriters have had their script on the market for several years and still continue to get reviews and make changes. It seems like an endless process. Writing is definitely about rewriting, but there has to come a point where you're confident enough in the material to proceed to market. If you're not confident enough about the material and continue to get review after review then one of two things is happening:

1) You're not being honest with yourself. Should the material be shelved?
2) You're looking for validation and Hollywood isn't a place you're likely to find it because one person will hate your script and the next one will love it.

The review process requires planning to be successful. This plan should include who reviews the material, how many reviews to get, determining what to change and what not to, a timeframe, a plan for making modifications and hiring an editor to help polish the script.

How you decide upon reviews is up to you, but having a plan and sticking with it is what's most important. Here's the plan I use. You can adopt it or create one of your own to suit your needs.

Review Plan:

Once a script is done to my satisfaction, I:

❖ Obtain 6 Total Reviews as follows:
3 from professional Hollywood readers
2 from aspiring screenwriters whose work I admire
1 from a complete novice

Let's take a look at these independently:
3 from professional Hollywood readers
-Professional readers charge a fee. I realize it can be outrageously high,
so I recommend only getting 3 of these. Professional readers read almost
daily and most have a sharp eye for what works and what doesn't work.

2 from aspiring screenwriters whose work you admire

-It's important that you've read their work and LOVE IT! You should

see this screenwriter as someone you expect to see up on the big screen

one day.

-Agree to swap reviews with the screenwriter. A word of warning: Don't

play Mr. Nice Guy because the writer is reviewing your script. Be honest

& give constructive feedback.

1 from a complete novice

-Wait a minute! Didn't I say earlier not to let anyone unfamiliar with scripts review the material? Yes, I did. However, we're not going to use

this review as part of the overall "change" process – explanation coming

up.

Note: Make sure none of the reviewers know each other or are in a position to compare notes. Some services give two reviews for the price of one. Don't do this. You want two separate, independent reviews. Two readers from the same company have the opportunity to compare notes.

The key to making these reviews work for you is to assure you do the following:

- ❖ Send for the reviews AT THE SAME TIME!
- ❖ Get a specific deadline from each party. The professional reader will probably take the longest. Mark a tentative deadline on a calendar for all reviews to be submitted to you.
- ❖ <u>DO NOT READ THE REVIEWS UNTIL ALL OF THEM HAVE BEEN SENT TO YOU!</u> This is extremely important!

Once ALL reviews have been received here's what to do:

- ❖ Get out a blank notepad. Write on the first page "MORE THAN ONE REVIEWER NOTED THIS." On the second page write "COOL STUFF."
- ❖ Without a critical eye, I want you to read all of the reviews except the one from the novice from start to finish and I want you to note on

259

the "MORE THAN ONE REVIEWER NOTED THIS" page any areas that more than one reviewer mentions about the script.

- ❖ DO NOT MAKE CHANGES YET!
- ❖ Next, I want you to read through the reviews again. Disregard the similar areas mentioned by the reviewers and on the second sheet marked "COOL STUFF" I want you to note anything a reviewer said that you knew you should have done, or something that sounds like a cool idea and you wish you had thought of it.
- ❖ Everything else noted by the reviewers is OPINION and should be treated as such!
- ❖ Now, I want you to read the novice's review. You're not looking for critique stuff. I want you to determine if the novice gets your story or not. Do they seem to get the gist of what's going on? Whether they liked it or not is irrelevant. What's most important from a novice review is whether they understand the overall concept. Do NOT make any of their suggested changes!
- ❖ Set all reviews aside because you're DONE WITH THEM!

Here's what to change and what not to change:

- ❖ CHANGE
  -Everything that more than one reviewer noted that implies something isn't working!
  -Anything that makes sense from one reviewer or you wished you had thought of yourself.

- ❖ DO NOT CHANGE
  -Opinion items just because they come from a professional reader and you want to be sure. Trust your gut instinct and stick with the plan!
  -Items recommended for change by the novice. No, no and no. Their opinion only counts for concept. By the way, don't tell them this. Ask them for the same review you're getting from everyone else. This is your little secret!

If you did an extensive outline in the beginning as I recommended you're not likely to be looking at a page one rewrite. It's more likely to be minor changes. Once you've made the modifications run the script back through the professional readers until the script receives a recommend. Once the script receives a recommend from ALL of the professional readers, then it's ready to market. NOT A MOMENT BEFORE!

I advised a writer to seek coverage from various sources to give a wide overview of her work. She plans to take the advice and asked me to refer her to produced writers for coverage. Like many aspiring screenwriters, she believes she has to get coverage from credited writers or it has no value.

Even after all these years in the biz, I'm still trying to figure out where this idiotic assumption comes from. I had a World History teacher who has never set foot outside the USA. I had a science teacher who has never worked in a science lab. Adored my cooking teacher and still use her recipe for sticky buns, but she's never been a chef or even a line cook. If I tossed out everything these folks have taught me, because they clearly lacked direct experience, I'd be one dumb blonde. In fact, I know chefs who couldn't teach a culinary school if their life depended on it.

With so many scam artists flooding the market who claim to be everything from producers to the next Mohammed Ali, I understand the concerns when it comes to determining the level of professionalism of a story analyst. Many different criteria can be put into place when considering which story analysts to use; how long in the biz, sample coverage, client successes, industry endorsements, etc. All of which are good criteria, but it can still be crap. I'm going to tell you why in a minute. With this in mind, I'd like to share with writers how I pick a story analyst and more importantly, why.

I have three readers for my material. One is a script coach. He has only optioned one script in 15 years, which means he has no credits to his name, but he's well respected in the biz and knows how to spot commercial screenplays. The second person I use is a reader for a top agency. She's never written a script in her life and hates to write anything, even Christmas cards, but she's recognized by the agency for her ability to spot a sellable script. The third reader I use is a produced writer with four films under his belt. He's the only reader I use who has credits and I only asked him to read for me because his style matches mine (I'll tell you why this is important in a minute).

Who would I pick if I could only use one of them? Would I select the script coach, the story analyst or the produced screenwriter? I value each of their opinions, but if I had to pick one it would be the story analyst who works for an agency. Why would I pick her? Frankly, she hates to write. She has no ambition to write, ever! Her goal is to become an agent, not a writer. I'd pick her because she knows what sells in this biz (on a daily basis) and her evaluation can determine whether or not my screenplay(s) can sell. Isn't that the real reason writers get an evaluation, to determine if their script will sell or not? I don't know about you, but that's why I pay $300 a pop to get the coverage! And I certainly want to be dealing with someone who knows what's selling on a daily basis!

In all fairness, good script coaches tend to follow selling trends and their advice can be invaluable. As for the produced writer, I'm quite sure he knows what's selling in the biz, but he's more focused on his genre and how it's doing in the market. While this certainly helps me because I've chosen a reader who matches my style of writing, I doubt it would help writers who write in different genres than he does. Don't take me wrong, I'm sure he'd give exceptional advice, but it's bound to be slanted to his own selling experience in the biz, which may not apply to every script's genre.

Also note that all three of my readers live in Los Angeles and work full-time in the business. With this in mind, the only question a writer needs to ask when considering a story analyst: Does the story analyst work full-time in the entertainment industry in a position where he or she knows what is selling on a daily basis? The key word is DAILY!

Forget all the other criteria. I don't care if the story analyst has sold 15 screenplays and has had 9 movies made! If he lives in Nebraska and doesn't work full-time in the industry, he's outdated and out of touch. Selling trends change fast in this biz. Writers need a story analyst in the heat of the action who knows what's happening daily, not yesterday, last week, last year or five years ago when they sold their last screenplay! That's why I'd pick the unproduced reader who works for an agency over a produced writer any day of the week! This person knows what's selling every single day and has an eye for commercial property. This person doesn't need a credit to be qualified to provide coverage and if you think he or she does, then you're a moron!

Still disagree with me, then here's a reality check for you. Due to the economy, I've noticed that some producers have started doing their own coverage. Nine out of ten of these producers have never sold a screenplay or even written one. Are you going to tell me they aren't qualified to provide coverage because they lack a screenplay credit? Are you nuts?

I don't care how many screenplays a story analyst has or hasn't sold. What I care about and so should you, is the day-to-day status in the biz and whether or not it puts the analyst in a position to know what's selling. If the story analyst is an accountant by day and a nighttime and weekend reader, kick his ass to the curb. If he's a produced writer from 1999 who lives in Omaha, forget it because he's old school.

Also, does the story analyst live in L.A. or NYC? If not, dump the loser. Don't try telling me he's in touch with the industry if he doesn't live in the industry. Impossible! This guy's a smuck trying to make a buck off a naïve writer who doesn't know better.

That's my criteria. Take it or leave it. Don't bother asking me to refer you to my readers. They're my gems. Find your own.

PROOFING YOUR SCRIPT

"Proofing Your Script" – Written by Guest Writer, Derek Ladd – Editor, Proof Edge

Terminating Terrible Typos - The Importance of Proofing

I watched an interesting film a while back called *The Prestige* with Christian Bale and Hugh Jackman. You may have seen it. A few months later I read the script (courtesy of dailyscript.com). There are more typos in that one screenplay than in all the screenplays I've edited combined. Do yourself a favor and read this script. Hopefully it will teach you how distracting typos can be and why you should be diligent in eliminating them. There seems to be a rule somewhere that says if you're an established screenwriter you needn't be concerned with your spelling and grammar. Maybe so, but I've never heard of a producer or agent being turned off by a script that was "too clean." Typos are like potholes in your screenplay: every time a reader hits one it jolts him or her out of your story. Your mission as a screenwriter is to deliver a script that reads like a freshly paved stretch of highway.

Typos aren't just obvious misspellings, either. Most of what I see are properly spelled words used in the wrong places: their in place of they're, were in place of we're, rode in place of road, etc. Spell check is a useful tool, but for this reason, relying on it alone to proof your work is a bad idea. Friends and family, including fellow screenwriters, can be a good resource of fresh eyes. But keep in mind that working for free (and knowing you) may impact the results.

Choosing Your Words – Editing 101

A screenwriter should not be scared by the concept of someone else editing his or her screenplay. A good editor uses a scalpel – a poor editor uses a chainsaw. Over the years I've made it my trademark as a 'word surgeon' to edit only when necessary in order to keep the writer's original voice intact.

When writing your screenplay, choose your words very carefully. Don't use a word like 'melancholy' when 'sad' or 'depressed' will do. I've seen writers

263

use words like 'erudite', 'obsequious', 'impetuous', 'feckless' and 'solipsistic' in their screenplays. It's great to have a large vocabulary, but with the exception of elaborate medical/technical terms used for realism, try to use shorter, simpler words whenever possible. The fewer syllables you use the faster the read. The last thing you want to do is weigh down your wonderful script with five-dollar words – especially if it forces a reader to crack open a dictionary every two minutes.

As most screenwriters know, unlike a novel, the page count of a screenplay is limited, which is why an editor can be a big help. You've crafted your precious baby and you love it to pieces: the characters, the plot, and every line of dialogue is perfect. The problem is, it's 147 pages and you can't bear the thought of cutting a single word. Enter the editor. If I'm asked to gently trim a little here and there without damaging your little darling I'll look for the following: large words, redundancy, unnecessary dialogue, dialogue that overlaps action (showing something AND telling about it in the same scene), and so on. My greatest feat to date is taking a 163-page script down to 120 pages. Don't ask me how I did it – a magician never reveals his secrets.

It's Developmental, My Dear Watson

Many writers are proficient at telling stories but need a little developmental assistance when it comes to distilling what they've written into what they really mean. This can be done with subtext (visual or spoken), or simply by trimming down information that isn't needed. For example, look at the lines of dialogue below:

TERRY
How are you and Dave getting along?

DIANA
How are we getting along? Not very well. He's
not around much anymore, spends most of his time
on the road. When he is home, it seems like all we do is fight.

What do you think, screenwriters? Eh. Right? Surely you could do better. The above is a mild example, but an editor might make the following suggestion:

TERRY
How are you and Dave getting along?

DIANA
Like a snake and a weasel. When he's not on the

road I usually spend the next day sweeping up
broken glass.

Notice how Diana doesn't repeat Terry's question and doesn't use 'seems
like' in the last sentence. The first Diana sounds passive and timid – her lines
sound dull. The second Diana sounds cynical and hardened by her situation –
her lines are more direct, angrier.

Once an editor gets a feel for a screenwriter's characters, suggestions like the
one above are much easier to make. If the writer establishes Diana as a jaded,
hard-nosed woman on page 5, the first lines of dialogue above wouldn't fit
and a good editor would point this out. A more common situation is one
where the screenwriter simply goes on and on and on with a chunk of
dialogue when a few lines will do.

Other times, parts of a script just don't work. Characters say or do things that
don't make sense, don't fit the story, don't move the story forward, or all of
the above. In these situations an editor will often make suggestions based on
where he or she thinks the writer wants the story to go. This is why
establishing the theme and tone of your story as soon as possible is essential
– without knowing the theme and tone, an editor might make suggestions that
aren't helpful. But if you establish that your script is intended as a family
comedy, an editor will probably tell you that having someone get shot in the
head in act 3 won't play (unless Quentin Tarantino is directing – he might be
able to make it work).

Know Your Stuff – Fact Checking

Adding factual realism to your screenplay can make for a more enjoyable
read, but only if you keep your facts straight. A good editor will look into
anything that seems askew in this area. If you're writing a thriller that opens
with the discovery of a dead body, make sure your lead detective doesn't
move the body (without good reason) until after the coroner determines a
time of death and clears it for processing. If you're writing a Vietnam-era
war movie set in 1968 make sure your soldiers aren't using M16A2 service
rifles. The devil is in the details they say, and while many readers might not
notice, if a factual error goes unfixed, someone will.

Over the past several years I've spotted and corrected many factual errors for
clients. Some were as simple as the name of a foreign city or landmark – a
misspelling or location – while others were as complex as the type of
treatment and medication given to convicted killers in an insane asylum.
How and when you do your research is up to you, but make sure you do it. If

you don't, the thriller you wrote that takes place in a hospital might fail to impress the producer who spent 15 years as a nurse.

Summary

The longer a screenplay sits on your hard drive the harder it is for you, the writer, to spot your own mistakes. The work 'hardens' like cement, and soon you've read through it so many times that the same mistakes you missed on the first, second, third and fourth passes become invisible to you. So enlist the help of friends, family, fellow screenwriters, circus clowns (if they're good readers, why not?) and professionals to help you polish your work until it shines. Producers and agents (and readers in general) will thank you for it.

Derek Ladd's Bio

Derek Ladd started Proof Edge in April of 2003 and has been editing professionally ever since. His clients include award-winning author and screenwriter, Chanrithy Him, screenwriter and film producer, Erin McNamara, and professional cinematographer and screenwriter, Jim Grieco. Many of Derek's clients comment on his ability as a long-time writer to offer helpful suggestions, and over a dozen have won or placed in screenwriting contests. Proof Edge offers competitive rates for Extreme Screenwriting's clients. To receive a quote for service, email Derek@proofedge.com

HOW TO WRITE A SYNOPSIS

If you've read this material from page 1 to this page, you should already have a one-sheet. See Chapter: Commercialize First – Create a One-Sheet. The one-sheet should include a synopsis. As I noted earlier, it's important to write the one-sheet BEFORE writing the script. But now I want you to go back and tweak the one-sheet, paying special attention to the synopsis portion. Why?

Because nine out of ten producers look at the one-sheet before asking to read the script. How can a screenwriter deliver a brilliant 120 page script, but fail to write an effective one-sheet?

The answer is simple; the writer is too close to the material. Every detail seems important to him. He can't sum it up without wanting to add some 'vital' piece of plot or character information. His brain is on story overload.

While writing the synopsis before the script will help the screenwriter stick to a summation of the story rather than bogging it down with unnecessary details, the writer still needs to learn a few sales/marketing synopsis techniques to tweak the one-sheet's synopsis after the script's completed. No, I'm not going to send you to a sales class. Let's talk real world. We all get junk mail. 99% of it is tossed in the trash. The same goes with query letters (that includes your synopsis). The query is basically junk mail and like the junk mail in your house, most of it gets tossed. Then one day you notice a catchy headline: Free Watermelons! Well, heck, you love watermelons. You hurry up and open the junk mail to see how to get free watermelons. The clever advertiser has lured you into checking out the ad – even if you hadn't really planned on buying watermelons!

Imagine you have a suspense thriller, serial killer story. You might open a synopsis with:

WARNING: HE'S COMING TO KILL YOU!

Or even open a synopsis with this line! Okay, I admit this could land cops at your doorstep, but I think you get the point. Think like advertisers and sales people. Look around your daily life. What catchy ads attract you and why? How can you apply this sales technique to your synopsis to land a read?

Next, think in terms of short, pithy sentences. This grabs a reader's attention. Instead of writing:

JOHN SMITH is a dangerous stalker who lures women to their deaths with his charming good looks and witty personality – write:

Ted Bundy's back! His new name is JOHN SMITH. He lives for the hunt. The kill. He's a new breed of stalker. Women beware!

Or you might want to open with a question:

What if Ted Bundy isn't dead? He isn't. His new name is JOHN SMITH.

In other words, your goal with a synopsis isn't to tell the story, it's to sell the story! Do yourself a favor and when it comes time to writing a synopsis, logline or query; take off the writer's cap and put on the salesman's cap! The first one-sheet you write probably reads with precise details to make the story clear. This is great, but you are here to sell a story, not tell a story.

Next, don't forget to slant the synopsis to suit the genre. I can't tell you how many comedy synopses I've read that aren't funny. Or how many horror synopses that aren't scary. The synopsis should paint a picture of the genre. Go back to the junk mail. We've all seen ads that use fear tactics: DON'T LET A HEART ATTACK CLAIM YOUR LOVED ONE'S LIFE – USE

267

THIS HERBAL SUPPLEMENT. Use this sales tactic to write a snappy opening horror teaser line: DON'T LET THIS STORY SCARE YOU FROM GOING TO BED TONITE.

By the way, you should NOT be writing each synopsis in the same way. You should be slanting each one based on the story and its genre. You might open a drama with a serious question; what would you do to save your soul mate's life? You might open a comedy with a funny comparison; Rambo's back and he needs a haircut! You might open a horror with a teaser line, like the one I wrote above.

Finally, don't be afraid to lay out the synopsis on the paper like it really is an ad. Guess what, it is! You might write WARNING: He's Coming To Kill You! in the middle of the synopsis centered in bold letters! Don't get carried away with this technique. You're only using it to grab attention. This technique may not be appropriate for all synopses.

Okay, I've taught you the importance behind writing a synopsis from a sales perspective! I've followed it with salesman techniques to use because the synopsis is a sales tool. And finally, I've provided a variety of techniques to help beef up a synopsis and turn it into a print ad that will lure every producer into asking for a read! Don't take this too serious. Have fun with it. Coming up with clever ad-style techniques to use in a synopsis is fun and will help you get closer to a sale than a thousand ordinary synopses and it'll gain more attention than a hundred well-written, ordinary one-sheets!

QUERY & MARKETING STRATEGIES

Have you sent out dozens or even hundreds of query letters with little or no response? First, go back and rewrite the query as a one-sheet and incorporate the sales ad techniques taught under the "How to Write a Synopsis" section, then try using a few new techniques to gain attention for your project as follows:

FAX QUERIES
The average screenwriter sends out letters via snail mail or email. This is an okay approach, but like the junk mail you receive everyday in your home mail or on the computer, most queries get tossed in the trash bin. BUT, faxes get closer attention. They're more likely to be read and more likely to be passed on to a producer. Why? Because an assistant probably can't determine if the query is solicited or not, so the assistant is more likely to add it to the pile of faxes for the producer to read. Locate directories that provide production company fax #'s and try this approach.

Extra Tip for faxes: I have a client who indicates at the end of his faxed one-sheet that he'll be calling tomorrow. He puts this in BOLD at the end of the query where most assistants will see it. The next day, he calls and seven out of ten times the assistant puts him through to the producer! He cleverly uses the fax query to set up a solicited phone call with the producer. Brazen, but it's landed him a dozen reads and an optioned screenplay!

HOLIDAY CARDS
Send Holiday cards on off-beat holidays, like Fourth of July, Labor Day, President's Day, etc. It'll probably get noticed, plus you'll be getting your name out there. Sounds weird. Well, I know a screenwriter who does this. He follows the card with a query and often gets request for reads because they've seen his name somewhere before – even if they can't remember where. Or right after the holiday, send the fax query and do a follow-up phone call!

YOUTUBE
Who doesn't have a video camera or phone with video capability? Even if you don't, I bet you have a friend who does. Have you ever thought of creating a skit 'bout your screenplay and putting it on YouTube? It doesn't have to be production-quality – just get a bunch of family or friends to help. Have some fun with it. You'd be amazed at the folks who've landed deals doing this. Recently, an aspiring director put his sci-fi/action video on YouTube and landed a $3million studio deal. That's the power of the Internet – why not use it to your advantage?. If you're squeamish 'bout this option, then ask your kids to help. Kids love this kind of stuff. No kids – then hire some local college students. Get creative with your career. At the most you'll have some fun! Send a fax inviting the producer to your YouTube Screenplay Query!

FACEBOOK, ETC.
Everything from food trucks to nannies have cult followings on Facebook, Twitter, etc. I wonder how many folks would love to follow the starving artist on his daily adventures while trying to break into the glamorous world of Hollywood? Honestly, I don't know, but I bet there are a few out there. I've always been amazed at how many Live Webcams watch everything from cute college girls to the Loch (Loch Ness Monster) to a pizzeria that makes homemade dough…it's crazy! Humans are naturally curious 'bout other humans and how they live their lives – why do you think reality TV is so popular? Give it a try…heck, send me your links and I'll publish them in the next newsletter. Be inventive with your career.

COLD CALL

269

I'm only adding this query-style option because so few do it. I know it's tough and 9 times out of 10 calls you're going to get a "NO!" or even get hung up on. But like a good salesman, you make it a numbers game and keep trying until you get a "yes". Or try the fax first, call second option noted above.

Keep in mind that very few writers dare to phone pitch. Do you know what that means? It means you have a wide-open area to query where few dare to swim. I know what you're thinking, "I hate phone solicitations. I can't do it". Some time ago, I took a marketing course, and what struck me the most about the course was the phone pitch portion. The assignment was simple. Prepare a phone pitch and call two producers and pitch them.

There were 20 other screenwriter participants in the course and I was the ONLY ONE who completed the assignment! I have tried phone pitching before taking the course and I hated it because people were rude or hung up on me. It was intimidating to say the least, but then I got to thinking. If out of 20 people I'm the only one doing phone pitches and most screenwriters I know WON'T DO IT, then here's a wide open market at my disposal.

So, I started to phone pitch. Out of 38 calls for a suspense thriller script, 9 asked to see a one-sheet, which I promptly faxed over and of those 9 a total of 6 asked to read the script! I received more requests to read the script from a dozen cold calls, than I did from a hundred written queries!

Still scared of cold calls? Use the fax first approach noted above and use the faxed query as a legitimate excuse to call the next day. Don't call on Mondays or Fridays. This is when production companies are swamped. Keep calls to Tuesday, Wednesday or Thursday after 10a.m. Hollywood doesn't officially open until 10a.m.

A majority of the time it'll still be a 'No', but keep dialing. What's the worst thing that can happen? You'll end up right back where you started from, but with some phone experience to boot. Plus, you'll be one of the very few screenwriters taking this approach and in the competitive screenplay market you'll need every advantage you can get.

ATTEND PITCH FESTS
If you can afford it, I highly recommend learning to pitch and attending pitch festivals like The Hollywood Pitch festival. It's imperative that you learn to effectively pitch first! Take the one-sheet to pass out and even though they will tell you not to bring scripts, tuck a few in your backpack or briefcase. I've given out scripts on the spot at a pitch fest. When they're hot for your idea you want the script in their hands asap!

USE THE ONE-SHEET

Don't try to write the query like a boring letter! Everybody does this. Start with the one-sheet and use the sales techniques outlined under "How to Write a Synopsis", then use unique ways to send the query, like via fax with a phone call follow-up.

SNAIL MAIL

It's a bit old school, but go ahead and keep sending out snail mail queries. Or, if you're smart, move from wasting stamps to sending out email queries. Producers are more likely to read an email than snail mail.

EMAIL QUERIES

Like snail mail, production companies get dozens of these a day! Most are trashed. My advice is to send email queries when you're a hot commodity. Wait until you've just placed in a screenwriting contest, then do the email queries. The email subject like might read something like: "Suspense Thriller Makes Finalists in Fade In Contest" – this type of email query is far more likely to gain the writer a read than an ordinary email query.

ATTEND FILM FESTIVALS

Even if you don't have a film or screenplay competing in the festival, attend! Take one-sheets for your material and copies of scripts. Pitch your material to anyone who will listen - okay, the guy behind the bar serving drinks doesn't count! Film festivals are filled with actors, agents, producers, etc. Any one of which could help take your script to the next level.

NETWORK, NETWORK, NETWORK

Start referring to yourself as a screenwriter wherever you go. The grocery clerk where you've shopped for 15 years might have an uncle who works at a studio in Hollywood or your hairdresser's kid might be an actor who just landed a role in a movie. Any of these folks could potentially help you get your script into the hands of people who can help take the script to the next level.

MARKETING MISTAKES

TRYING TO GET AN AGENT FIRST

Nine out of ten aspiring screenwriters that I know think if they get an agent they're guaranteed a sale or at least they're marketing worries will be over. Most also focus on trying to get an agent and don't bother with the queries and other marketing strategies. I guess they think this is the agent's job. Having had three agents, I can tell you that they consider selling your script a collaborative effort, meaning they'll expect you to pitch, market, attend festivals, etc.

In today's market, it's highly unlikely an agent is even going to consider an aspiring screenwriter without a track record. So what can you do? Read the Chapter titled "Marketing the Writer" because agents look at more than the screenplay when consider a new writer client!

Or forget having an agent at all. What? Have I gone nuts? If you think you need an agent to make a sale, you haven't my hero, Bill Martell. He's the screenwriter who runs Script Secrets at www. ScriptSecrets.net and he's sold 17+ screenplays WITHOUT AN AGENT! Bill sells CD's and books on his website on how to market without an agent titled "Guerilla Marketing". It's worth the money!

WAITING FOR CONTESTS

Sitting around waiting to see if you've placed in a contest and hoping it'll jump start your career is like waiting up on Christmas Eve to see if you'll catch Santa in the act of delivering presents. It isn't likely to happen. Only a handful of writers have landed deals from script contest placements and my hats off to them, but there are hundreds more where they came from. Keep entering contests because placements are important to show that your script stands above the rest, but keep marketing! Don't wait around for results. When the results are in and if you've placed, then use the placement while it's still hot off the presses to market your script via faxes, email, etc.

SUBMISSION BASICS

When submitting a screenplay the only thing that should stand out is the writing. That means no fancy covers, exotic fonts or bolts instead of brads. Here are the basics:

BINDING

*Front/back 20lb. stock covers; white or a neutral color.
*Three-hole punched covers and pages.
*Use standard, industry brads. Don't buy at an office supply store because those are too long. Buy from industry stores, like The Writer's Store on-line. Purchase washers with the brads.
*Don't write the title on the spine. This is done by the production company or requesting party.

COVER PAGE

*Do not write contact information or anything on the 20lb covers.
*Use courier font 12 on the cover page, including the title. Nothing larger!

*Put contact information on the right hand side at the bottom, no where else. On the left hand side it might get hold punched and be missing information.
*Be sure to include screenwriter's name, phone and email on the inside title/cover page.
*Do not include WGA or copyright information on the cover page. This information is requested on standard release forms.

SCRIPT PAGES
*Do not include a page number on page 1. All other pages are numbered.
*First page should open with FADE IN. Last page should end with FADE OUT. This distinguishes the material as a screenplay, separate from a radio or stage play.
*Check all pages. Make sure they've printed straight, not crooked or with information cut off or left off the page due to printer error. Check for missing pages.
*Check top of each page. Is the page # showing?
*Check bottom of each page. If it breaks at a straight point, then fix.

FORMAT
Read the Format chapter in this material to assure you're using the current industry standard.

MISCELLANEOUS:
*Include a cover letter and indicate who requested the material.
*On package, be sure to write REQUESTED MATERIAL. This way the mail room won't toss the submission.
*Use the post office's flat rate envelope. It's sturdy and fits one screenplay perfect. This package comes with a tracking # so you'll have receipt of delivery.
*Only include a SASE if you want the script returned.

RESPONSE TIME

It's a great feeling to have a production company request your script. You can't wait to hear from them. Then four weeks go by without a word, then two months and six months. What's going on? Have they passed on the script and left you hanging in silent agony? Should you follow-up? How much longer should you wait? Is no response an automatic "no thanks"?

To be frank, this is the most unprofessional industry in terms of responding to a screenwriter. While many production companies are courteous enough to contact the writer with a pass, many never reply at all. There's an assumption that if you haven't heard back, then it's a pass. How rude! Well, I for one don't let them off that easily and neither should you. Assuming you submitted the script in a professional manner then you deserve a professional response, preferably in a timely manner.

Here are a few guidelines to help you follow-up until you receive a 'yes' or 'no':

First, be aware that larger production companies and studios take the longest because they are the busiest. I wouldn't recommend bothering to follow up with them until two months after the submission. If it's a smaller production company, then six weeks is a good time to follow-up.

Do follow-ups via phone or email. Production companies keep logs of submitted scripts and the log should reflect what's happening with the script. If calling, ask the assistant who answers if they could check their log for a script you submitted 6 weeks ago. Most will oblige and will often tell you it hasn't been read yet. Thank the assistant for taking time to check for you, indicate you'll check back in 6 weeks, then mark your calendar and forget about it until 6 weeks later and repeat the process. For email, thank the producer for the request, indicate the date submitted and say you're wondering if they've had time to read the script yet. Often they haven't read it yet. Again, say thanks, mark your calendar and repeat the follow-up 6 weeks later. Keep doing this until you get a 'yes' or 'no'. If it's the third follow-up, I usually politely remind them that I've followed up twice.

Please keep in mind that if you submit a script during November, Hollywood shuts down for the holidays, usually Thanksgiving through the New Year. So, don't start the clock until January and the first follow-up should be mid-February of the following year.

If you followed-up for six months with no response, it's probably a pass. The exception is larger production companies and studios. It's standard for them to take up to 6 months or more to respond.

The key to making this work in your favor is patience and persistence. Mark your calendar, forget about it and keep marketing the script. Do NOT wait for the production company to respond or you'll waste valuable time. Consider your script for sale on a first come, first serve basis.

A few real-life response times: While I've found smaller production companies take around 2 months to respond, the mini-majors and studios take 4-6 months or longer. However, I've waited 8 months for a response. I recently read an article where the writer heard back a year and a half later with good news, an option! The shortest time I've waited was one weekend.

274

Guess anything can happen in Hollywood. No matter how long or short the wait, the key is patience and persistence!

NO RESPONSES? TRY THE BOOK ROUTE

For months or years, you've sent out snail mail queries, email queries, placed in contests, attend pitch festivals, made cold calls, etc., and still no luck. You're ready to toss your script in the trash and go back to pretending you love your day job. Wait! First, let's try another approach. If there's one thing Hollywood loves it's a built-in audience. What's a built-in audience? It's something that comes with a following. Like the stage play "Driving Miss Daisy" that later became an Oscar winning film. It already had an audience, which attracted Hollywood's attention and help it become a movie. A book can accomplish the same thing. But wait a minute, if you can't even get producers to read a screenplay, how are you going to get a publisher to put out a book? You aren't! Instead, you're going to self-publish the book via a self-publishing website. I'd recommend Amazon.com's do-it-yourself book publication Create A Space. After all, Amazon has 220 million customers. If even a fraction of them buy your book, you'll have a built-in audience and the screenplay will become a thousand times more marketable! Obviously, this only works if the book is based on the screenplay.

Producers Love a Built-In Audience

Novels are attractive to producers because they come with two things built in: a specific genre and an audience. It's very difficult to transcend between these two mediums because novel writing and screenwriting are two very different talents. Many writers are incapable of moving between the two with ease, which is why the Oscars have a category for Screenplay Adaptation. The norm is for a novelist or producer to hire a screenwriter to adapt the novel into a work known as a screenplay, which means the story has been translated from its internal monologues to an external story that can be filmed.

What I'm proposing is screenwriters do the opposite; transfer their screenplay story into a book format. Suddenly, you may find that producers who wouldn't give you the time of day are interested in looking at the screenplay because it's 'based on a novel'. It's a cruel irony that it works this way, but it's something to consider.

I don't recommend this route unless you're 100% comfortable with novel writing or prepared to hire a ghostwriter to do it for you. It can be a daunting task for those who are used to writing visually. A few of Extreme Screenwriting's clients have gone this route, like Cindy McDonald and the book based on her screenplay *Deadly.com*, Diane Hanks *Grove Rats* based on her *Summer Camp: A Memoir* and Lee Chambers best-selling teen thriller on Amazon titled *The Pineville Heist*.

If you're concerned that you'll do all the work, then be unable to get a publisher, you're behind on modern technology. It's time to turn off reruns of "The Golden Girls" and get with the program. Books can be self-published for a minimal cost and go live at places like Amazon.com's Kindle or via Amazon's Create a Space. You can pay for hardcopies and/or linked downloads. And guess what? You get to keep the profit! This doesn't involve an agent, manager, producer or anyone else......just you, your book and a distributor.

Keep in mind, this technically isn't being done so you can become the next great American novelist and be rich and famous. This might happen along the way, which is great. But you're doing this to market a screenplay. It may sound nuts, but considering screenplays can fetch six figures or even more, it may be worth considering.

One word of advice: since going this route involves an investment for the book publication, I suggest you only do so for screenplays that have a franchise potential. This means there can be sequels, prequels and/or TV spin-offs from this work that could total into the millions for the writer. I believe you'll find it worth the time and effort to go the book route.

The screenwriter has written a killer script, won a contest and he's gained the attention of agents and producers, then he shows up for a Hollywood meeting (in person or via phone) and he blows it! The screenwriter has worked long and hard to quit his lousy day job and become a career screenwriter. What happened?

I'll tell you exactly what happened; the writer became so focused on marketing the perfect script that he forgot – or never realized – he has to market himself too! The script isn't the only commodity agents and producers are looking for when it comes to making a movie. They want a writer they can work with long term, who understands this is a collaborative business, who isn't an arrogant, pompous ass who thinks the script must be made via 'his vision' or nothing and most importantly, a writer who understands how the business of show business really works.

Failure to understand how this business works is the stupidest thing a writer can do. I've heard the arguments from writers who only want to focus on the 'creative' side of the business. They have the illusion that agents, entertainment attorneys and producers will handle the rest. These same writers often complain when they're cheated out of their fair share of a sale or back-end profits or not being allowed on a movie set or when they're never invited to a premiere of their own movie or have to purchase their own movie from Amazon.com because they didn't even know to ask for a copy of the DVD in a contract. I've seen all of the above happen. All I have to say to these writers is I'M GLAD YOU GOT SCREWED! YOU DESERVE IT FOR BEING STUPID ENOUGH TO DO BUSINESS IN ANY BUSINESS WITHOUT KNOWING HOW THINGS WORK!

Think about this a minute. Remember the first job you ever had? Maybe it was flipping burgers at a fast food joint. Did you just show up one day and start flipping burgers? Heck no. You were trained on how to handle meat, how to properly cook meat, how to test if it's done, how to properly place it on a bun, how to make sure it stays hot for the customer, etc. Not to mention the details stuff you learned that goes along with this job, like hygiene, how to wear your uniform, hairnet, etc. Knowing all these things made your life easier, didn't it? All you had to do was show up each day and you were capable of getting the job done with a confident level of professionalism. Imagine if your teenager told you he got a job at the fast food joint, but planned to skip the 'training' he needs to do the job. The teen figures he's eaten at fast food joints before so how hard can it be to cook a burger. Of worse, he figures he doesn't really need to know how to cook a burger; he'll

277

leave it up to the head cook, the line cook, the assistant manager, the manager…..or hey, maybe the customer can cook his own burger!

Get the point? Focusing solely on the creative aspects of being a screenwriter makes you the stupid teenager. I'm not saying you need to go out and get a degree in film, financing or anything or the sort. I believe that the best way to learn is from reading everything you can get your hands on. Read more than just the books on screenwriting. There are fantastic books on the market that give an insider's look into the industry. Read books on producing films. This can really help a writer learn what it takes to make a film. Soon the writer will find himself making correct choices of what to add and remove from a script because he'll know it'll get cut in production if he leaves it in the script. Learn what scripts really go for (see more information on this under INSIDER INFORMATION). Know the players in town. You should NEVER take a meeting with anyone in this town unless you've done a thorough check on who they are, what they've produced, what they are working on, their track record in terms of sales, etc. Believe me when I say they'll be checking on you.

In fact, producers routinely use simple questions to gauge how savvy a writer is. In terms of screenwriting, one of the first questions a producer will ask is, "What's the script's theme?" It's amazing how many writers can't answer this question. If a writer can't rattle off the theme to a producer in one sentence, the producer will know he's dealing with an amateur who doesn't understand this biz. Why? Because theme is a primary ingredient a producer uses to sell the story to an audience. If the writer doesn't get this, then the project is already in trouble.

For the business end of things, producers will often test the waters with the script's price by making a low-ball offer for the script. This isn't necessarily being done because the producer is cheap or trying to cheat the writer. Many times he wants to see how the writer will respond. If the writer comes back with a smart-ass remark about how he'll never sell his script for under a million bucks, then the producer knows he's talking to an amateur who won't go far in this biz because it's extremely rare for a first sale to be a seven-figure number. Plus, it's obvious the writer doesn't even know the base pay, per WGA. This spells trouble from day one!

If, however, the producer gets a one-line response to the theme question and the writer responds to the price offer by thanking the producer for the offer, but quoting the proper price, per WGA, then the producer will know he's dealing with a savvy, professional writer. And this is the type of individual the producer can work with long term for this sale and potentially future sales.

278

As much as I hate sounding negative, I'm going to add a few sections for those writers who don't have a freaking clue how the biz really works. Instead, they have massive attitude, they're arrogant and are plain stupid. Let's start here....

LOSE THE JACKPOT MENTALITY

From the late 1980's to present day, every time a screenplay from a new writer sold for $1million or more it was splashed all over the press. This resulted in every Tom, Dick and Harry writing a screenplay. Every cab driver, hairdresser, alligator hunter to mailman has a script; 99% of which are crap. It reminds me of the casinos. Millions of people visit casinos yearly, yet only 1-2 big winners emerge. Even so, people keep on going – keep on hoping and believing they're that 'special' person who will hit the jackpot. This 'jackpot mentality' spilled over into the screenplay arena, resulting in hundreds of thousands of screenplays – a literal slush pile – from individuals with no formal training and frankly, with no clue what they're doing hitting the market with crap for 20+ years. This slush pile is the reason it's so hard to get scripts read. Industry professionals have had to set restrictions to help weed out the crap. They often won't read a script unless it's referred to them or has won a contest or has somehow proven it's a diamond in the rough.

But like the casinos the odds of hitting a jackpot are rare. If a script from a new writer sells for a million bucks it's most likely due to a bidding war between competing parties, usually studios. In fact, I did a quick check (don't quote my numbers), but between the year 2000-present, only around a dozen scripts from new writers sold for $1million or more. That averages out to less-than-one a year. Do you think you're the next one? I bet you do. Do yourself a favor and stop wasting your time screenwriting and go hit the casinos or play the lotto, the odds are better.

The reality is that the Writers Guild of America receives roughly 60,000 scripts a year for registration. Most scripts have been on the market for 3+ years. That would give a total of 180,000 scripts circulating at any given time, although I've seen articles that report this number to be closer to 800,000 to 1,000,0000 scripts at any given time being marketed to Hollywood. But there are only 5 major studios, a handful of mini major studios and around 900 production companies. Only around 200-300 productions are made a year, so what are your odds of making a million dollar sale? In fact, your odds of making any kind of a sale aren't in your favor. But don't worry – that's why you're reading this material; to help you break through the slush pile. But that doesn't mean you'll make a million dollar sale and expecting or even demanding it will only serve to make you look like a stupid idiot.

In order to break through the slush pile and assure you're ready for the market, you have to go beyond having a great script. You have to be market-ready. The writer does this by knowing what to realistically expect from a screenplay sale. How? Go to the Writer's Guild of America website (www.wga.org) and look under Writers Resources, click on Schedule of Minimums. This is the REAL rates paid for screenplays. Notice how the million-dollar figure suddenly shrunk to under a hundred thousand or a low-six figure. Print this schedule of minimums and know what to really expect from a sale. I know writers who are on their third and fourth sales and are nowhere near being paid a million bucks! They've been paid fair market value, they're fulltime writers and I guarantee most would laugh at the newbie writer who actually thinks he's going to make a million bucks on a script!

Even when I tell screenwriters this I still get unrealistic responses. Let's review some of them....

- ✓ "I'm entitled to a percentage of the total budget."
  -No, you're not! All things are negotiable, but for a first sale this is most unlikely. In fact, most first sales aren't with big studios; they're with smaller, non-signatory producers who can offer any amount. I know a writer who was offered $4,000 for a script she thought was worth $500,000. A signatory company would have offered her around $125,000, but a non-signatory company (not a member of WGA) can offer any amount!

- ✓ "My script is worth more because it's a big budget action/adventure."
  -I know screenwriters who've sold numerous big budget flicks and have never made a dime over $50,000 on each sale. A big budget flick doesn't guarantee big bucks, especially if it's a first sale. As I noted above, if the company (or producer) making the flick isn't signatory, they can offer any amount.

- ✓ "I'll only make a sale to a signatory company, then I'll be guaranteed the big bucks".
  The likelihood of making a first sale to a signatory company is rare. It's more likely a first-time writer will sell a small project to a smaller production company.

✓ "I know of a first-time screenwriter who made $1million on a script that isn't half as good as mine."
-Seven figures for a script is a RARE EXCEPTION, even for many A-list writers. Read what I wrote above about the odds of making a million dollars. If you're still holding out for a million bucks, then read into your pocket, pull out a dollar and go play the lotto – you're more likely to win the lotto long before you'll make a million dollar script sale.

✓ "I'm entitled to a royalty of the film's profits."
-There are only a handful of A-list screenwriters who get this and even they don't get it on every deal. There is absolutely no way you'd receive royalties on a first sale - maybe never! Okay, some producers do offer it, but again it's rare. Most first-time sales are an outright purchase. What you get upfront is all you get, ever!

Print the WGA's Schedule of Minimums. Learn the real price to expect from a sale and lose the jackpot mentality.

LOSE THE HACK MENTALITY

I liked those quirky comedy shows that say, "You know you're a redneck if…." They fill in the blank. So, let's have some fun with this same type of question by asking, "You know you're a hack screenwriter if…"

You know you're a hack screenwriter if you believe you're going to retire after a first script sale with a million bucks in the bank.
Reality: As noted under LOSE THE JACKPOT MENTALITY, it's rare to see a first-time writer hit the jackpot with a first sale. A writer is more likely to have to work years making multiple sales to even come close to a million dollar figure (see WGA's Schedule of Minimums).

You know you're a hack screenwriter if you believe producers don't really do anything.
Reality: Producers do everything on a film from securing talent, negotiating contracts, obtaining permits, arranging schedules, working with the unions, etc. If anything goes wrong, guess who gets to fix it; the producer. Long after the director's gone, the producer is still there….selling the film to distributors, etc. I can't think of anything they don't do on a film! Without the producer there is no film! Ever wonder why producers receive the Oscar for Best Film rather than the director, actors or writers? Now you know.

You know you're a hack screenwriter if you believe the director doesn't really do anything.

Reality: The director's responsible for the look of the film, which involves every single shot...not scene...I said SHOT...in a film – every frame of every shot, which includes every angle, every detail of the look from the coloration down to when the credits roll. Anyone who's ever edited a home video knows the detail and amount of work involved...imagine doing this on a feature film level times one thousand. It's an awesome responsibility.

You know you're a hack screenwriter if you believe formatting doesn't count toward a sale.
Reality: It's as important as the entire story because it determines the writer's style and level of professionalism. A producer can immediately tell if a writer is a professional or an amateur based solely on format.

You know you're a hack screenwriter if you think typos don't count. After all, you can't film a typo so why does it matter?
Reality: So, let me get this straight; you expect to get paid what lawyers get paid, but you don't think typos matter? Really? Do us all a favor and stop pretending you're a screenwriter and go back to your day job. Pros have flawless scripts that have gone through editors because getting paid the big bucks means providing a product that shines on every level.

You know you're a hack screenwriter if you think you'll land a sale when you land an agent.
Reality: Most sales come from the writer's own networking contacts and agents merely close the deal. Or most often the writer gets a producer interested in the script and then an agent comes along.

You know you're a hack screenwriter if you think it's entirely the agent's job to land a sale.
Reality: Most screenwriters land their own deals via their networking contacts. Agents do shop scripts, but even if a producer is interested in a script he'll want to meet with the writer first. The writer will have to pitch the story and the two will have to determine if they can work together long term. This means the writer is still the final factor when it comes to selling a script, not an agent.

You know you're a hack screenwriter if you think you can show up to a Hollywood meeting in a three-piece suit.
Reality: Writers have a uniform! Yes, I said uniform. It's simple: Jeans, jacket, t-shirt (or nice blouse for the ladies) and tennis shoes (or comfortable shoes)...us ladies can get away with high-heels.

You know you're a hack screenwriter if you balk at wearing the Hollywood uniform for screenwriters.

Reality: Let me ask you a question: What do you wear at your day job? Most likely you have to wear business attire, dresses, suits, nylons, heels…oh God…stop me…I typed the word nylons. I don't know about you, but I hate those things. I'd much rather dress casual…how 'bout you?

You know you're a hack screenwriter if you think big A-list talent will flock to your script because you wrote the perfect story for George Clooney.
Reality: Unless you know George, forget it.

You know you're a hack screenwriter if you think commercializing a script means giving up your creativity or 'compromising your art'.
Reality: Real writers can become creative under any circumstances, including commercializing a script. Hack writers use it as an excuse not to write. They say things like, 'I'm not going to compromise my art'. Art? This isn't art business; it's show business. If you want to be an artist, take up painting. A screenwriter is a skilled worker who has mastered his trade and can deliver a marketable product known as a screenplay. He can be 'creative' under any circumstances!

You know you're a hack screenwriter if you think it's okay to take a year to write a script.
Reality: This might seem okay if you're writing on spec, but if you're serious about a Hollywood career, then you must realize real screenwriters have real deadlines placed upon them by producers and studios. This can mean a 1-2 week timeframe to re-edit an entire script! Or if you're lucky enough to eventually get to the point where a studio purchases an idea (pitch), you'll have around 6 weeks to deliver the final product. I've heard the arguments, 'No problem, I'll have more time when I'm a pro writer to devote to writing in such a short timeframe from my previous 1 year stint'. Wrong! Unless you're used to writing on tight deadlines, you'll find yourself making excuses to try to get a deadline extended and the studio will end moving on to another writer who can deliver.

You know you're a hack screenwriter if you think it's okay that you already have your Oscar speech written.
Reality: I'd advise you to mail it to the Academy of Motion Picture Arts and Sciences, because that's the closest you'll ever get to an Oscar.

You know you're a hack screenwriter if you think once your script sells that you'll never have to make changes. After all, it's an ace script that's won awards and received recommends from a number of story analysts.
Reality: I've never seen a script that didn't have some kind of change – ever! Even writer/directors end up changing something in their own scripts due to changes in the production.

You know you're a hack screenwriter if you think your job on a movie set will be to 'guide' the director on how the story should unfold.
Reality: Did the director come to your house and tell you how to write the script? Nope, I didn't think so. You're in his house so don't think for a minute he's going to let you tell him how to film the story!

You know you're a hack screenwriter if you think your story is the next big blockbuster film.
Reality: If Hollywood knew what the next big blockbuster was going to be they'd hire an A-list writer with a proven track record to write it. Get the picture? Nobody knows what the next hit movie is…nobody!

You know you're a hack screenwriter if you think you can never be replaced as the script's writer because it's your script.
Reality: Once you sell it to a producer it's his script! If you're inflexible and holding up a production, he'll hire a writer who can get the job done and the WGA will back him, not you! You'll still get the credit, but it'll be a shared credit. Pro writers are good at collaborating and are flexible. They can take a love story and turn it into a shoot-out at a 7-11 if they have to.

And finally...my personal favorite…

You know you're a hack screenwriter if you think you can write an ordinary story and sell it.
Reality: It doesn't matter how well-written it is or how many contests it's won or how many times your spouse has bragged about it. If it isn't fresh, original and have a WOW factor, then you're wasting precious trees (paper) and ink! Keep your day job and stop wasting time on a pipe dream. Pros know how to take the ordinary story and make it extraordinary! Extra Note: Recently, an article featured George Clooney talking about how difficult it is to get ordinary, character-driven material made. If George has a tough time getting this type of story made, what do think your odds are?

MUZZLE THE DEFENSIVE DOG

I'd like to take this opportunity to compliment the majority of aspiring screenwriters I've worked with. You're hard working, handle yourselves in a professional manner and maintain an open level of objectivity about your work. I wish you all the best in your careers.

There are, however, a few out there who will fight tooth and nail about why a reviewer's opinion is dead wrong. Instead of comparing reviews to see what more than one reviewer might have said that's consistent with a problem area, this type of writer becomes defensive and argues every point. They maintain that their type of work has been done before and theirs is just as good. If a writer is this argumentative with a reader, then how is the writer ever going to work with a producer when the first thing producers do after making a sale is hand the writer 'story notes'. For those of you who don't know what story notes are, they're notes for changes the producer wants made before the story heads into production. Try arguing with the producer and he'll bring in another writer to make the changes.

Why the Defensive Posturing Doesn't Work in Your Favor

✓ A pro will get more than one review and compare notes and will know if more than one person says the same thing about a problem area that they MUST make changes. They don't simply assume everyone is wrong because similar material has been made. That's naïve and makes the writer look like an amateur.

✓ Burning bridges in Hollywood is a very bad habit. Today's reviewer could be tomorrow's producer, director or agent. And let me assure you that Hollywood is a very small town where word spreads like wild fire. Don't burn bridges!

✓ Reviews are highly subjective. This is why I'm such a strong advocate for receiving multiple reviews all at once so you'll get a real perspective of what works and what doesn't work. Unleashing the defensive dog on any reader is a waste of time and makes you look unprofessional and out of touch with the fact that some people will love your stuff while others won't. It's just part of the biz, so get a grip!

✓ Defensive writers tend to be difficult to work with and most producers steer clear of them. This only serves to work against making a first sale or any sale, ever! In fact, most producers will gauge a writer's flexibility before purchasing the writer's script. If the writer is argumentative from day one, it's unlikely the producer will purchase the material. Even if the producer does purchase the material, he'll quickly bring in another writer to make changes.

✓ Taking things personal means you're too attached to the work! The work isn't you and a negative review (or one you perceive to be negative) isn't an assault on you personally. How could it be when it's unlikely the reviewer knows who you are? Pro writers know there are a million different opinions out there and none of them are meant to be taken personally! Same goes for the moment the writer

285

receives story notes from a producer. The producer just purchased the script, doesn't he love it? Yes, he does, but he wants it to be the best commercial product possible. Do you think he's in this business because he wants a pretty story? He's in this business to make money. If you don't like that fact, then go work somewhere else.

Do you simply agree with every review? Of course not, but take the position to thank others for their time and ask constructive questions about areas you're unclear about and remember - one person will love your stuff while the next person will hate it! Get used to it. It's just part of this biz and it's also part of real life as well. How often have you seen a movie you loved only to have a family member or friend say they didn't like it? It's all part of this biz!

Even if you disagree with a reader or a producer, always maintain an air of professionalism because the defensive dog will only leave you leashed to the dog house for the rest of your years.

STOP WAITING FOR INSPIRATION

I know countless writers who spend years working on a script or worse, they don't write unless they're inspired. So, here's a reality check for you. Let's say you get a pitch in Hollywood. Here's how it works:

-You pitch a producer a feature-film idea. Let's say he buys it!
-This was only an "idea" when you walked in the room = you have nothing down on paper.

Here's where the reality check comes in....

You and the producer shake hands to seal the deal and he says he'll see you back **at the studio in 6 weeks to look at the first draft!**

Did he just say 6 weeks?

YES, HE DID! (By the way, selling a pitch only is only realistic once you're an established writer – I'm just using this as an example so a writer can learn to train himself NOW, so he'll be prepared for a career in screenwriting).

This is the average time a studio gives for a first draft. It could be longer or shorter depending on the deal, but this is STANDARD! Professional screenwriters have 6 weeks to deliver a first draft!

If you've spent three years writing a screenplay you could be in serious trouble in Hollywood. Take a look at the next topic to learn how to resolve this issue.

HAVE REAL GOALS NOT PIPE DREAMS

Professional screenwriters are consistently churning out new material. I realize most of you still have day jobs, so let's take a realistic look at what's **not** realistic if you want to be a pro:

- ✓ 1 completed screenplay in 3 years
- ✓ Continually working on the same spec for years

Here's the reality of what it'll take to work like a pro:

- ✓ 3 to 4 completed specs per year. This gives you 3 months (12 weeks) to complete a spec. That's double the time a pro has to deliver material
- ✓ Complete a script and move on to the next one
- ✓ Consistently churning out new material

The goal is simple: To produce new material on a consistent basis! The best way to do this is as follows:

- ✓ Stop thinking of a certain screenplay as your "baby." The reality is your "baby" will probably get chewed up and spit out during the Hollywood development process. Try this instead: Think of a script as your "baby" while you're writing it, then let it go and move on to your next "baby." Don't you consider all of your writing to be "special" or are you just capable of producing one good piece? Are you nothing more than a one-hit wonder? If so, forget a career in Hollywood because producers and agents want to work with career screenwriters, not one-hit wonders.

- ✓ Once you've completed an outline use a red pen to assign dates to the margins for when you want certain sections of a screenplay to be completed. Coordinate with your calendar so you're not running over the 12-week period. Does the 12 weeks include review time once you're finished? No. You can get started on another script while the most recent one is being reviewed. This will also help eliminate the urge to rush a script to market.

    Constantly be looking for ideas. I keep file boxes with index cards in them. I write down anything of interest to me: ideas, pieces of

287

dialogue, scene locations…everything. <u>This will keep the creativity flowing to the point you won't have to wait for inspiration</u> because it's at your fingertips.

Stop dreaming of what it'd be like to be a full-time screenwriter and start living like one! Don't bother telling me you can't do this because you have a day job, the kids, the errands, the house to run, etc. Don't try to convince me you CAN do this when you're a full-time writer because you can quit your day job. Most writers have to sell 2-3 scripts, maybe more, before they can quit their day job and scripts 2-3 have to written on a deadline. So, I'd strongly advise you to stop making up excuses and find a way to make this type of deadline work. Get up earlier. Stay up later. Give up a Saturday out or a Sunday sporting event. You'll thank me when you're able to meet a producer's 4-6 week deadline with ease, even while you're still working a day job, toting the kids around town, shopping for groceries and cleaning the house. By the way, clever writers find ways to weave writing into their busy schedules. I can't tell you how many times I've dusted while talking through a scene with a handheld recorder taking my notes. I don't think I've ever made an entire home-cooked meal without jotting down notes between mixing sauces and checking on the pasta.

STOP WORRYING ABOUT THEFT – LET THEM STEAL IT

This might sound crazy, but take a look at the reality of copyright theft. There have only been a few lawsuits filed and a few wins. Of those "wins" the screenwriter was awarded multi-millions of dollars. One figure is around $10 million! There is NO WAY you'll ever make $10 million on a script.

Hollywood folks know this. They aren't stupid. Does this mean theft never happens? It does happen, but more than likely if someone's interested in your material they'll go about obtaining it via the proper option or purchase channels rather than risk a multi-million dollar lawsuit.

What can you do to prevent theft? Three things:

1) Don't discuss ideas until you have a completed screenplay because you can't copyright an idea only the execution of the idea. I continually see screenwriters asking other screenwriters on message boards what they think of an idea – STOP DOING THIS! You're giving away your ideas - for free!
2) Keep a record of everyone who views the script. Not the logline or synopsis, these don't count. The entire script. Note when they requested the material, the date requested, who requested the material and any follow-up notes. If you ever do have to file a

288

copyright lawsuit you have to prove the party in question had access to the material, so keep records.

3) Do WGA Registration AND a copyright. You can't file a copyright lawsuit if you didn't copyright the script in the first place. WGA is mainly for arbitration in the event of a dispute. Do both! Plus, if you sell the script, the producer will need to transfer the copyright to his name because he's the new owner. He can't do this if you didn't copyright the material!

RESUMES & BIOS

Part of making sure the writer is market ready involves presenting a resume and/or bio. The problem arises because Hollywood isn't really interested in how long you worked at an accounting firm or how many years you've been a doctor unless your screenplay's topic is derived from your expertise. For example, it would be worth noting that you're a prominent physician if your script is a medical thriller.

But what if you're just an ordinary guy living in New Jersey with a wife and 2.5 kids? Again, Hollywood doesn't care. What they want to see is industry-related accomplishments, especially in the area of screenwriting. This includes contest placements, recommendations from script readers, IMDB credits (including shorts), YouTube videos (crazy, but true), college degrees (if industry-related), completed writing courses (on-line or in a college setting), industry-related jobs (PA on a film, Associate Producer, etc.), or other writing achievements, like a published novel, short stories or even poetry.

Don't forget volunteer work, like the time you helped out at a film festival or took part in a theater read or helped actors in an acting coaching class rehearse their lines. Or maybe you developed websites related to the industry or poster or videos, etc. Anything industry-related should be listed.

Be careful with college degrees. While it's always impressive that you've gone to college and shown you can complete a degree, a degree unrelated to the industry could raise eyebrows from producers. I've often heard producers ask, "Why does a guy with a degree in Engineering think he's a screenwriter?" If you have a degree that's unrelated to the industry, I'd be sure to mention in a bio or briefly on a resume why you're interested in screenwriting. For example, I know screenwriters who are doctors or lawyers in their day job who want to share their 'expertise' via the visual medium known as feature films. Mentioning you're a doctor who's written a medical screenplay can actually help sell it!

What if the writer doesn't have any of the above? Then I'd strongly recommend building a resume. Send your screenplay out to review services and try to obtain a recommend, enter contests and start volunteering at local film festivals in your area. Does your town have a theater? Volunteer to help actors read lines or make costumes or do cold calls to sell tickets. Build a Hollywood resume.

The most impressive thing producers look for on resumes is recommends and contest placements/wins. Why? Because it shows you're a serious player and you are not a member of the crappy slush pile of amateurs who are trying to use the industry to strike it rich.

An extra note on contest placements: I advise against listing the year your script placed. Just mention the placement. A script can look outdated if it placed in a well-known contest five years ago. Only mention the year if a producer directly asks you.

As for contact information on a resume have a special email for industry-related contacts, like MikeScreenwriter@aol.com. Keep it separate from your personal email. If you have a website, list it on the resume. Be sure to include a cellular phone number. I advise against listing day job number. Do you really want a producer calling with the answering partying saying, "Hello, thank you for calling Kentucky Fried Chicken?" I don't think so! Plus, most employers frown upon personal calls and you'll need to keep that day job until you've sold several screenplays. Yes, I said several. Quitting for one sale isn't likely since WGA minimums rarely hit six figure numbers and a first sale is most likely to net (after taxes) less than you'd make at KFC.

Extra note on websites: This is a great way to promote yourself and your accomplishments as a writer, but a word of caution. When putting up a screenwriter promotional website, please don't include pictures of the kids and pets – unless you're trying to sell a true-life story about them. Keep it screenwriter-related.

Keep the bio brief; a paragraph or two. Again, it should be industry-related. We don't need to know about your job at Kohls or how long you flipped burgers at McDonalds or that you're the Lead Supervisor at a Waste Management facility. What you don't want to include is unprofessional crap. I've actually seen bios that proclaim the writer to have the next big, undiscovered blockbuster screenplay! For the record, that writer still hasn't sold his so-called 'blockbuster'. If you're applying for a computer job, would you write a cover letter announcing you're the world's greatest computer programmer? You'd look like a fool! So stop being arrogant on bios. Keep it simple. Keep it professional and keep it industry-related.

Extra note on bios: If you have a unique background that lends itself to the stories you've written, I'd advise the writer to include this information. For example, if you're a veteran who's written several military-type stories, then I'd add the veteran information to the bio. The goal is to keep the bio restricted to things that relate to your screenplays. Also, include unique experiences that relate to what you've written. Perhaps you're a bio scientist who's written an apocalyptic germ warfare screenplay. Personal experience or expertise can lend credibility to a screenplay.

AGENTS VS. MANAGERS

It's important for an aspiring screenwriter to understand the difference between an agent and a manager. It's also important in helping the writer determine which one best suits the writer's career objectives. Let's take a look at the differences:

COMMISSIONS
Signatory agents with the Writers Guild can only take a 10% commission. Managers can take any amount and usually take from 15-25% commission.

SOLICITATION CONSIDERATIONS
Signatory agents can solicit any producer in town – even ones who indicate "no unsolicited material". Signatory gives them this status.

Managers can not solicit producers directly. Even if they do – based on established relationships - a final deal must go through a signatory agent. This applies to producers who are signatory and many are with the guilds. This means the writer has to pay the agent and the manager's fees for a total commission of 25% or more. If this happens to you, be sure to negotiate a deal BEFORE THE SALE where the agent and manager split a lower commission rate of say 15-20%.

WRITER KNOW-HOW CONSIDERATIONS
Signatory agents prefer industry-savvy writers. They don't have time to hand-hold; that's what managers are for. They'll expect a screenwriter to know how to pitch, how to network, know who's who in the industry, know what's in development, know what's in production, etc.

On the other hand, managers cater to writers. They'll help the screenwriter understand the industry, how things work and guide the writer every step of the way. If a writer needs the extra level of assistance, inspiration and recognition, then a manager is the way to go.

MATERIAL CONSIDERATIONS

Signatory agents come in two forms; boutiques and big agencies. A new writer is 99% times more likely to end up in a boutique agency to start out than a big agency. The main difference is the way they solicit material. Big agencies 'go wide'. This means they call up 50-100 production companies and say they're sending over a hot script, then give a specific deadline for purchase or the company loses out. They build 'hype' for the script, which can lead to bidding wars and big sales. Sounds ideal, but it can backfire if no one buys the script because it'll have to be taken off the market for some time before it can go wide again.

Boutiques do NOT go wide. Instead, they tend to work with a closer net of established industry contacts and via referrals to get their client's material sold. Clients at boutique agencies often bring in their own deals and the agent closes the deal. This is done via networking, pitches, etc.

Managers do NOT go wide. Instead, most use their own networking base for solicitations. Many can avoid signatory requirements due to strong established industry relationships that allow them to go directly to producers, directors and actors with a script. If considering a manager, check out his industry contacts and background. Does he have direct access to talent and producers? If not, he'll have a hard time selling a writer's material.

PITCHES

All managers and agents want screenwriters to pitch. As noted above, managers will guide screenwriters through this process while agents expect the screenwriter to know how to pitch.

Agents or managers do not attend pitches with the screenwriters, so honing this skill is imperative prior to becoming a client. What if you plan to strictly sell spec scripts and don't plan to pitch? Then you need a reality check and don't expect to get signed by anyone. Pitching is the way 99% of scripts are sold. Don't think it's only the agent or manager's job to pitch. Wrong! Even if an agent/manager sends out a script and the producer likes it, the producer will want to meet with the writer to discuss the project in detail. In other words, to convince the producer he really wants to spend years on this project. In other words, the final sale almost always depends on the writer's ability to sell the product! You can't be a fireman without knowing how to work a hose and you can't be screenwriter if you don't know how to pitch.

TIME CONSIDERATIONS

The longer an agent/manager has been in the biz, the more clients he's likely to have. An agent or manager can have 50 or more literary clients, can receive 100 or more calls and emails a day! They're busy people. If the screenwriter's insecure and has to ask a million questions before being comfortable enough to function in his/her career, the writer's not likely to last long in the biz. Agents are simply too busy to deal with a writer who hasn't taken the time to understand the industry.

I'm amazed how many screenwriters ignore the business basics of how the industry works. Yet in a day job, they'll prep like crazy; discover a company's history, know its product, how many years in business and even slant their resume to get the job. But when it comes to Hollywood, they ignore the basics and for some bizarre reason they think the 'creative' side is enough to see them through. Don't be a moron! Being a screenwriter is no different than any other day job and it requires you know everything about the industry.

Ask how many clients an agent has. What's the response time to emails and calls? Some agents or managers may want you to call in once a week with an update. Why? Because they want to know you're working. This tells them whether you're a serious writer or just looking to score a big sale, then retire. Agents and managers want career-minded screenwriters, not lotto seekers. They also want writers who understand what the industry really pays and who understand that six figures is a rare deal as most writers make far less.

If you land at a big agency, you'll most likely be assigned to a junior agent as opposed to a more established 'senior' agent. This has its benefits. Their career is younger and they're hungrier for sales and will be more aggressive in promoting the writer and the work. They'll also have fewer clients to start out with and will have more time for the individual writer.

If the writer needs hand-holding, then find a manager. Managers specialize in guiding and inspiring writers. They tend to take on fewer clients to assure they have time to mold a writer's success. Many writers prefer this career advantage over the hustle and bustle of the Hollywood 'norm'.

THE EDGE FACTOR
Screenwriters know a script needs 'edge' to sell, but the trend with the big agencies is seeking clients with edge. Perhaps it's the economy, but agents have to be able to sell both the script and the writer. This is the trend primarily of the bigger agencies and bigger boutiques, but an important enough factor to warrant mentioning.

What is client edge? Like a script's selling point, it's the screenwriter's selling point. The basics help, like a degree in a field related to film, background in TV, film or writing, etc. However, edge can be anything that makes the writer stand-out from the crowd. Perhaps the writer lost 100 pounds last year, survived a rattlesnake bite at the age of ten, lives in a haunted house, or claims to have been an alien abductee. Don't laugh because edge sells. Can't find anything interesting 'bout yourself? Try friends, family, old college buddies, former lovers or even neighbors. I bet someone remembers the year you spent in Minnesota looking for meteorites or the time you won that hotdog-eating contest at the county fair.

The edge can also be related to the work. Maybe you're a doctor who's written a medical thriller or a rock climber who's written a hiking/murder mystery? Your day job might make you uniquely qualified to sell the screenplay, but be careful as it could work against you. After all, is a doctor or a rock climber really willing to become a career screenwriter? Only you can answer that question.

FORGET THE AGENT – THE DIY APPROACH

I have met so many screenwriters who complain how they're ignored by the industry, how they can't find an agent to look at their work and believe they'll never make a sale without an agent. Frankly, I have no idea why screenwriters think they need an agent to make a sale.

Have you ever considered quitting the agent hunt completely? Are you really that naïve to think you must have an agent to make a sale? Then you haven't met my personal hero; screenwriter Bill Martell. He's sold dozens – that's right – dozens of screenplays and has dozens of films out and he did it without an agent or a manager! He's the King of the DIY (Do-It-Yourself) approach. No, he didn't make his own films. He's not a filmmaker, he a screenwriter.

He's done it successfully because he knows this biz inside and out. He's savvy and knows how to think outside the Hollywood box! He's the guy who'll tell you to get over thinking screenwriting is an art and get down to business because if a script isn't commercial, it won't sell. See his amazing website at www.scriptsecrets.net.

For the record, I'd like to say that all of the ghostwriting projects I've done over the years, most of the scripts I've sold (produced and unproduced) were without an agent. I'm no Bill Martell, but I know that having an agent is a bonus in this biz, not a necessity. Does this mean you should stop looking for an agent? That's up to you. Just be aware that it is possible to make a sale without one.

HOW TO GET AN AGENT TO CALL YOU!

Five years ago, I would have told a screenwriter the way to get an agent is to get a producer interested in the screenplay. This is still true to some degree because producers work directly with agents and have the ability to make referrals. It's also much easier to get a producer to read a screenplay than an agent. There are different books put out yearly like the Hollywood Screenwriter's Directory that provides lists of producers who'll accept unsolicited queries. If you land a read and the producer likes the script, whether he buys it or not, ask him to refer you to an agent. If the producer is interested in the script and makes the referral, there's a good chance the agent will call you. Isn't that easier than sending out hundreds of unanswered queries?

But times are changing. Fewer movies are being made due to economic considerations. This means fewer producers are interested in work from untried sources. It's hard to hear, but a lot of producers are sticking with seasoned writers who are a sure bet at the box office. Do you blame them? They need to make a profit. Is this true of all producers? No. Others prefer the new writer because in today's tough economic times they can negotiate to pay a lower rate for the script, which could help minimize any potential loss on the film.

Yikes! Did I just scare you off? Have you decided to keep your day job and forget this biz? Keep in mind that most successful people became successes in times when others didn't believe it was possible. So, your best bet is to be aware of what I just told you, then totally ignore it and push ahead!

Is there another way to secure an agent and make a living as a writer without a producer being interested in the script? Yes, but first let me tell you what recently happened to a writer I know. He landed an option and got the attention of an agent. They had a face-to-face meeting. During the meeting, the agent asked if the writer was interested in doing writing assignments (rewriting someone else's work). The writer said 'no'. Several days later he called me stunned that the agent turned him down as a client.

Agents who used to live off screenplay sales are finding their bread and butter in today's market comes from assignments. So, if a writer isn't willing to do assignments, he's unlikely to get an agent.

Here's how to use this economic consideration to your advantage and get an agent to call you even if you don't have a producer interested in your script.

295

Start ghostwriting. Ghostwriting isn't just for novels. You can rewrite another writer's dialogue, description, characters, TV pilot bibles, synopses, loglines or entire scripts. Do it for a fair rate and make sure to have a written contract that states you have the right to inform a signatory agent that you were a ghostwriter on a project (but no one else). I'm advocating doing this as a ghostwriter instead of for a credit for a number of reasons; 1) most writers don't want to share credit 2) many producers don't want to step on established writer's toes with shared credits. Here's how this works:

Instead of sending a general query to producers, like ten thousand other writers, send a query to producers that highlights a contest placement or script awards and put in BOLD, CENTERED text – Experienced ghostwriter available for film/TV assignments! I guarantee that after years of sending out countless queries with no response, the phone will RING! They probably won't want to buy your script, but will want to read the placement script as a sample writing and might hire you to ghostwrite for them.

Now, you've moved up from ghostwriting for a writer to ghostwriting for producers. Next step, send out queries again, this time to agents! Again, highlight a contest placement or award and write in BOLD, CENTERED TEXT: Experienced Ghostwriter for Producers Seeks Agent. I guarantee the phone will RING! That's right – the agent will call you!

If you're willing to ghostwrite for writers and producers, then you'll be willing to take assignments while the agent attempts to sell your script(s). This is the client today's agent is seeking! When he looks at you all he sees is dollar signs! You'll make him happy by doing assignments and you'll be happy that you have an agent who's marketing your script! It's a win/win situation backed by real money. Ghostwrite your way into an agent calling you!

Don't tell me it can't be done! Do you know what it means when someone tells you "It can't be done?" It means they can't do it. I'm here to tell you I've done it and I know others who have too! Stop making up bullshit excuses and start writing!

But you're not interested in rewriting someone else's stuff and prefer to wait until your script sells. Let's look at what you're missing. The ghostwriters I know, myself included, can build up a client base and be doing 2-12 projects a year, roughly every 4 weeks. Let's say you make $10K per ghostwriting gig (could be more or less) and this year you do 5 jobs. Obviously, that's $50K. This might sound low compared to selling a script. Let's say you sold a script for $200K, but don't sell another one for 5 years. That breaks down to roughly $40K a year, meaning you would have made more ghostwriting.

Better yet, if you'd done both, which agents will expect you to do; over the five year period you would have made $450K.

Why would you ghostwrite and not demand a credit? Some assignments will have credits, others won't. As noted above, writers don't like to share credits and producers often back them. Besides, you're not doing this for the credit, you're doing it to land an agent and put real money in the bank. In other words, to move you from your lousy day job to being able to proudly call yourself a writer; there's nothing wrong with ghostwriting for no credit. The definition of a professional is someone who gets paid to provide a service, not someone who gets a credit.

The most famous ghostwriting gig in town with no credit was for "Good Will Hunting". To this day, many claim it was actress Carrie Fisher (yes, she's a ghostwriter) who rewrote the project. When it hit the Oscars, it's rumored she was paid millions in 'hush' money. Like many writers, Affleck and Damon didn't want to share the credit. It's very common. Here's an example from my own experiences:

A CBS showrunner hired me to rewrite a pilot as a ghostwriter. He didn't want to step on the original writer's toes by forcing a shared credit. We cut a deal and I ghostwrote (rewrote) the pilot. Without giving precise figures, I will say I was paid nearly double the norm. In other words, it was 'hush money'. The showrunner was shooting the pilot independently and plans to take it into the studio during the 2014 pilot season. I'll never see another dime and I won't see a credit if it makes it on the air. Do I care? No! Why? Because I'm too busy laughing all the way to the bank!

Does this mean you should do all rewrites as a ghostwriter? No, but it's a great way to get the attention of producers who are seeking ghostwriters and agents who want writers willing to take assignments. Plus, it's money in the bank.

But how do you do this? Okay, I admit that you aren't likely to start off ghostwriting for a CBS showrunner. First, you can't do this unless you have contest placements or have won awards. You have to show that you have the ability to deliver. These scripts will become your sample writings. Start by advertising on places like Craigslist or Done Deal Pro or anywhere screenwriters hang out. This is the easiest group to start with. Or you could go straight to sending out the queries (as noted above) to producers. WAIT until you've done ghostwriting for several producers before approaching agents.

Another bonus is the contacts. These producers you're ghostwriting for might buy one of your scripts in the future. The ghostwriting assignment gives you a direct 'in' with the producer for future work. Remember the CBS showrunner? I just wrapped my first sitcom and after receiving three recommends for it, I called him and asked if he'd look at it. He said, "Send it over".

If you don't have the necessary placements or wins, then hone your skills, enter contests and get noticed. Continue to market your scripts like normal, but follow the steps outlined above and I guarantee you will get an agent to call you!

THE SCREENWRITER'S UNIFORM

Were you one of those kids who hated high school because you didn't have the cool, trendy designer clothes or didn't quite fit in? Were you intimidated by all those stuck up, arrogant, pompous kids who thought they were better than you? Well, Hollywood is ten times worse than high school because Hollywood is high school with money! And YES, the way you look and especially the way you dress means something.

There's a book on the market called "The Hollywood Rules." It's a shocking insider's look at how things really work in Hollywood. I consider it MANDATORY READING for anyone seriously considering a career in tinsel town, especially if you hated high school.

This might be shocking news to those of you who don't work in the biz, but Hollywood has uniforms! In a corporate setting, men wear suits and ties, while women wear skirts and high heels. At McDonalds they wear those hideous colored uniforms with funny little hats. It's just part of doing business and in Hollywood it's no different. In Hollywood, specific designer clothes "reveal" who you are!

The Screenwriter's Uniform: Jeans, t-shirt, jacket and tennis shoes!

I'm amazed at how many writers I've told about the Hollywood uniform scoff with comments like, "I'll wear whatever I want." Here's a true story I'll share with you...

My friend, I'll call her "Amy," landed a meeting at a Hollywood Studio. Amy's used to the corporate world where she'd worked for 15+ years prior to her first big Hollywood meeting. I promptly informed her to tone it down to jeans, t-shirt, a jacket and tennis shoes - all designer names, of course! She laughed me out of her house. This was an important meeting and she was

298

going to look her best. She had a nice dress picked out. I assured her she was making a mistake, but I couldn't convince her that wearing casual designer jeans, a t-shirt, jacket and tennis shoes was the screenwriter's uniform.

In Hollywood, it's actresses who wear the long skirts and dresses, not screenwriters.

Amy went to her studio meeting and on at least two occasions someone asked her what role she was auditioning for. When she told them she was a screenwriter they gave her a funny look. Amy now wears designer jeans, jackets with t-shirts underneath and her tennis shoes. Now she's asked, "What did you write?"

Here are the Hollywood uniforms:

Screenwriters
Jeans, business jackets with a t-shirt underneath and tennis shoes.
Writers can get away with replacing tennis shoes with high heels for the ladies and boots or dress shoes for the men.

Actresses
Dresses or long skirts.

Actors
Slacks, nice jacket with no tie.

Directors
Jeans, leather jackets. Directors often have a fetish for baseball caps.

Producers
Jeans, slacks, suits…they're the combo guys …easy to mistake them for actors.
Their lingo gives them away. The more dramatic they speak, the more likely they're actors.

Studio Executives
Suits and ties.

This isn't an absolute, but 9 times out of 10 you can immediately recognize what someone does on the studio lot by the way they're dressed. I'm amazed at how much flak I hear from screenwriters about this.

Hollywood's a dream job when it comes to attire. What other job can you get up, slip on your jeans, t-shirt, jacket and tennis shoes and you're off and running? I don't know about the rest of you, but I HATE NYLONS! Thank goodness for the Hollywood uniform!

There is one catch to the uniform! <u>Everything you wear has to be designer</u>. Think I'm kidding? I'm not! Hollywood folks know designer clothes. I'm not even into fashion and I know what someone is wearing. I know, it sounds shallow. It is. But think of it this way - if you landed a job at a corporation would you think twice about going out and buying that suit and tie or those skirts and heels? It's how you're expected to dress and are often required to wear.

What if you can't afford all the designer labels? I shop at designer outlets – they're great and you only pay a fraction of the cost for your Hollywood uniform. If you live in the middle of nowhere, try eBay. Don't fret about it. If you worked at McDonalds you'd have to wear one of those silly hats. I'd rather wear designer duds than a silly little hat, how about you? No need to buy an entire wardrobe. Most writers meet with different producers on different days, so you can probably get away with 2-3 outfits to start. Make them interchangeable by selecting t-shirts that go with all your jackets and jackets that go with all your jeans, etc.

DON'T BE A HOLLYWOOD WHORE

A screenwriter told me I had no idea what I was talking about when I warned him against rewriting a script FOR FREE for a producer without some kind of commitment in writing from the producer. After all, the producer had agreed to shop the material around town if he was happy with the rewrite and the screenwriter wasn't about to pass up the opportunity to get his material sold.

What happened? Six weeks later the screenwriter e-mails me saying he completed the rewrite and the producer claimed to like the new version, but wasn't interested in pursuing the material at this time. This same writer hooked up with another producer who wanted completely different changes with no commitment on the table. Fortunately, he'd learned his lesson and is no longer the Hollywood whore.

Producers know they can get free rewrites out of screenwriters; at least from the hungry and desperate writers. This isn't a derogatory statement about producers. Many are honestly attempting to help the writer create the best material possible, but here's a reality check for those considering doing a rewrite with no commitment…

If a Producer is Interested in a Script he will Option it on the Spot!
He WILL NOT RISK losing it!

If he doesn't make a bonafide offer, but tries to get the free rewrite first, it means he's interested in the script's concept and that's it!

If he were really interested in the entire script, he'd make an offer. This doesn't mean you'll get a big fat option check and be able to pay off your mortgage. It might be enough to pay the electric bill and that's about it. A written offer means the producer is SERIOUS about the project. Anything else is Hollywood bullshit and you're a sap if you fall for it!

This doesn't just apply to producers. Here's a recent example: A screenwriter e-mailed me about a romantic comedy she wrote. A manager was interested in representing the work "only if it had a darker edge" and asked for a rewrite. I told her to get the commitment to represent the work "if it meets the criteria laid out" in writing. Guess what? The manager wouldn't do it. Sounds like the manager wasn't that interested after all.

There's nothing wrong with being open to rewrites. In fact, it's a major part of the biz, but writing without a written commitment from the requesting party is stupid. Test the requesting party's real intent by asking for a preliminary commitment in writing that should the rewrite meet their criteria, they will market or represent it as they said they would.

For the record, I'll say that I've seen many, many, many screenwriters make these freebie changes and 99% of them have never landed the deal! Don't be the Hollywood Whore!

HOLLYWOOD MAKES CRAP

There are screenwriters who think Hollywood makes nothing but crap! They hate most movies or have more negative opinions about films than positive ones. Frankly, they believe they can do better.

Reality check! There is no industry in the world that creates so-called "crap" that can survive and still make multi-billions of dollars a year! They MUST be doing something right!

Come on folks! We all have movies we love and we all have movies we aren't wild about, but I have noticed a trend with real pros. They tend to respect all films made - even the bad ones - because they know how difficult it is to get ANYTHING made in Hollywood.

Besides, most pros eat, sleep and drink film. They love it and live for it! Frankly, I love to watch a horrible film - - it gives me hope and shows me what not to do in my own work.

If you're one of the "know more than Hollywood" screenwriters I have one question for you....

Why do you want to work in a "crap" industry?

If you really want to make yourself market-ready you'll need to lose this attitude quick! Have some respect for those who have been successful at getting something made...it isn't an easy thing to do. You don't have to like it – but you also don't have to badmouth it! Act like a pro – discuss what works and what doesn't about a film and make yourself a more marketable commodity!

PLAYING THE GAME WITH ONE SPEC

Every time I go around a mountain curve I see a sign that reads "DANGER." If you're a screenwriter trying to play the big Hollywood game with one spec you're in DANGER!

Why? Let's say you actually succeed in selling the first script you ever wrote. It's happened, but it's rare! You'll become what's known in Hollywood as "The Flavor of the Month." In other words, you'll be a hot commodity. Everyone will want to know who you are and most importantly what else you've written.

Oooops...you haven't written anything else!

Career's over before it's even begun. You might get lucky and get pitches and assignments to write and rewrite material, but had you played the game with several marketable specs you might have landed a 3-picture deal or sold all those specs!

There's an old saying to "strike while the iron's hot" and this is very true in Hollywood. My advice is NOT to play the game until you have enough material to look like a pro. A pro in for the long haul!

A quick note: Often screenwriters ask me if they have to have material in different genres. It's a good idea to show your flexibility to transcend the genres, but many of you will find there's a specific genre that suits you best. My advice = stick with what works for you. If you try to force material that

302

you're not really interested in it'll show in the writing and won't be marketable.

SCREENWRITING MEANS REWRITING

A producer or studio loves your script and purchases it. Next thing you know you're being handed script notes and being given recommendations for changes from the people who are supposed to <u>love</u> your script. What's up with this?

You did everything you were supposed to. You had the script read professionally, had it professionally proofread, did the necessary rewriting and managed to land as a finalist in several top contests. Why are they asking for changes?

In my opinion it's because Hollywood doesn't trust itself. With all that money on the line and the script coming from a first-time writer there has to be something they can do to make it work even better. They may be right or they may be wrong. It doesn't matter.

What matters is that you're aware this is most likely going to happen so you'll minimize the shock when it does.

Usually you'll be given the opportunity to do the first changes. After that they'll bring in other writers. Sometimes they automatically bring in other writers. Why? Well, with all that money on the line they want to make sure they have the best dialogue, so they bring in a top-dog dialogue writer to touch up the dialogue. This is followed by a top-dog plot writer, etc. The only problem with this script manipulation is that everyone is going to see a story from a different angle and it could easily result in a great script being reduced to a pile of crap.

I've seen some great scripts get chewed up and spit out in the process. By the way, this process is often referred to as development hell. Isn't there a way to avoid this from happening?

In my opinion, your best chance is to get a producer interested in the script who loves more than just the concept. Find one who loves the characters, the plot, the scenes and the dialogue. This is the producer who'll help keep the script intact. He may or may not be successful, but it's your best chance! He might even recommend changes, but overall you and the producer should share the same vision and be on the same page in terms of how you see the project.

Do all scripts get put through the development hell? The majority, unfortunately, do.

Even if a story makes it through development hell without any other writers being called in - usually because it originally came from an A-List writer who Hollywood trusts with delivering quality material – it's bound to have changes.

Here are two examples of A-List writers whose scripts were drastically changed from their original story to the big screen:

> *Gladiator*
> In the original script the Gladiator lives!
>
> *American Beauty*
> The original script is a crime drama where two teens are framed for a murder!

If you go to www.script-o-rama.com you can read both these original scripts. The changes are significantly different than the screenwriter's version!

This is why it's so important not to become attached to your "baby." Save the attachment for the writing process. When you're done writing your "baby" let it go because it's just another commercial product subject to development hell.

Take it personally and you lose. Remain flexible and even grateful for getting the credit and you might survive a near drowning in the Hollywood pool. For those of you who haven't seen the film "Swimming with Sharks" I can assure you the Hollywood pool is full of sharks! Be sure to watch this film before going for a swim.

MEET THE PRODUCERS

From page 1 of this book, I've talked about how to sell a script to producers, but who are the producers? What do they do? What's the difference between the various types of producers, like Executive Producer, Associate Producer, Co-Producer, Line Producer, and the Producer?

Let's take a look at the producers and their function in Hollywood, starting with the lesser-known types of producers:

ASSOCIATE PRODUCER
This is a person who introduces a party with funds to a party in a position to make a movie, but lacks funds. By bringing the two together, a movie is made! This position rarely gets paid, but sometimes receives a finder's fee for referring one party to another. Most of the time, this person just receives a credit.

EXECUTIVE PRODUCER
This is the money man! This is the person who brings the funds to the movie. The funds may have been allocated to him by a studio, his own bank account, an investment group, etc. It might be all the funds for the project or partial funds.

CO-PRODUCER
Often in larger films that only have one or two main producers; a person is hired to pick up the slack. In other words, the co-producers fill-in and help out the producers, but unlike the producer, the co-producer doesn't own a stake in the film.

LINE PRODUCER
This is the person who cuts the checks for a film. He's in charge of overseeing the day-to-day budget on the set and cuts checks for the crews, equipment, etc. It's usually a hard-nosed person who won't let the film go over budget with unnecessary expenses. He's basically the film's accountant.

PRODUCER
This is the person who's going to decide whether or not to buy your script. This is the person who'll make it happen by bringing in the talent, the director, the location scouts, the wardrobe, the makeup, the art department, the special effects, the film permits, the equipment, the cinematographer, the assistants, the other producers, etc. Unlike the other producers listed above,

the Producer owns the film…if it wins an Oscar for Best Movie it's the Producer who receives the golden statue because somehow, almost magically – well, with a whole lots of sweat, tears and perhaps a little screaming – the Producer coordinates everything into one seamless moment where a director can finally say "Action!" -- not to mention all the stuff the Producer does after a movie's done filming.

So, hats off to the Hollywood Producers and all their hard work in helping the screenwriter's story make it to the big screen!

Extra Tidbit: Many aspiring screenwriters are confused by the credit "Script Supervisor" and wrongly believe this is someone who 'fixes' the script. This is actually a production position involving film continuity. A Script Supervisor is the meticulous person who makes sure the hero's tie isn't straight in one shot and crooked in the next shot.

THE HOLLYWOOD MEETING

A producer read a script and has called the writer in for a meeting. The writer would make a big mistake if he quits his day job. Understanding what this meeting is about and how to prepare for it is very important.

First, it's unlikely that this meeting is to talk about a sale. The initial meeting is usually to size up whether or not the producer believes he can work with the screenwriter. It's what is often referred to as the 'meet and greet' meeting. A producer will be spending many months, maybe even years working with the screenwriter, so determining whether or not the producer can work with this individual is priority number one. It's basically a job interview. Is the screenwriter flexible? Can the writer attend meetings on a short notice? Is the writer available and/or willing to do rewrites? How does the writer handle story notes? Is he open to changes, small and radical?

Keep in mind that this meeting may have nothing to do with the screenplay the producer read. Instead, he might want to hire the writer for an assignment to rewrite another script he's already optioned or purchased. The producer knows from reading the writer's script that the writer can deliver. He's called that writer in for an assignment meeting.

The first meeting is rarely a sale! Be prepared to go to numerous meetings regarding a screenplay before it'll get to the sale phase. This is a major reason why learning to market the script via pitching and learning how to market yourself as a screenwriter is very important. As a producer, I can assure you that I'd be less likely to work with an unprepared, inflexible writer than the writer who is industry savvy and ready to do whatever it takes to make a successful film.

THE THEME MEETING

Earlier I mentioned how producers weed out the pro writers from the amateurs by asking one simple question, 'What's the story's theme?' Amateurs can't answer this question, pros can. Two successful writers sent in a screenplay to Extreme Screenwriting that had previously been given a recommend because they had a distributor-backed financing meeting for the screenplay; meaning they could land a sale. The producer of the project was asking for a 'theme meeting' the following week. While the story has a strong theme, the producer wanted it to be even stronger. The writers had beefed up certain areas and wanted to be sure they'd hit the mark before taking the meeting. A very smart move!

Producers have gone beyond just asking the simple 'What's the story's theme?' to requesting theme meetings. Why is this so important? Because theme is what the producer uses to sell the story to an audience. By this I mean, the story has to be about more than a boy who saves his dog, it has to be about a boy who learns to be a man while saving his dog. Smart producers know theme creates emotion and emotion is what involves the audience in the story on a deep level that assures the film's success. We go to the movies to laugh, cry, etc. We might think we're going for the big pyrotechnic effects, but if that's the case, then films like 'Battleship" wouldn't have bombed at the box office! We're going to connect to a hero and his story and that connection is made via the theme.

While I've never personally been called to a theme meeting, I have had many producers ask me the theme question. However, while marketing my feature film I have had distributors (studios and others who put movies into theaters, etc.) ask me for the story's logline and theme logline.

Most writers could easily answer a producer if asked, 'What the story's logline?', but what if the producer asks, 'What's the theme logline?' If a writer can't answer this question as easily as the story logline, then the writer will never sell a screenplay. In fact, the writer shouldn't have written the screenplay in the first place. Theme is the most important story component.

Pro writers start with a theme and build a story and its characters around the theme! A pro writer might decide he wants to explore a redemption theme and create a story about a man who betrayed his only son and is given a second chance to make things right. Or he might want to explore the many aspects of a coming-of-age theme for a young adult audience. The possibilities are endless, but the story should always start with theme to assure its success.

The Theme Logline

Let's get back to the theme logline. My gut feeling is that I'm going to have to explain this because some of you are still scratching your heads and looking at a stack of scripts you've written that you have no idea what the theme is for any of them. The easiest way to deal with the theme logline is to start with the story's logline. If you don't know the story's logline, stop reading this and get back to your day job because you're not a screenwriter. Let's stick with the generic example I provided earlier regarding the boy and the dog. The story's logline might read something like:

A teen boy encounters bandits while on a cross country road trip to find his lost dog.
This logline states the story's premise and provides a visual of the story. It's the story's logline, but it's NOT the theme logline. To be a theme logline, the writer has to tell us what the teen boy learned while on the road trip to find his pet. In other words, the theme is the arc or the lesson learned by the hero. Here's how the theme logline for this story might look:

A teen boy becomes a man while on a road trip to save his beloved dog from animal bandits.

Notice the theme logline mimics the story's logline, but takes it to another level. This new 'level' exposes the story's emotional core, thus its theme.

Does your story have a theme logline? Do you even know your story's theme? If not, then stop everything you're doing right now and go find your story's theme. Without it, you'll never sell a screenplay in Hollywood and if by chance you do, it'll be because the producer likes the idea. In this case, the producer will dump your sorry butt and bring in a real writer to rewrite the story and add a theme! If there's one thing I know about writers is that they hate to be rewritten….avoid this nightmare by knowing your story's theme and being fully prepared for the theme meeting.

THE EASY WAY TO MAKE A FIRST SALE

Besides knowing proper format, the easiest way to make a first sale is something I rarely see from screenwriters; it's a low-budget script. Nearly 99% of scripts I read from aspiring screenwriters fall into the category of medium to high-budgeted films. Yet, 99% of first sales from a new screenwriter come from low-budgeted screenplays.

Could this by why you haven't made a first sale?

If it's this obvious, why do screenwriters continue to crank out scripts that aren't likely to help them break into the biz? I've heard a few arguments; 1) they prefer a certain type of story and it just happens that this 'type' is high budget, like a big action/adventure that takes place in many remote locations 2) they think their story is low-budget and don't truly understand what the term 'low-budget' means 3) they can't come up with a concept that is this limited in its parameters 4) they believe writing for a specific budget hinders their creativity – really? 5) they want the big bucks so they'll only write big budget flicks.

We'll take a look at each argument individually, but first let's clearly define what is considered low-budget in Hollywood. Here is the key word to remember – LIMITED! Limited locations – no more than three. Limited cast – 3-7 (more okay if killed off or only used in part of the film). Limited stunts, SPFX, etc. (usually none is better). Limited page length, usually around 90 pages (no less). This doesn't mean you have to write a Woody Allen style movie where everyone talks around a table. It means you have to really dig deep into your creativity to come up with concepts that you can use within the confines of the 'limited' restrictions of low-budget screenplays. Extra note: Sound effects are cheap to produce, Special Effects are expensive! Bring on the HOWLS, THUNDER, etc., but stay away from MORPHS, DISAPPEARING ENTITIES, etc.

Let's take a look at each argument individually:

1) They prefer a certain type of story and it just happens that this 'type' is high- budget

-The story is an action-adventure with many, remote locations. How do you make this low-budget? Can't you narrow down the story to its most important character components and find a way to make it adventurous in 1-3 locations? Is your creativity this weak or limited that you can't come up with something? Or do you prefer to keep writing high-budget flicks that will never help you break into Hollywood? Save the high-budget stuff for after you've made a sale and become an established writer because it won't benefit you until then.

2) They think their story is low-budget and don't truly understand what the term 'low-budget' means

I've defined what low-budget means. If your story doesn't fit into the 'limited' confines I've mentioned above, then it's medium or high-budget! Also, see the HOW TO WRITE A LOW-BUDGET FILM section of this book.

3) They can't come up with a concept that is this limited in its parameters

Again, I have to ask is your creativity this weak or limited? If so, I recommend you keep your day job. Screenwriting is about coming up with many different stories, big and small – very small! What if a producer buys your high-budget script, then hands you story notes with recommended changes to reduce the budget by 80%? If you can't do this, I guarantee the producer will bring in a writer who can and you'll end up with a shared screenplay credit.

4) They believe writing for a specific budget hinders their creativity – really?

What a cop out! Don't call yourself a screenwriter if you prefer this excuse because I can't think of anything that challenges and reveals a writer's ability to be creative more than coming up with a low-budget concept that works!

One of my favorite low-budget films is a supernatural thriller titled "Dead End". 98% percent of the story takes place in a car and involves a family going to a holiday dinner. It has 3 locations, small cast, no SPFX, etc. Rent it today and get inspired to create something unique, low-budget and most importantly something that will help you finally break into the industry.

5) They want the big bucks, so the writer will only write big-budget flicks

Name one job where you started at the top ranks with the top pay? I don't care if you work at a fast food joint flipping burgers, when you start a new career you start at the bottom and work your way up. Besides, almost all of the big-budget flicks were written by established writers with ability to deliver at the box office. Until you join their ranks the odds of selling a big-budget flick is zero!

Get a reality check and write a low-budget script that helps you break into the biz. Keep in mind, Hollywood isn't looking for jackpot seekers who want to make a sale and retire. These types of writers are delusional and have no idea how the biz works. Hollywood is seeking career-minded screenwriters who know they might have to 2, 3 or even 4 sales before they can leave their day job and even then they risk never selling another script and could be back looking for a day job in a few years.

A spec script is a screenwriter's calling card. It can land the screenwriter a sale, help the screenwriter obtain representation or be used as a sample writing to get the screenwriter assignments. Unlike the produced script, a spec script doesn't have camera angles, scene numbers or any type of directorial references.

Most screenwriters understand the spec script's purpose and how its appearance is different than a produced script. However, what many fail to grasp is that a spec script needs to 'play by the rules'. If a script mixes many genres, comes in at 150 pages or 80 pages or the hero has no arc (except for horror), or the script only has two Acts, etc., then the script doesn't 'play by the rules'. Why is this so important? Because before you can break the rules, you'll need to show Hollywood that you can write a script that adheres to the rules!

I've heard the arguments against playing by the rules. My favorite is the comparison game, where the screenwriter says, "I can write a script like this because a movie was made that breaks the rules in the same way." I'm sure we can all name films that have broken the mold, but rarely are they from first-time screenwriters! They're more likely from established writers who can get away with bending the rules because they have a proven track record and the producers will take the risk on them!

Here's an example: A screenwriter sent me a script several years back that started out as a Crime Thriller and ended as a Horror. There wasn't a single hint that the story was going to be about werewolves until the very end. Extreme Screenwriting gave the script a PASS. The script clearly had a genre identification problem! The screenwriter was furious at the 'pass' and compared the script to Quentin Tarantino's screenplay, "From Dusk Till Dawn", that starts out as a Crime Thriller with two brothers on the run from the law and ends as a Horror with the brothers taking on vampires in a remote Mexico bar. What the screenwriter failed to understand is that Tarantino is an established A-list writer. He doesn't have to get past studio readers and stringent coverage to get his script made! I informed the screenwriter that once he's an established writer he can break the rules too, but until then he'll need to play by the rules!

If you're going to compare your script to a produced film and use it to argue why your script could be made, then be sure to do your homework. Knowing how a script got made can help you understand what it'll take to get yours made. If a script required an A-list actor before the studio would consider it, then your script will require the same. If it required private financing, then your script will most likely have to be done independently to get it made! If it was written by an established screenwriter, then you'll need to be an established screenwriter before your 'rule-breaking' script will be taken seriously.

If you refuse to play by the rules and prefer to scoff at Hollywood, that's fine. Make your own films! But if you have to rely on the funding of producers, production companies and/or studios, then you'll need to show them that you can play by the rules before they're going to play ball with you.

This in no way means compromising your art, individual voice, style or originality. It means understanding what it really takes to get a spec script from an aspiring screenwriter made! Once you're an established writer then whip out those rule-breaking scripts! Until then, you'll need a commercial-quality script that adheres to the rules!

Oh no, I said the evil word "commercial". I know screenwriters hate this word. I'm not sure why. Perhaps because they truly believe it means selling out to the establishment. When it really means is showing the business – and this is a business – that you can deliver a marketable product. The number one thing a producer is looking at when he reads your material is its market viability. Don't believe it? Why else would he purchase it? Sure, he has to love the story, the characters, etc., but the bottom line is the script's market potential. Many producers send scripts to companies to have the script's commercial potential evaluated! The script goes through a rigorous checklist of items like; does the script have enough 'trailer' moments, will the story's characters attract A-list talent, is the dialogue 'meaty' enough to attract talent, does the story have wide appeal for its market, who is the audience, will the budget fit a specific market, can the script be sold under one genre, etc.

Producers rarely run a script from an established screenwriter through a 'marketing' test, but nine times out of ten times they will test the marketability of an unknown writer's script to gauge whether or not it's worth their time and money to pursue. The number one way an aspiring screenwriter can pass the 'spec' test is to understand the rules, play by the rules and write a marketable script.

ACTORS & THE SCREENPLAY

Understanding how an actor sees a screenplay can help the writer make commercial choices that will increase the potential for a sale.

As a producer, when I get an actor to agree to read a screenplay for a lead role here's what he (or she) requests or wants to know:

1) Actor wants the producer to list what pages the role/character appears on. This is easily provided via a report run in Final Draft.
Writer reality check: If an actor doesn't believe his role appears enough in the movie, he won't bother to accept the role. The lead character should appear the MOST in a story. He should appear more than any other character!

2) Actor wants a list of pages he appears on so he can read his role only.
Writer reality check: Actors often only read their role to determine if they're interested in pursuing the part. If it isn't a meaty, well-developed character who steals the show, the actor will pass.

3) Actors want to know when their character first appears; sooner the better.
Writer reality check: If the lead role doesn't appear until page 15, 21, 34 or later, I guarantee an actor, especially the A-list actors, will pass! Most actors want the opening scene or close to it if they're the lead role, which means the role appears by page 10, no later!

4) Actor wants to determine if he's been given a grand entrance.
Writer reality check: If the writer has provided a typical day scenario where we see the hero get up, brush his teeth, shower and eat breakfast, I guarantee the actor will pass. If however, the lead character does all this naked in Times Square; I think you get the picture. Providing a grand entrance makes the character memorable and it guarantees an actor will fight to play the naked guy in Times Square.

5) Actors often flip to the last page before reading a single word.
Writer reality check: Why would an actor do this? He wants to see if he gets the last scene and last line. I know actors who'd pass on a script if they don't get this. They're the hero! They want a grand entrance and a grand exit! This is especially true of A-list actors. There are exceptions to this 'last scene scenario'. For example, a horror story might use a last scene to show the killer is still alive, thus promising a sequel. This is okay because it's really seen as a teaser-for-a-sequel scene and as long as the hero gets the last big scene, then the actor won't toss the script.

6) Actor refers to pages his role appears on and only reads the dialogue on those pages.
Writer reality check: If another character has better lines, then forget it. The actor doesn't want to be upstaged and he'll pass. The meaty, good lines should go to the lead.

313

7) Actor wants to know what page the theme appears on.
Writer reality check: A staggering number of writers don't even know their story's theme. What the actor is really asking is, 'When does the arc happen?' A lead actor wants to see how the hero's change is handled and if it appeals to him. It should be an emotionally-driven, tough moment that tugs at our heart strings. If not, it's likely an actor will pass. The top-dog actors want roles that challenge them.

8) Actor wants page information for the antagonist.
Writer reality check: This one's tricky because the actor's looking for two things: 1) is the antagonist initially stronger than him. The answer should be 'yes' 2) even though the antagonist is initially stronger, he shouldn't upstage the lead role. If the hero's upstaged by the antagonist, the actor will likely pass. The good news is that A-list actors often request page information for the antagonist because he wants a buddy-actor to play the bad guy.

These are the items I've personally had lead actors request or want to know. I think it's important for writers to have this insider information so they can understand how their material is being viewed by lead actors. Hopefully this will inspire writers to write with the lead actor in mind to assure their screenplay has the best chance at being accepted by name talent.

ATTRACT A-LIST TALENT

A well-written and memorable story will attract producers, but another deciding factor on whether they purchase a script is whether the material can attract A-list talent. A medium to high-budget project (and most fall into this category), will require recognizable talent to market.

The screenwriter should be aware of this commercial requirement when writing and create a hero that will attract a leading actor or actress to the role.

Here are a few ways to attract A-list talent to a role:

GRAND ENTRANCE
Remember Indiana Jones' entrance in "Raiders of the Lost Ark" or Johnny Depp's entrance in "Pirates of the Caribbean"? Give the hero a grand entrance worthy of a big star.

BEST LINES
The best lines should go to the hero, not a supporting role. This is one of the most likely reasons talent will turn down a project. They don't want to be upstaged by another actor who gets better lines.

LAST LINE
The lead role should get the last line in the story. He should come in as a hero and leave as one!

MAJORITY OF SCENES
A lead role should be in a majority of scenes throughout the screenplay. No one should have as many scenes as this character. He's the star!

BIG MOMENTS
The climatic, emotionally-charged moments should go to the hero. If a supporting role gets these moments, the A-list talent will turn down the role.

CHARACTER RANGE
A-list talent prefers to play roles that have range. By range, I mean the hero changes and/or has a defined arc. If he started out being a coward, by the end he's courageous. It must be a clearly defined and dramatic range to attract worthy talent.

DON'T SHARE LEAD
There are plenty of buddy movies and ensemble pieces on the market, but if you're trying to sell a screenplay and you're still an aspiring screenwriter, then you'll need to write a strong hero lead. Save the buddy and ensemble pieces for later in your career.

EVERYTHING MEATY
Every meaty piece of dialogue, every meaty scene, moment, crisis, emotion, etc., should go to the hero. If not, it won't sell to an A-list talent and a producer will either pass on the project or hire another writer who understands how to write for talent.

STRONG ANTAGONIST
The antagonist should initially be stronger than the hero. Don't confuse this with upstaging the hero. By stronger, I mean he should outsmart, outwit and outplay the hero because this forces the hero to change to defeat him. Be careful while creating a strong antagonist that he (or she) doesn't get more screen time than the hero.

Writers hate to be told how to commercialize their screenplays, but if you're going to break the mold and make that first sale it'll require adherence to what a producer needs to market a story to talent.

If I ask screenwriters how they'd make money from a script, they'd answer with an obvious response, "From the sale of the script". Sure, that's the big bucks, but there is more than one-way to make money from an initial sale.

Let's discuss a few ways:

BUY THE WEBSITE
Every time a writer registers a screenplay with WGA, the writer should go to www.GoDaddy.com or another site and purchase the website associated with the script's title www.MyScreenplayTitle.com. If you sell the script to a producer, you can also sell him the website. Obviously, you're not going to ask millions or even six figures, but you would ask for a percentage of what was paid for the script, say 5%. If you were paid $100K for the script, then ask $5K for website rights. Be sure to purchase as many of the sites' as you can, such as .biz, .tv. .org. etc. I'd also recommend the script title, plus "THE MOVIE", which is popularly used by studios www.MyScreenplayTitleTheMovie.com . Do NOT ask for 5% for each website just a flat 5% fee for rights to all associated sites you own.

TRADEMARK THE TITLE
Go to a T-Shirt shop and have T-Shirts made with the script's title. You have to have a product in order to trademark a name. Use the T-shirts to apply for a trademark, then use the same technique above to sell the trademark to the producer. Again, I'd ask for 5% of what was paid for the script. Assuming the script sold for $100K, that's another $5K in your pocket.

SECURE THE TITLE
To assure the producer doesn't simply change the title to avoid paying you fees, have written into the Literary Deal Memorandum that should the producer change the title, he must pay a nominal fee to cover the costs you've accumulated by holding ownership to the website and trademark. For example, if you paid $20 a year for the website for 2 years = $40, plus you put $400 into a trademark, then the producer should pay you $420.

MERCHANDISING
Producers never discuss this with the writer because they plan to keep merchandising money for themselves. Not every script will have merchandising potential, but if you know your character's special lunch box could end up being a marketable product, then add to the Literary Deal Memorandum that you receive a few percentage points of merchandising, say around 1-2%.

ADVERTISING PROMO

Do you own a company? Have written into the Literary Deal Memorandum that your company gets a 'thank you' in the film's end title credits. It's free advertising and you can use it to promote your business. Customers love doing business with folks associated with Hollywood.

WEBSITE RIGHTS

Not the rights mentioned above that a producer purchases from the writer, rather the writer's own personal promo, screenwriter site. If you have one, then write into the screenplay's Literary Deal Memorandum that you have the right to use the film's poster, logo, etc., on your site to promote yourself as a screenwriter. Remember, once you sell the script, you no longer own it and would have to ask for these rights. Putting a poster up on your site for your movie is a powerful visual that could help land future reads, get an agent, etc. It's worth its weight in gold.

LOCATION MONEY

I know many of you have written scripts based on actual locations associated with the story, like a tavern or the house you live in. Offer the location to the producer for a fee, say around $500-$1K a day, that's a cheap rate, unless it's an ultra-low budget production, then scale down the amount to a suitable price. If you don't own the location, write up an agreement (before you sell the script) with the owner. Offer to promote the location to the producer and if the producer uses the location, the two of you will split the monies. If the owner balks at this, remind him of the millions of dollars in free advertising he's going to get by having the location used in a Hollywood movie. All you want is half his location fees and he can keep the advertising payoffs.

Okay, let's do a tally of how much extra money I made for you:
$5,000 website rights
$5,000 trademark rights
$5,000 estimated merchandising percentage
$5,000 potential business revenue (from your biz advertised in film's credits)
$7,500 a 15-day shoot @ $1K per day location, divided by 2 = $7,500
$27,500

The $100K movie sale is now increased to a $127,500.

SMALL TOWN ADVANTAGE

Do you live in the backwoods of the Appalachian Mountains? Perhaps you live in rural New Jersey, a hick town in Maine or a lumber-jack burrow in Oregon. This can be a disadvantage when trying to sell a screenplay. Why?

Because Los Angeles (or NY) is a meetings town and it usually takes meeting after meeting to make a screenplay sale.

However, you do have one huge advantage over those living in the Los Angeles, New York or other metropolitan areas. You have a small town advantage. Long before you have to fly to L.A. or N.Y. to make a sale, you'll have to write the screenplay. It can be well-written and even won awards, but it'll need a fresh spin to land a sale.

Before I opened Extreme Screenwriting, I worked at Walt Disney Studios for four years in the press room. In addition to writing press releases, press kits and scouring news reports for the studio, I'd help go through literally hundreds of magazines and newspaper articles from around the country. Primarily to find Disney-related articles, but if the press room ran across anything interesting, say a unique story, we'd hand it off to the TV and Film Story Development Departments. Today, studios have entire departments that do nothing else but look for stories. They weed through the Internet, newspapers, books and magazines from around the world! They even send out scouts to investigate stories based on associated press articles!

Talk about competition. Let's do the numbers. If you've seen a story in a local newspaper and it has the words 'Associated Press' at the top of the article, it means the article has circulated around the globe. It has literally been seen by millions, including the studios! Let's say you decide to write a screenplay based on one of these articles. I'd wager to guess 200-2,000 other writers got the same idea. The numbers are probably higher. Worse, the studio might have liked the idea and passed it along to an A-list writer, which means the other 200-2,000 aspiring writers don't stand a chance at a sale. The sale goes to the established writer.

This is the reason I tend to see trends in spec screenplays. Before the turn of the millennium (year 2000), the market was inundated with doomsday scripts, then it was the 2012 doomsday scripts. These writers may have given the mainstream media story a twist, but they never made a sale. Why? Because these type of trend movies are written by established writers. Don't believe me? The movie *2012* starring John Cusack wasn't written by a first-time writer! Get the picture? Ever wonder why or how the studios come up with the same type of concept you spent months writing? Well, now you know! And now I'm going to tell you how to beat them at their own game!

Here comes the small town advantage. Let's say you live in the backwoods of Oregon ten miles from the nearest hint of civilization. Then you must know the local folklore, the monster stories, the nearby town's legends, the

318

myths, the mysteries? No? Shut up already! Yes, you do! You probably have a story of your own, right?

When I was on location filming in a rural high desert town outside Los Angeles, everyday the crew and I drove past Lake Elizabeth. One morning a crew member mentioned he'd lived in the area and told us how the lake was supposed to have a flying monster in it called 'The Thunderbird'. I'm watching TV one night and the cable network hit series *Ancient Aliens* had its season premiere and guess what they did a piece on? You got it, Lake Elizabeth's 'Thunderbird'. The local folklore of a small desert town was being featured on a hit cable show. I'm quite sure the network and/or the show's producers have people scouting the world for these 'ancient alien' stories, but you have the advantage of already living in a small town.

You don't have to go looking for the stories. You already know them. Remember the 1984 hit movie *Footloose* starring Kevin Bacon? A writer combing through old, legal ledgers in a small-town courthouse came across a law still on the books that made it a crime to dance in public. The law could have resulted in a modern-day arrest. This find resulted in the hit film.

The cult sensation *The Blair Witch Project* was based on Maryland folklore that was fictionalized. Even today, tourists stop by Maryland 7-11 convenience stores and ask where the Blair Witch house is located. There's no such place! It's fiction loosely based on local folklore.

Still think your small town has nothing to offer? Think again. And remember, the studios don't have access to your information! Only you do! If there's another screenwriter in your town, kill him! I won't tell.

Here's an exercise I'd like you to try. Go to your local library or courthouse. Plan a few days to go through old ledgers and old newspapers dating back as far as the town has on record, probably mid-1800's to present day. What are you looking for? Anything that sparks your interest or that you find odd, mysterious, unique, etc. I'm not advocating writing a historic screenplay, but rather using the story as a basis for something modern and fresh, just like the writers of *Footloose*, *The Blair Witch Project* and many other stories have done.

You don't even have to go to the courthouse or library. Look around. Remember that house at the end of the road you believed was haunted as a kid? What about the stories of a lake monster or Big Foot roaming the forest? What about the sheriff who suspects everyone's a drug dealer or a terrorist? Or the strange girl who dropped out of high school and seemed to disappear

319

– was she pregnant, a runaway or something more sinister? Get a notebook. Start writing this stuff down!

Even if you live in a small town and have already written several scripts, take a look at them. Where'd you get the idea? If it's from mainstream media sources, you may need to rethink your approach to storytelling and take a closer look at your small town.

By the way, if you ever sell a TV show, MOW or screenplay and the producer asks where you came up with the idea, lie! The last thing you want to do is tell a Hollywood producer your small town secret. Why? Isn't it obvious? The studio will send scouts to your small town to find other stories. Bastards! That's your secret stash. Keep the treasure trove of stories to yourself! You'll thank me later.

So, the next time someone puts you down for thinking you're a screenwriter when you live in a hick town, just smile because now you know that you have something Hollywood doesn't have; a small town advantage.

BIG CITY ADVANTAGE

The big city advantage is obvious; proximity to the action! If you live in Los Angeles or NYC, you're within driving distance to studios, agents, managers, directors, producers, actors, etc. You can attend meetings at the drop of the hat without having to book airline tickets, hotels and rental cars. Your only expense is gas and time. This can be a huge advantage if you have a successful lunch meeting on Tuesday and you're called back for a follow-up meeting on Friday, then a pitch on Monday. Considering it takes a succession of meetings to sell a screenplay, consider yourself lucky.

Another advantage is trends. Big cities often set the pace for the country in terms of hot new trends. For example, if the Goth kids are steering away from vampires to werewolves, you'll probably know it before the small town folks. Music, fashion, dance, art, etc., often have trends that start in the big cities. This can make you first to the information and ahead of the game when it comes to writing a screenplay based on a hot new trend. There can be one disadvantage; the ten thousand other screenwriters who live in the big cities too (probably higher than ten thousand). Unfortunately, they have access to the same trends as you do. So, unless you're a writer who can write and market a script within 4-6 weeks, the trends won't do you much good.

Now I'm going to let you in on a secret Hollywood doesn't want you to know and neither does your spouse who has become used to the privy lifestyle of the big city; it is OKAY to leave L.A. (or NYC)! Trust me, there is another world out there and it's waiting for you! In other words, stop sitting around whining because small town folks have you by the balls when it comes to original stories. Leave the big city and get a piece of the small town advantage for yourself. The hit movie *City Slickers* starring Billy Crystal came from a screenwriter's vacation to a dude ranch. An L.A. screenwriter visiting a relative in the desert was in awe when he saw a cargo plane landing at a prison; a plane his relative referred to as *Con Air*.

It's time to move beyond your comfort zone. It's amazing how we drive around day after day and never notice the details. I guess we're just too used to them, but go someplace unfamiliar and the senses come alive! Don't make the mistake of going somewhere 'comfortable'. If you hate being cold, then go where it snows! If you hate heat, then go to the desert.

If you're in Los Angeles, then you're literally an hour away from the beaches, deserts and mountains. You could have breakfast in the mountains, lunch in the desert and a sunset dinner at the beach all in the same day! Get a map (or go to Google maps) and find some obscure place you've never heard of and go there. Make it a day trip, a weekend getaway or plan a vacation. Don't go to the franchise places you could go to in the city. Instead, visit the local mom-and-pop shops, the family-run pubs, the one-of-a-kind restaurants and pawn shops. Ask questions. Waitresses, bartenders and shop owners love to brag about their small town. They'll tell you the notorious and heroic stories that can fill your screenwriting schedule for years to come!

Here are a few other places you might not have considered; truck stops, police stations (ask for recent police reports), libraries, lodges, local coffee shops (not Starbucks!), courthouses, wineries (or take a wine-tasting tour) – remember the movie "Sideways"? Where do you think they came up with idea? For L.A. writers, try state line. You don't know what that is, do you? Okay, time to get out of L.A. It's the 'state' line between Arizona and California. There's more there than a border stop. Go beyond the state line and instead of sticking to the freeways, drive through Desert Center. Miles and miles of nothingness…why the hell I am suggesting this place? I've never been through there without coming out the other side with a story from the flashflood that almost swallowed my car, to the strange lights at night, to the heat lightning when there isn't a cloud in the sky, to the eerie van following too close, to the one and only gas station on the road (boy do they have the stories to tell!), to the wooden crosses from the accident victims (each one is a story in itself). Also, don't forget to pick up a local newspaper – a treasure trove of local information.

Okay, you get the picture! Head off the beaten path, get the hell out of the big city! Here's a bonus: take the recent hot city trend and combine it with an idea you came up with while on your trip and you could end up with the next hit movie!

I advised the small town writers not to tell Hollywood people where they came up with the idea because Hollywood will swarm the writer's small town and steal all the ideas. I have different advice for big city writers. Tell them! Let them follow your lead and leave Los Angeles or NYC because that means less competition for you!

LIMITLESS HELP

What do the movies *Limitless* and *The Help* have in common with movies like *Secret Window*, *Adaptation* and *Throw Mama from the Train*? They're all movies written by writers about writers. I'd wager to say that this is the most difficult type of spec script to sell. But wait a minute, if all these movies have been made, then how can this be true? Doesn't this mean it's easy to sell? After all, there's even a hit TV show *Castle*, which involves a writer.

In Hollywood, producers know that every writer has a script about a writer. It's a given, which means it's grossly overdone. So overdone that when pitched to producers watch closely and you'll see the producer cringe. The reality is that among the hundreds of films made a year, it's rare a film written by a writer about a writer gets made. When one does get made, it's because it was adapted from a novel (*The Help*) that has a built-in audience or the writer has a proven track record (A-list) of films under his belt. Let me make this 100% clear: a spec script written by an aspiring writer about a writer has NEVER sold! Of all the tough genres, premises, etc., to sell, scripts about writers are on the bottom of the purchase barrel. It might be fair to say this type of script isn't even in the barrel.

Should the writer toss a script where the hero is a writer? No. Instead, consider how the other rare sales of these kinds of scripts came about and go the same route. For example, adapt the script into a book and use the sales to show the material has a built-in audience. It won't guarantee a movie, but it will help the script get more serious attention. Maybe the script got made because a big actor became attached, then the writer will need to try to get an actor interested. The actor will need to be A-list or at least a household name for the spec to sell. Or the writer can wait until he has a hit movie or two under his belt, then he has a decent chance at getting this type of story made. By the way, notice I said 'hit movie', not just a film. It takes more than a produced writer to get this type of movie made. It takes a hit movie writer to get it done.

Or the most likely scenario is the script written by a writer about a writer will become nothing more than a writing sample. It's better to use it to land an agent than tossing it in the trash. But the trash is another alternative since you and approximately two million other writers have the exact same premise; a script written by a writer about a writer. Cliché, overdone and it's the last type of pitch a producer wants to hear.

A VERY BERRY PROFESSIONAL WRITER

99% of writers know the WGA has a list of signatory agents available on their website. But let's take a look at how to utilize the WGA, whether you're a member or not, to help you look like a professional writer.

First, let's start with a fictitious scenario:

INT. STARBUCKS – DAY

A MALE CUSTOMER, 30s, enters. A CLERK takes orders behind a counter. Five JOB SEEKERS sit at a nearby table filling out applications.

The Male Customer steps up to the counter.

MALE CUSTOMER
I'd like a Venti Very Berry Hibiscus.

The Clerk glances around, confused.

CLERK
Do you know how much it costs?

MALE CUSTOMER
What? Don't you work here?

CLERK
Well…yeah, I work here, but I don't really
know how much it is.

MALE CUSTOMER
You don't know the cost of your own product?

The Clerk glances over at the Job Seeker's table.

CLERK
(to Job Seekers)

Hey, do any of you guys know how much the Very
Berry Hibiscus is?

JOB SEEKER #1
It's like $10.99.

JOB SEEKER #2
No, it's more than that. Charge $15.99.

JOB SEEKER #3
You guys are all wrong, it's no where
near that amount, it's $1.99.

The Male Customer grins from ear to ear.

MALE CUSTOMER
Yeah, it's $1.99.

Clerk ponders this information a beat.

CLERK
Okay, I guess I can take $1.99.

The Clerk rings up the order and moves to the mixing station.

CLERK
(to Male Customer)
How do you make a Very Berry Hibiscus?

*****
The CLERK is no different than an aspiring screenwriter who's marketing a
script when he doesn't know how the business works. The Male Customer is
the Producer who sees the opportunity to take advantage of the CLERK,
screenwriter, and he ALWAYS ends up paying less for his drink (script) than
it's really worth and the only one to blame is the naïve writer.

An aspiring screenwriter has probably never seen an option agreement and/or
really doesn't know what it entails. And he's guessing at the value of his
product, the screenplay. Worse, if he's lucky enough to get a producer
interested in optioning or purchasing a script, he runs to every wanna-be
writer on every message board on the Internet (like the Clerk asking the Job
Seekers for advice) and asks what he should do, how does he handle the
option, what price should he ask? He's the idiot CLERK from Starbucks!

324

When the real question he should be asking is, what the hell is he doing in this biz if he doesn't know how it works?

I already hear the excuses: 'Oh Barb, give me a break, I'll let my agent or entertainment attorney handle the legalities of a deal'. Do you have an agent? Can you afford an entertainment attorney? Do you think none of these folks are unscrupulous?

You're telling me you've walked in blind to job interviews you've had in the past? I bet you didn't. I bet you did your homework (company info, products, sales, etc.) and were prepared (resume, salary expectations, etc). Seeking a career in screenwriting shouldn't be any different. To really consider it a career, you need to know how the business works. This will make you look professional and more importantly, it makes it difficult for producers (screenplay buyers) to take advantage of you.

Case in point: I often get calls from producers to fix scripts on a ghostwriting basis for pay. A producer left a voice mail message for me a few weeks ago for a dialogue-fix script. I wasn't going to call him back because he's known for getting writers to do 'freebies' for him and I'm no Hollywood whore. One day, I accidentally answered the phone without looking at the caller ID and it was him. He told me what he needed and offered $7,500 for the work with a 4-week deadline. I asked him why he didn't try to get a freebie out of me. He laughed and said, "Hey, you know the biz". When I asked how he manages to get freebies from writers he said, "Because I can". In fact, he'd gone through a dozen freebie writers for the dialogue-fix before he finally paid me, a professional, to do it right. For those of you doing freebies you're nothing more than desperate wanna-be writers who don't know the biz because the definition of a professional is someone who gets paid to deliver a product or service.

Writers who do freebies RARELY sell a script and if they get lucky, they always end up being rewritten. Face it, if a producer has asked for more than one freebie rewrite and you still haven't delivered a solid draft, I guarantee the producer already has another writer in mind. Also, freebie writers, who ironically undervalue themselves, will often want an above-market value for a script. Why would a producer pay above-market value or even market value when you're willing to work for free? I guarantee if you get the sale that you'll be low-balled into accepting a fraction of the script's value. If you still think it's okay because you'll only do this for the first sale, then you're an idiot! You've set the precedence for your entire career! Don't fall for producers who tell you they need free rewrites until they raise funds. Rewrites are only a couple grand. Most of us have this sitting around on a

325

credit card. If they can't come up with a couple grand they shouldn't be in the game.

Producers can smell desperation and naïve writers a mile away! So let's fix this issue once and for all! I want you to stop being the CLERK at Starbucks. Back to the WGA. As I noted above, all of you know the WGA has a list of signatory agents, but their website www.wga.org has more than the list. Did you know they have every option agreement you can imagine available to download? You can stop guessing what goes into an option, download a few sample templates (MOW, feature length screenplays, TV teleplays, etc.) and familiarize yourself with what goes into an option/purchase agreement. Next, they have a section titled Schedule of Minimums. Click on this area and you'll be able to view the rates film and TV writers are paid! There it is in black and white. No more guessing what your script is worth and no more dreaming of million dollar figures when the WGA minimum says something different. By the way, these minimums have high and low scales – a first-time writer is obviously at the low-end of the scale. Last, the WGA has a newsletter. It's free so sign up and have it emailed to you. Don't assume you can't get these rates if you're not a member. Why not? If you're planning to be a professional writer, then start acting like one by asking for professional rates.

WORK FOR PRO RATES

The first thing a producer is going to say is that the writer can't get these rates unless he's a WGA member. Writers have fallen for this lie so long in Hollywood that I hear writers say it! They actually believe it's true! It is NOT true! Here's the truth: The producer doesn't have to pay signatory rates unless you or the producer is a signatory member. It doesn't mean he shouldn't pay it! Why should you be treated like anything less than a professional? Remind the producer that by going non-union, you're actually saving the producer thousands of dollars in signatory fees, pension and benefits. With this in mind, why is he expecting you to under-price the script when you're already taking less than your value as a writer? I guarantee you that when it comes time for profits, he won't take less!

PRODUCER CAN'T AFFORD RATES

In all fairness, some indie producers legitimately can't afford even the WGA minimum. What now? I'm not advocating that you blow the deal, just cut a better deal. Tell him you understand the low-budget considerations and you'll take less, but only if you're brought aboard as a producer. Be warned: Most producers will balk at the idea. This means they don't plan to profit share. I'm not talking about taking back-end as a writer. I guarantee you'll never see a dime. Producers own the project. They're paid upfront. You want part of this share or no deal.

Don't hesitate to become a producer. Yes, you'll have to get permits, schedule craft service, coordinate actors, etc., but what a great way to learn the biz. Plus, you'll be on the set every day and can make fantastic contacts from actors to directors. It's rare for a writer to be on the set – most are never allowed near the set!

Okay, here comes the argument from the aspiring screenwriters who have the brains of the CLERK:

Argument #1 – "I need this deal to break into the biz and I need the credit". Credits don't put food on the table. I know screenwriters who've sold a script and five years later are still hoping for another sale. All the while, the producer from the first movie is still making money. What is the writer making five years later? Nothing. Plus, every script doesn't get made. So much for the credit.

Argument #2 – "I'd only deal with signatory producers, so I don't have to worry about unscrupulous people; I don't need to know all of this".

Case in point: A few years ago, a producer with 30+ credits to her name offered to purchase a screenplay from me. Her production company was WGA signatory, so I didn't anticipate any issues. When she arrived at my agent's office, the contract she presented to the agent and I was under a different company name than her 'signatory company' (she had a side, non-signatory company) and out of a $5mil budget, she wanted to pay $50K for the script. The amount under her signatory company would have been $250K. A desperate, wanna-be writer would have been stupid enough to take the deal. My agent said it was up to me – agents want commissions so they're not likely to stop a writer from doing a bad deal. The producer's excuse to devalue my work was my lack of credits. My agent quickly clarified that I had sold dozens of teleplays (equivalent to credits) and at the time had 2 scripts under option. Then the producer claimed she needed the funds for the production. She tried to convince me it's everyone's job to take cuts to get the film made. I politely corrected her because this isn't the writer's job to do everything possible to get the film made, that's the producer's job. I suggested if she wanted to under-value the script by $200K, I'd take the deal, but only if I was brought aboard as a producer (entitling me to profit share, residuals, etc.). No way would she go for this!

I know there are only three things she could be doing with the extra $200K: 1) putting it toward the production – as she claimed 2) setting it aside to pay

327

another writer to rewrite the script and take half the credit 3) line her pockets with extra 'producer salary'. Well, she's done dozens of films, so I didn't believe she shortchanged the budget and needed an extra $200K for production. I also knew she planned to immediately send the script out to actors who were waiting to read it, which meant she wasn't hiring another writer for a rewrite. This left only one possibility: A producer with dozens of credits to her name was going to pocket the $200K that should have gone to me! The CLERK writer who doesn't know this biz wouldn't understand this dynamic and would be stupid and desperate enough to take the deal.

I turned the deal down flat! This producer was livid. She even threatened to blacklist me as a writer. I knew she was bluffing because she couldn't blacklist me without exposing her unscrupulous practices. I saw her a few years ago at a film festival and made it a point to say 'Hi'. She made one mistake: she assumed I was desperate for the credit. A film credit doesn't pay the bills. And I've since had people ask how I could have walked away from $50K. I didn't. I walked away from being cheated out of $200K! The way to assure you know how to handle this type of scenario is KNOWLEDGE of this biz, how it works and what's truly fair to you as a writer and NEVER accept less!

Knowledge is power! The only one in this biz who is going to look out for you is YOU! Learn the biz and stop acting like the CLERK at Starbucks! If you appear professional, it's far less likely anyone will try to take advantage of you and if they do try, you'll know how to spot and stop it quickly!

Don't think I'm bad-mouthing producers. I am a writer, producer and a director. I've dealt with upstanding producers and shady producers. Knowledge of the industry and how it works on every level gave me the ability to deal professionally with both kinds of producers and the confidence to know when to say F-off.

By the way, the correct price for a Venti Very Berry Hibiscus is $3.60 plus tax. If my fictitious scenario had been real, Starbucks would have been out of business years ago. Don't let yourself be out of the business before you're in the business. Whether you accept a deal or not, you'll have the confidence to know that your knowledge of the industry makes you A Very Berry Professional Writer.

****

Is screenwriting an art? This question has been pondered by many screenwriters. It seems it is an art, but one where the screenwriter provides a specific "artistic" talent to deliver a commercial product. Like any talent, it must be practiced, disciplined and honed down to a specific market before it can be appreciated by the masses.

I sincerely hope the Extreme Screenwriting book has provided you with the tools you'll need to commercialize your art so all of us can share in it.

Sincerely,
Barb Doyon
Owner/Founder
Extreme Screenwriting
www.extremescreenwriting.com

16057913R00191

Made in the USA
San Bernardino, CA
16 October 2014